Cognitive Self-Instruction for Classroom Processes

Cognitive Self-Instruction for Classroom Processes

Brenda H. Manning

STATE UNIVERSITY OF NEW YORK PRESS

Production by Ruth East
Marketing by Theresa A. Swierzowski

Published by
State University of New York Press, Albany

Printed in the United States of America

For information, address State University of New York
Press, State University Plaza, Albany, N.Y. 12246

Library of Congress Cataloging-in-Publication Data

Manning, Brenda H., 1946–
Cognitive self-instruction for classroom processes / Brenda H.
Manning.
p. cm.
Includes bibliographical references.
ISBN 0–7914-0479–X (alk. paper) . — ISBN 0–7914-0480–3 (pbk. :
alk. paper)
1. Learning. 2. Cognitive psychology. 3. Cognitive learning.
4. Study, Method of. I. Title.
LB1060.M33 1991
370.15'23—dc20 90–32701
CIP

10 9 8 7 6 5 4 3 2 1

CONTENTS

Part Two: Related Research in Cognitive Self-Instruction

Part Three: Classroom Application of Cognitive Self-Instruction

PREFACE

This educational guide consists of three parts (i.e., theoretical/conceptual, research, classroom application). The intent of this work is to describe cognitive self-instruction (CSI) as a teaching/learning model for classroom use. The main thrust is application of CSI in the regular classroom setting to improve memory, comprehension, problem solving, and self-control of both teachers and students. These processes are informed by an account of their theoretical and research bases. Areas such as spelling, reading, and mathematics are tied within the CSI classroom suggestions. CSI strategies to aid classroom self-control of stress, anger, and panic are included. Age appropriate activities by grade level and guidelines to begin and maintain a CSI program are detailed.

After reading this book, a motivated reader should have ample resources to teach cognitive self-instruction at the university/college level, and/or use it as a basis for metacognitive instruction in a preschool to high school classroom (regular and special education), and/or use it as an administrator to understand and promote metacognitive instruction, and/or as a parent to become more knowledgeable about children's metacognitive skills. In summary, those involved in teacher education, educational psychology, early childhood education, elementary education, special education, parent education, counseling education, and child study may find this a valuable text.

It should be noted, however, that the best ideas for classroom practice will be those creatively developed by informed individuals who understand the theory and research foundations and who know the strengths and limitations of their students. The classroom examples provided in this text are prototypic ones found successful by various teachers, at various times, under various conditions, with various populations of students. These examples were born in the minds of professional teachers who knew CSI theory, research, and how to formulate and match instruction based on student needs and curriculum/methodological knowledge. Therefore, the classroom suggestions in this book should be analyzed, synthesized, and modified for specific classroom use. It is hoped that the CSI suggestions will stimulate the creativity of teachers to go beyond them.

ACKNOWLEDGMENTS

Foremost I acknowledge the patience and love of my family. To Stewart, Jill, and Ginger, who reside with me and spent at least a year talking to me at my desk, while I listened halfway, I thank you. Your steadfast love, and pride, and belief in what I was doing made my work possible.

To my mother, Lucille Holcomb and sisters Judy Alford and Kim Turner, I express my sincere gratitude. The four of us have always pulled for one another. Thanks for one more "pull." In addition, I must say to my father, James Holcomb, who died in 1984, you were right: "Go to school, make a scholar, wouldn't miss it for a dollar." Your dialogue became my guiding monologue.

To Stephanie Bales, a very bright and creative person: she typed this entire manuscript (more than once) from a handwritten copy on a legal pad, while my department head stood by mortified that I had not typed it "on the computer." Stephanie, without you, I would not have met the deadlines or kept my tiny shred of sanity.

I am indebted to all the teachers, who as my students, contributed to my understanding of CSI from a classroom teacher's perspective. Many of their ideas are contained within this text.

Gratitude is expressed for permission to reprint passages from the following works:

Improving Attention with Self-Monitoring: A Manual for Teachers, by D. Hallahan, J. Lloyd, and L. Stoller. Unpublished manuscript prepared 1982 by University of Virginia Learning Disabilities Research Institute. Permission granted by Daniel P. Hallahan.

The Utility of Cognitive Self-instruction in Altering Teacher Expectations and Locus of Control Orientations, by P. L. Dagley, p. 163. Unpublished Doctoral Dissertation written 1988 at University of Georgia.

A Guide to Rational Living, by A. Ellis and R. A. Harper, p. 23. Copyright 1975 Wilshire Book Company, North Hollywood, CA. Reprinted by permission of Albert Ellis.

Adapted from "How to Incorporate Comprehension Monitoring Strategies into Basal Reading Instruction," by M. C. Schmitt and J. F. Baumann in *The Reading Teacher, 35,* (10), pp. 28–31. Copyright 1986 by International Reading Association, Newark, DE.

Metacognition, Cognition, and Human Performance, edited by D. L. Forrest-Pressley, G. E. MacKinnon and T. Gary Waller, pp. 115–116. Copyright 1985 by Academic Press, Orlando, FL. Reprinted by permission of Michael Pressley and the publisher.

"Think Aloud—Modeling the Cognitive Processes of Reading Comprehension," by B. Davey in *Journal of Reading,* October 1983, pp. 44–47. Reprinted with permission of Beth Davey and the International Reading Association, Newark, DE..

"The Turtle Technique: An Extended Case Study of Self-Control in the Classroom," by A. Robin, M. Schneider, and M. Dolninck in *Psychology in the Schools, 13,* pp. 449–453. Copyright 1976. Reprinted with permission of Clinical Psychology Publishing Company, Inc., 4 Conant Square, Brandon, VT 05733.

Figure 1 from "Application of Cognitive Behavior Modification, First and Third Graders' Self-Management of Classroom Behavior," in *AERJ., 25,* no. 2, pp. 193–212. Copyright 1988 by the American Educational Research Association, Washington, D.C. Reprinted by permission of the publisher.

"Knowledge Systems for Realistic Goals," by S. Goldman in *Discourse Processes, 5,* pp. 289–290. Copyright 1982, by Ablex Publishing Corporation, Norwood, NJ.. Reprinted with the permission of Ablex Publishing Corporation.

Talking to Yourself: Learning the Language of Self-Support, by P. E. Butler. Copyright 1981 by Harper and Row, San Francisco, CA. Excerpts reprinted with permission of Pamela Butler.

Cognitive Behavior Modification: An Integrative Approach, by D. Meichenbaum. Copyright 1977 by Plenum Press, New York, NY. Excerpts reprinted with permission of Donald Meichenbaum.

"Knowing, When, Where and How to Remember: A Problem of

Metacognition," by A. L. Brown in *Advances in Instructional Psychology* (vol. 1), edited by R. Glaser. Copyright 1978 by Lawrence Erlbaum Associates, Inc., Hillsdale, NJ. Reprinted by permission of Ann L. Brown and the publisher.

"Metacognition, Executive Control, Self-Regulation, and Other More Mysterious Mechanisms," by A. L. Brown in *Metacognition, Motivation, and Understanding*, edited by F. E. Weinert and R. H. Kluwe. Copyright 1987 by Lawrence Erlbaum Associates, Inc., Hillsdale, NJ. Excerpts reprinted by permission of Ann L. Brown and the publisher.

"Teaching Adolescents the Skills of Self-Management," by L. Nielsen in *Clearing House*, September 1984, pp. 32–35. Reprinted with permission of the Helen Dwight Reid Educational Foundation. Published by Heldref Publications, 4000 Albemarle Street, N.W., Washington, D.C. 20016. Copyright 1984.

Metacognition, Cognition, and Human Performance edited by D. L. Forrest-Pressley, G. E. MacKinnon, and T. Gary Waller, pp. 57–109. Copyright 1985 by Academic Press, Orlando, FL.. Reprinted by permission of Wolfgang Schneider and the publisher.

What to Say When Your Talk to Yourself, by Shad Helmstetter. Copyright 1986 by Grindle Press, Scottsdale, AZ. Excerpts reprinted with permission of Shad Helmstetter.

"Metacognitive Strategy Instruction" by A. S. Palincsar in *Exceptional Children*, vol. 53, no. 2, 1986, pp. 118–124. Copyright 1986 by the Council for Exceptional Children. Reprinted with permission of Annemarie Palincsar and the publisher.

"Teaching and Self-Regulated Learning," by L. Corno in *Talks to Teachers*, edited by D. C. Berliner and B. V. Rosenshine, pp. 249–266. Copyright 1987 by Random House, Inc., New York, NY. Excerpts from this material are reproduced with permission of Lyn Corno and McGraw Hill, Inc.

INTRODUCTION

As classroom teachers, we often tell our students to THINK, to STUDY, to CONCENTRATE. It has been my experience, upon years of investigation that often students do not know what it is teachers are requesting when teachers ask them to think, or study, or concentrate. Of course, some students understand. However, in most cases, it is not because teachers clearly model for them their definitions of "thinking," "studying," and/or "concentrating." In fact, when I have asked for these definitions, or for teachers to demonstrate how to concentrate, teachers often are unable to respond. Most frequently their response is to laugh. They laugh, I believe because they see the absurdity of asking students to perform processes, we, as educators do not understand ourselves. How do we expect our students to engage in a cognitive process that we as teachers cannot model, define, or demonstrate for our students? This was made very vivid for me, when my daughter brought home her social studies book and notebook to study for her first major quiz in social studies. I was preparing dinner and she sat down in the kitchen with all her "study" materials. She said, "I have this big test tomorrow and the teacher told me to study," I said, "Go ahead then. Get your studying completed before dinner." I watched her as she flipped through her notebook, closed it, flipped through her book, closed it. Ginger turned to me and said, "I need to study; the teacher told us to study hard; I want to make a good grade. What am I supposed to do?" It became very obvious to me that my daughter and probably many like her do not know what cognitive behaviors are associated with studying. She was not aware of metacognitive strategies for aiding recall (e.g., rehearsing aloud or grouping the key points to be remembered). The same is true for "thinking" and "concentrating" and "paying attention." Teachers tell students to "really think." What is the difference between "think" and "really think"? One first grade child thought "really think" meant to look seriously, as her teacher looked when studying her plan book.

The reason some students fail in school is not always because the material is too difficult, it is often because students are not taught how to become monitors and regulators of their own learning and classroom behaviors. One component of cognitive self-instruction as a teaching strategy, is to model learning and self-control for students by thinking aloud. The teacher allows the students to take a front row seat inside of his/her head. Teachers talk aloud as they demonstrate memorizing, comprehension monitoring, problem solving, and self-control of behavior, through self-verbalizations. Part of the difficulty is that these self-verbalizations for these processes have become automatic and routinized for most teachers. We are not fully aware of what it is we do cognitively when we learn and control our behavior. Therefore, as educators we have to reconnect with these cognitive behaviors in order to teach our students the cognitive steps we take when learning, whether it is for the purpose of recall, self-control, etc.

Cognitive self-instruction as a learning strategy occurs when students instruct themselves through speech-to-self during independent learning tasks. This self-instruction (Meichenbaum, 1977) includes problem definition, focusing attention, guiding, coping, and reinforcing self-statements and self-questions during independent cognitive assignments. Students are taught how to use cognitive self-instruction through teacher and peer modeling, student guided and independent practice, and teacher-student cueing. Therefore, cognitive self-instruction is a teaching and a learning system. It is hoped that via this book, I will provide a thorough knowledge base in both how to teach CSI and how to use it as a way to learn.

Part One

Theoretical and Conceptual Framework of Cognitive Self-Instruction

Overview of Part One

Part One is composed of five chapters that reflect a theoretical/conceptual framework of cognitive self-instruction. The topics presented in Part One are historical/theoretical perspectives, metacognition as a concept, types of other-regulation (i.e., dyadic instruction, cognitive behavior modification, informed training and reciprocal teaching), theories related to verbal self-regulation, and cognitive psychologies. This framework is presented to structure the understanding of CSI for classroom use. It is against this backdrop that CSI becomes more than isolated recipes for teaching methodology and curriculum.

1

Historical/Theoretical Perspectives of Cognitive Self-Instruction

Overview

Vygotsky's major goal was to develop a psychology of the mind. One aspect of this psychology is Vygotsky's theory of verbal self-regulation. Assumptions that are the building blocks of this theory are delineated. Definitions of the "zone of proximal development" and the "concept of verbal mediation," according to Vygotsky's writing are provided. Briefly, the contributions of A. R. Luria and A. N. Leont'ev, followers of Vygotsky, are described. These contributions are limited to those specific to understanding CSI.

Self-Questions

1. Knowledge. What year was Vygotsky born?

2. Comprehension. Explain the difference between the motoric and the semantic aspect of speech.

3. Application. Based on the motoric aspect of verbal self-regulation predict why restaurant owners who want customers to eat quickly might play rock music, and restaurant owners who want customers to linger and dine for a long time may choose slow, classical music.

4. Analysis. Describe the discrete stages in the development of verbal self-regulation, as outlined by Vygotsky. What is the significance of each stage?

5. Synthesis. Defend and refute the following statement: although Luria did not intend to stray from Vygotksy's major thesis of verbal self-regulation he, in fact, did.

6. Evaluation. In my opinion, was the work of Vygotsky-Luria-Leont'ev (a) psychological, (b) sociological, (c) anthropological, (d) combinations of "a," "b," and/or "c"? Document answer with specific reasons for my choice. If I choose "d," develop a term to describe this unique approach.

Lev Semenovich Vygotsky (1896–1934) considered language the substance of thought, which directs action. According to Vygotsky, meaningful words spoken to one's self guide and regulate human behavior. This idea is the key to understanding cognitive self-instruction.

After Vygotsky died, his work *Thought and Language* was published in Russian in 1934. It was not translated into English until 1962. Vygotsky's motivation was to describe a general theory of the development of the human mind. His ideas are complex, varied, and many. In this particular text, I am interested in describing how students direct their own learning as a result of social transactions in the school setting. Therefore, Vygotsky's ideas are restricted to those related to this goal.

Theory of Verbal Self-Regulation

The primary difference between humans and animals is that humans develop planful speech. In animals, thought and speech originate from different sources and develop differently. Koehler's experiments with apes substantiate that thinking in animals is not related to their speech. The ape language functions apart from the intellect. On the other hand Premack (1976) provides evidence of the ape's capacity to learn and use symbolic representations. Since 1976, even more advances have been made in understanding the language of apes and other animals that might produce a variety of opinion about the relationship between thought and speech in animals. However, because Vygotsky's focus on intentional self-guiding language is embedded in social context and spontaneity, it is doubtful that Vygotsky would change his claim that "The primary difference between humans and animals is that humans develop planful speech," regardless of these recent findings. To explicate further, the vocal reactions of apes are a part of emotionality—an emotional reaction that fulfills a biological and psychological need. However, these reactions are not at all akin to the purposeful verbalizations used by humans to inform and direct themselves.

The thought and speech of animals compared to humans have different genetic roots. During the entire life span, animals' thought and speech continue to develop independently of each other (biologically). In contrast the thought and speech of humans converge whereupon thought is verbal and speech is rational. There is a qualitative shift at this convergence point from biological to sociohistorical.

In childhood, there is evidence (Vygotsky, 1962) of a prespeech phase when thought is functional. The actions during the prespeech phase of thought development have been noted in the tenth, eleventh, and twelth months. Examples of prelinguistic thought are purposeful play with toys, planning motor functions such as crawling to a parent, throwing food on the floor.

In addition to the prelinguistic phase of thought, there is also the preintellectual phase of speech development. The child's word play, babbling, perhaps even first words repeated without thinking are examples of emotional forms of behavior, separated from the development of natural thought. Verbal thought is not predetermined (phylogenetically) but is dependent upon the specific social/linguistic history of each individual (ontogeny). This verbal thought is not subject to the characteristics preset in the natural forms of thought and speech. Knowing this helps us to understand the individuality of inner speech (thought) as it regulates and controls specific human behavior. Once we understand that our self-language possesses the power to motivate, guide, limit, control, and reinforce our actions, we have a concrete means for restructuring education.

The cognitive development of humans is determined by language, in particular the social/linguistic experiences of a child. The development of inner speech (verbal thought) is determined by outside factors. The outside factors are outside the natural development of the child, and are usually the social interactions between parent and child. Children's intellectual development is framed by the verbal environment created within the social transaction between adult and child. If children have parents who are excellent language users, who model verbal problem-solving, who cope and reinforce themselves verbally; then these children will be more advanced intellectually than those in a deprived verbal environment. "The speech structures mastered by children become the basic structures of their thinking" (Vygotsky, 1962, p. 51). This is similar to the idea that expressive language is influenced by receptive language—what goes in, comes out, or garbage in, garbage out! But Vygotsky takes this a step beyond, when he contends that the language of significant adults during the social/linguistic experiences of children becomes the means for children to verbally guide their own lives.

Speech becomes verbal thought through a development of three stages: external, egocentric, and inner speech. When children are born, they do not live alone. They develop in a typical social milieu of parents, grandparents, sisters, brothers, aunts, uncles, and cousins. These more experienced members of the family unit talk to the child, labeling the world and directing the child's activity. The child comes to know the world through the verbalizations of these others. The child is being externally directed through verbalizations. For example, the child soon learns that the configuration of sound "Come here" means a corresponding motoric reaction of walking toward the speaker. The child may come to associate car keys with the parent's directive, "It's time to go ride." The jingle of the keys may prompt the child to find his/her coat even without the usual parent verbal directive. When parents say "bath time," the child may start to shed clothes on the way to the tub. In any event the activity of the child is directed by the verbalizations of an external agent. This is what is termed the "External Stage" of Vygotsky's theory of verbal self-regulation (Stage 1).

The second stage of development is called the "Egocentric Stage." This is when children have internalized the parents' verbal messages in Stage 1 to the point that they are talking aloud to themselves. They are using words that strikingly resemble the parents' messages in Stage 1. This second stage has been referred to as the "Private Speech Stage." Private speech is defined as overt speech-to-self. Some researchers object to the name of this stage, "Egocentric," because it is confused with Piaget's meaning of egocentricism. In actuality it is far removed from Piaget's meaning that children see themselves as the center of the universe and are unable to role-take. Vygotsky was interested in the development of verbal self-regulation, instead. I will refer to Stage 2 as the "Private Speech Stage." Within this stage there are three substages. The progression of these stages illustrate the movement of the child from impulsivity to reflectivity. This progression is also an account of the term *internalization.* Internalization of the parent message into the cognitive constructs of the child's intellect begins during Stage 1. It is impossible to parcel out exactly when internalization begins and ends. Wertsch and Stone (1985) defined internalization as the relationship between external and internal activity when external activity is transformed into internal activity. The external verbal messages from others are internalized to become an integral part of children's internal cognitive directives.

In Stage 2, children first act and then describe their activity verbally.

Next, they act and talk to themselves aloud simultaneously. Finally, they verbally direct, then act in accordance with their verbal guidance. In Stage 2, all substages are in the form of overt self-verbalizations. The child is talking aloud. Gross predictions of age have been ages three (substage a), four (substage b), and five (substage c). Of course, as with any developmental theory, the specific ages are less important than the order of events.

To give several examples a child in substage 2a will go to a television, turn the knobs, step back, and tell him or herself "no," "no." This self-direction is actually the parent message which has been internalized by the child, from the External Stage. During substage 2b, the child goes to the television and tells him or herself "no," "no" while at the same time turning the knobs. Finally, in substage 2c, the child has the capability to go to the television, to say "no," "no" prior to turning the knobs, and to follow this self-direction accordingly.

Another example can be illustrated when asking children to draw a picture. A child in substage 2a will impulsively make scribble marks on the paper and then label the scribbles as "tree." A child in substage 2b will talk to self as he/she draws: "Here's a tree, a sky, under here, etc." A child in substage 2c will cognitively direct self prior to drawing anything, "Now, I will draw a tree, a house, and a bird on my paper." Only in the last instance is the child verbally planning the drawing. The child has moved from impulsivity (substage 2a) to purposeful, planned behavior based on self-verbalization (substage 2c). Stages 1 (External) and 2 (Private) are alike in the form of verbalizations: both are overt verbalizations. They differ in the source of control: Stage 1 is an external, other-regulation; whereas Stage 2 is self-regulated, overt speech-to-self.

Stage 3 is called "Internal Verbal Self-Regulation." In this stage the verbalizations have become covert. They are silent. It is important to note that mental problem-solving and verbal thought are occurring just as in Stage 2. However, the self-regulatory speech is now spoken inaudibly, rather than audibly. Vygotsky says that the speech-to-self has gone "underground." I prefer to think of it as taking a different form but being in every way just as instrumental in determining behavior outcomes. Therefore Stage 2 (Private) and 3 (Internal) are alike in that they both are characterized by verbal self-regulation of behavior. They differ because Stage 2 is overt; while, Stage 3 is covert speech-to-self.

To sum, the three stages of verbal self-regulation are external, egocentric (private speech), and internal. External is when children are regulated by the verbalizations of a more experienced member of society; private speech is when children talk aloud to themselves to bring behavior under verbal control. There are three substages in the private speech stage. First children act, then verbalize about the activity. Next they act and speak to themselves simultaneously. Finally they use self-verbalization in a purposeful, deliberate way to regulate their subsequent behavior. It is not until "2c" that children are exercising cognitive planning. In the final stage they continue to verbally regulate behavior; however, language to self is covert, silent, inhibited speech-to-self. Nonetheless, the power of self-verbalization is still operating in Stage 3 and planful thought is now inner speech.

When individuals are stressed or in disequilibrium, they revert to Stage 2, private overt speech and they talk aloud to attempt to establish equilibrium. Examples are "lost keys," "heavy traffic," or "finding a new location." In all three examples we often talk aloud to ourselves to regulate our behavior: "Where did I have those keys?" "Crazy drivers, look at that!" and "Where was I supposed to turn?" These verbalizations spoken to self are aides to equilibrium or problem resolution.

The progression through the stages is often referred to as movement from an interpsychological to an intrapsychological plane of functioning. In reality, I believe individuals move from intrapsychological, to interpsychological, back to intrapsychological during initial growth and development. To explain, first children are growing from a biological pre-set timetable in speech and thought (phylogenetically). They are very much "within themselves." This is the intrapsychological development. As children shift to the ontogenetic verbal thought as a result of social transaction, they also shift to an interpsychological plane. As they internalize the social messages needed to regulate behavior, they shift back to intrapsychological functioning.

It appears that the progression from intra- to inter- to intra- is more cyclical than linear. Throughout life as we interact with others, especially when learning a new area of study, we move from what we bring uniquely to the learning situation (intra), to what we learn from someone else (inter), back to how we internalize this information for ourselves (intra), to how this new internalized knowledge impacts on future social transactions (inter). This progression has implications for learning and teaching. It will be used for the foundation of cognitive self-instruction in classroom processes.

The major characteristic of verbal self-regulation is purposeful, self-directed speech aimed inward to promote human accomplishment of goals. Although there are many areas of confusion and disagreement about Vygotsky's theory of verbal self-regulation, one area of consensus has been goal-directed, planful behavior based on verbal thought. Inherent in the definition of verbal self-regulation has been the concept of goal-directedness. If a human purpose is not present, then another area of cognition is operating. Verbal self-regulation does not encompass the entire study of human cognition. It relates to the area of metacognition, rather than cognition. Metacognition is awareness and regulation of one's own thinking. Verbal self-regulation is intrapsychological awareness and control of human behavior via speech-to-self as a goal is sought. While studying this book, it is important to remember that verbal self-regulation is not referring to all of the mind's functioning. The characteristics to remember are awareness, purposeful self-directed speech on an intrapsychological plane aimed at goal achievement.

Zone of Proximal Development

The zone of proximal development as defined by Vygotsky in *Mind in Society* (1978, p. 86) is "the distance between the actual developmental level as determined by independent problem solving and the level of potential development as determined through problem solving under adult guidance or in collaboration with more capable peers."

This Vygotskian concept has important implications for parenting and teaching. Inherent in the definition is that instruction should precede cognitive developmental levels of children. This learning by social transaction is the means by which children reach higher, more abstract levels. These new levels create more awareness, consciousness, and control over the environment. Vygotsky promoted the idea that social interaction is the means to educating our young. He did not view "good learning" in the paradigm of children, left unaided, struggling to bring about sensible, rational answers that may be meaningless without adult explanation and guidance.

From a Vygotskian perspective, children advance in consciousness and control through the aid of adults and more competent peers. Bruner (1985, pp. 24–25) termed such aid "scaffolding." "The tutor in effect performs the critical function of scaffolding the learning task to make it possible for the child, in Vygotsky's word, to internalize external knowledge and convert it into a tool for conscious control." In this way knowledge and skills are mastered first in collaboration with others. Once the knowledge and skills are mastered, children internalize this information as part of their verbal thought. At this point children are able to use speech-to-self dialogues to exercise conscious control over new related learning. The child's language becomes a tool for further learning and deliberate control over the ever-widening environment.

Many researchers (e.g., Ann Brown, James Wertsch) used the "zone of proximal development" concept to formulate systems of educational evaluation and instruction. Brown encourages the use of the zone as an aspect of intelligence testing, beyond the usual way intelligence is tested (see Brown & Ferrara, 1985 for a complete discussion). She points out that a measure of intelligence is possible when child A (CA = 10; MA = 8) deals with problems up to a twelve year old level with adult guidance, and child B (CA = 10; MA = 8) only deals with problems up to an eight year old's level with the same adult guidance. This is a measure of the capability of children of the same chronological and mental age varying to a high degree under teacher guidance. Brown proposes that this capability with adult guidance becomes an added dimension to understand and assess learning potential. Traditional IQ measures do not indicate what a student may be capable of when learning is structured and/or aided by a more capable person. Since the instructional process in classrooms is often one of teachers structuring, guiding, and controlling the learning environment to insure optimal gain from learners, it would seem very important to know a student's potential for learning, when aided. As Brown and Ferrara (1985, p. 275) state; "the substantial improvement over initial response (working independently) that is achieved via the interaction of the adult and child (working jointly) is precisely what learning potential methods aim at measuring." These authors discuss three programs which address such an assessment of learning potential. These three programs are Feuerstein's Learning Potential Assessment Device (LPAD), Budoff's Learning Potential and Educability Program, and the Soviet clinical assessments of the zone of proximal development. Readers who wish to know the specifics of these programs are referred to the Brown and Ferrara (1985) reading.

Two important educational implications should be emphasized when considering the zone of proximal development. First, consideration should be given for using this idea in diagnostic intelligence testing previously discussed. Second, instruction should be aimed at the upper, not lower limits of a student's zone. If educational methods/curricula are reserved for only what students can perform independently, then they may be denied the challenge necessary for educational advancement. Both of these implications are extremely important for educational practice.

Concept of Mediation

Verbal mediation is the fundamental unit of analysis for cognitive self-instruction processes. For this book, mediation is word(s) spoken-to-self to reconcile between stimulus and response. In the case of tutors, the tutors' verbalizations can serve as a social mediator of learning. Later, the verbalizations of the tutor are internalized by the learner and become the learner's self-structures of mediation.

Vygotsky called word meanings, "psychological tools." For him, the word is a "symbol with a definite meaning that evolved in the history of culture" (Davydov & Radzikhovskii, 1985, p. 54). This approach enabled Vygotsky to add a third dimension to the S-R of behaviorism. The "psychological tools" were an intervening link in the behavioristic chain. Meaningful words serve as the determiner that mediates mental functions.

A. R. Luria and A. N. Leont'ev Contributions

The work of Vygotsky was disseminated by A. R. Luria (1902–1977) and A. N. Leont'ev (1904–1979). Luria is credited with bringing Vygotsky to the Western world. In addition, Luria tested the development of the "other- and self-regulated" motoric aspect of speech upon behavior in a laboratory setting.

In Luria's bulb-press experiments, children pressed a bulb as the experimenter issued commands to start, stop, or simultaneously press with a flashing light and/or with their own speech. Luria was able to document a stage-like progression of abilities from 1 1/2 to 5 1/2. At 1 1/2 to 2 1/2 there is: "1) the initiating function of speech by another person, but there is not yet the 2) inhibiting function of speech by another; and there are neither 3) initiating nor 4) inhibiting functions of children's own speech . . . at three to four years there are both initiating and inhibiting functions of another's speech and the initiating function of the children's own speech, but the inhibiting function of their own speech has not yet developed: they can do the two tasks the younger children failed . . . if the three or four year olds are asked to say, 'shall press twice', they will verbalize correctly, but make one protracted press that lasts for the duration of the utterance; on the other hand if they say 'Go! Go!' they will press correctly" (Zivin, 1979, pp. 31–32).

When children reach 4 1/2 to 5 1/2 Luria's experiments show that they can easily perform (1), (2), (3), and (4). They are then able to inhibit and initiate behavior response by means of the rhythmic motor patterns of speech spoken by others or by themselves (Luria, 1961). Therefore, Luria believes that by 4 1/2 to 5 1/2 children have fully transferred from the first to the second signal system. Once the control is apparent, Luria did not study silent verbal planning. His interest went in the direction of clinical study of how to reteach verbal control to patients who had lost this ability. Luria's experiments document the beginning of the internal stage of verbal self-regulation at age 5 1/2, while Vygotsky's naturalistic studies indicate age 8. This discrepancy is most likely due to the fact that the two men were studying two very different phenomena: Luria, the motoric and Vygotsky, the semantic, as well as two different research settings: Luria, the laboratory and Vygotsky, naturalistic, as well as two different forms of verbalizations: Luria, induced and Vygotsky, spontaneous.

The third member of the sociohistorical school with Vygotsky and Luria was Leont'ev. Leont'ev promotes that goal-directed activity is central to a cultural theory of cognition. Leont'ev believed that knowing human motivation is critical to understanding a culture's activities. He defines activity as "the goals, means, and constraints operating on a person" (Cole, 1985, p. 151). Leont'ev's contributions include illuminating the concept of activity that was previously "fuzzy" and also for demonstrating the weaknesses in Luria's cross-cultural research. In addition, he is credited with the Soviet theory of activity which has dominated the "major theoretical underpinnings for psychology in the USSR since 1969" (Wertsch, 1979, p. 85).

Cognitive Analysis: Definition of Terms

Bulb-press experiments Luria's laboratory experiments whereby children, ages $1^{1/2}$ to $5^{1/2}$, pressed a rubber bulb at the verbal command of the experimenter or themselves, or in rhythm with a flashing light, to initiate and inhibit motor behavior.

Covert speech-to-self Speech spoken silently to self. The form of speech in the third stage of Vygotsky's theory of verbal self-regulation.

Cultural theory of cognition This is another reference to Leont'ev's approach to Vygotsky's ideas. The concept of activity is the central thesis in this theory.

Disequilibrium This is a term used in Piagetian theory. For this book the term does not keep with a strict Piagetian definition. Here it simply means that an individual is not in a state of balance. Some factor has caused the individual to experience a feeling of maladjustment.

Equilibrium This is a term used in Piagetian theory. For this book, a strict Piagetian definition is not used. Here it simply means that an individual is in harmony with the forces present in his/her life. There is a balanced state between conflicting desire, interests, etc.

First signal system Pavlov (1927) termed as the perceptual signal system. This term is categorized as part of the Soviet theory of activity developed by Leont'ev. The way an infant responds to the environment which is conditioned by physical contingencies. The young reacts and controls behavior based on the physical properties of conditional stimuli such as touches, sights, and perceptible sounds of words (Zivin, 1979).

Goal-directed behavior Vygotsky's concept of speech-to-self is to direct one's behavior toward the accomplishment of a goal.

Impulse part of speech A synonym of the motoric aspect of speech. A stimulus transmitted in a muscle or nerve, which causes or inhibits activity in the body.

Inhibiting function of speech The power of verbalization to stop a behavior response. Luria used this function as one of the conditions in his bulb-press experiments.

Inner speech Covert speech-to-self, spoken silently to regulate behaviors. The inner speech form is used during the third stage of Vygotsky's theory of verbal self-regulation. Vygotsky says that the speech has gone "underground." During this stage the inner speech is considered "verbal thought." Inner speech continues to direct behavior even though the form now is covert, rather than overt.

Internalization The process by which children draw information into their existing cognitive structures. At this point they are able to use the knowledge to serve their individual purposes.

Interpsychological functioning When psychological functioning occurs between two people and one is being mediated by the other. The adult or more experienced member of the two is serving as a substitute cognitive guide for the less experienced learner. This interaction is on an interpsychological social plane. These interpsychological processes are the basis for higher mental processes in human learning.

Intrapsychological functioning This term was a part of Vygotsky's "general genetic law of cultural development." Any functioning within humans, including learning, first appears on a social plane between people and later within the human. When learning from social interactions is internalized, within the human, we say it has moved from an interpsychological plane to an intrapsychological plane. When the learning is internalized, (intrapsychological) the individual can now use it to govern his/her own environment. Therefore a transformation in structure and function occurs as the psychological function (e.g., voluntary attention, formation of concepts) goes to an intrapsychological plane.

Metacognition Mental awareness and regulation of one's own thinking (including cognitive, affective, and psychomotor mental activity). Flavell (1987) defines it as knowledge and cognition about anything cognitive (p. 21). One of my third graders defined it as "spying on your own thinking."

Motor system of speech A synonym of the "motoric aspect of speech."

Motoric aspect of speech The nerve carrying impulses from the central nervous system to a muscle producing motion. That part of speech which Luria studied in laboratory experiments; the rhythmic, excitation, physical aspect of verbalizations.

Neuropsychologist The branch of science dealing with disorders of both the mind and the nervous system integratively. A. R. Luria was called the greatest neuropsychologist of the twentieth century.

Ontogeny The life cycle of a single organism; development of the individual.

Other-regulation Much of learning occurs in the presence of others who promote cognitive advancement. Vygotsky argues that all psychological processes are initially social. This socialization/regulation by others before a child is able to gain conscious use of a particular bit of knowledge is referred to as "other-regulation." Other-regulation occurs on the interpsychological plane, prior to internalization of the knowledge by the learner. In addition, other-regulation occurs in the first stage of Vygotsky's theory of verbal self-regulation.

Other-regulated motoric aspect of speech When the motoric aspect of speech originates from an external agent. The external agent's verbalizations regulate the motor response of someone else.

Overt speech-to-self Speech spoken aloud to self. The form of speech in the second stage of Vygotsky's theory of verbal self-regulation.

Physical/regulatory effect upon motor behavior Another way of referring to Luria's focus on the motoric aspect of speech as it inhibits and initiates behavior. The physical/regulatory effect refers implicitly to overt, verbal regulation from the excitation, rhythmic part of speech as it impacts on an inhibitory or initiatory motor response.

Phylogeny The racial history of evolutionary development of any plant or animal species.

Planful speech Goal-directed speech spoken to oneself. Private or inner speech that purposefully guides, directs, and controls human activity. According to Vygotsky the most important means for self-regulation is through self-directed or planful speech.

Preintellectual speech Speech without thought. Examples are babbling, crying, and word play.

Prelinguistic thought Thought without the regulation of word meanings. Examples are purposeful play with toys, planned motor functions such as crawling to a parent, or throwing food on the floor.

Private speech The second stage of Vygotsky's theory of verbal self-regulation. During this stage children talk aloud (overt self-verbalizations) to regulate behavior. There are three developmental substages: a) children act first and then speak b) children act and speak simultaneously and c) children speak first and then act in accordance with their own verbal directions. These verbal self-directions are a result of internalized parent verbal messages received during Stage 1, the External Stage. It is not until substage "c" that the child's overt speech-to-self is serving a planning function.

Scaffolding Jerome Bruner's term used to describe how the more experienced member of a social team structures learning tasks to promote higher mental processes. In Vygotsky's terms, scaffolding causes internalization of external knowledge as it is transformed into mediation for conscious regulation by the learner.

Second signal system Pavlov (1927) termed this system the "linguistic signal system." This term is categorized as part of the Soviet theory of activity developed by Leont'ev. When the meaning of words becomes understood to the point that individuals can use their own spoken words to guide behavior. The second signal system begins when verbal self-regulation directs purposeful goal-oriented activity.

Self-regulated motoric aspect of speech When the motoric aspect of speech originates from individuals whose behavior is being regulated by their physical act of speaking.

Self-regulation Although much initial learning originates in the context of the social setting; "continuous adjustments and fine-tuning of action occurs via self-regulating processes" (Marshall & Morton, 1978, p. 227). Self-regulation occurs in the second and third stages of Vygotsky's theory of verbal self-regulation. After internalization of parent messages, the child has moved to the intrapsychological plane of functioning and is capable of verbal self-regulation.

Semantic aspect of speech The meaning factor of verbalization; that part of speech which Vygotsky studied, mainly during spontaneous, natural occurrences.

Social-cultural/historical This term is in reference to Vygotsky's explanation for the psychological development of the mind. It refers to the context in which intellect is born. It is where nature meets nurture, and there is a qualitative shift to a higher plane of mental functioning in light of the social context of interaction.

Social/linguistic experiences These experiences are comprised of an individual's social, verbal interactions with the more experienced members of a culture. It is through these verbal dyads that children initially develop their knowledge of the world.

Social transactions The interaction between the more experienced members of society and the learner. According to Vygotsky social transaction is the vehicle through which individuals are able to move from a lower to a higher level of mental functioning.

Theory of verbal self-regulation Another name for Vygotsky's theory. It means the conscious awareness and control of one's actions or behavior through the medium of word meanings spoken initially by others, internalized, and spoken later by the child, first overtly and then covertly. The child's overt and covert verbal messages to self have a regulatory effect upon his or her own behavior.

Verbal mediation The use of words to intervene between stimulus and response for the learner. Lee (1985) explains how words can be mediators: "Speech is reversible because words can be both stimulus (heard word) and response (spoken word is a reflex producing the same stimulus)" (p. 76). Lee says that the first property of language is a "mediating device" (p. 76).

Vocalized speech Egocentric speech (private speech) is in the form of vocalized speech. It is audible speech spoken by self. In addition vocalized speech may be spoken by others. Luria's studies were confined to the study of vocalized speech.

Zone of proximal development "The distance between the actual developmental level as determined by independent problem solving and the level of potential development as determined through problem solving under adult guidance or in collaboration with more capable peers," (Vygotsky, 1978, p. 86).

Cognitive Synthesis: A Summary

One aspect of Vygotsky's notion of cognitive development is the theory of verbal self-regulation. As per this theory the sociolinguistic experiences of children are internalized by the children and used later as cognitive self-guides. Therefore, individuals' ability to serve as competent cognitive self-guides is dependent upon the linguistic richness and social soundness of a particular individual's history. Students in school who lack the ability to direct themselves at developmentally appropriate times may be suffering from a lack of qualitatively rich, sociolinguistic experiences in their past. Teachers may need to fill this gap by serving in the role of a strong verbal mediator and emotional supporter for these children until such students have sufficient direction to be enabled to internalize the teacher mediation for their own use as a cognitive guide. Without such social and linguistic support, some students may be deficient in school autonomy and social responsibility.

2

Metacognition

Overview

In chapter 2, Flavell's definitions, concept, and taxonomy of metacognition are described. Components are metacognitive knowledge and metacognitive experiences. These divisions are explained, defined, analyzed, and applied via real-life examples. A detailed explanation of the five situations which promote metacognitive experiences are provided. The final section is a discussion of comprehension monitoring, a metacognitive skill.

Self-Questions

1. Knowledge. Name the two major divisions of Flavell's taxonomy of the metacognitive domain.

2. Comprehension. Define the person variable of metacognitive knowledge.

3. Application. Give three personal examples of intraindividual-person variable illustrating metacognitive knowledge.

4. Analysis. Draw a schematic rendition of Flavell's taxonomy.

5. Synthesis. Provide an example of an interaction among person, task, and strategy (metacognitive knowledge) variables.

6. Evaluation. In two paragraphs, (1) evaluate Flavell's impact on the domain of metacognition and (2) predict future research trends and questions related to metacognition.

When Flavell and his colleagues conducted their metamemory studies in the early 1970s, the term *metamemory* was introduced. As a result of this introduction, the term *metacognition* became popular around 1975 (Brown, 1987). Flavell became known as the founding father of the concept "metacognition." He defines metacognition initially as "knowledge and cognition about cognitive objects, that is, about anything cognitive" (Flavell, 1987, p. 21).

Flavell's Concept of Metacognition

Flavell (1987) states that metacognition can reasonably include anything (1) psychological, (2) any kind of monitoring, and perhaps even (3) processes that are not on a conscious level. An example of (1) psychological is cognition about emotions or feelings; an example of (2) monitoring is cognition about a motor activity, such as dancing; an example of (3) the lack of consciousness level is cognitive self-regulation activities occurring without conscious awareness. Therefore metacognition, according to Flavell, is broadened to mean knowledge and cognitions about cognitive, affective, perceptual, or motor human characteristics.

Flavell created a taxonomy for the domain of metacognition. The two main categories are metacognitive knowledge and metacognitive experience. The following section will include the details of this taxonomy.

Flavell's Taxonomy of Metacognition

Flavell first divides metacognition into metacognitive knowledge and metacognitive experience. Metacognitive knowledge is "one's acquired world knowledge that has to do with cognitive matters" (Flavell, 1987, p. 21).

Metacognitive knowledge is further divided into three categories: person, task, and strategy knowledge. Each will be discussed separately, even though they interact within individuals.

Person variables refer to one's knowledge about what individuals are like as cognitive organisms. There are yet three more categories to explain person variables: intraindividual, interindividual, and universal. An intraindividual-person variable occurs within persons. For example, knowing that you are better at math than reading is an example of an intraindividual-person-metacognitive-knowledge subcategory. It is knowing yourself as a thinker. Interindividual variables are comparisons between, rather than within, individuals. Examples are knowing you are better at math than the teacher, or that your teacher is more reflective than the principal. The final subcategory, universal variables, is the acquired knowledge we gain from living within a culture. Flavell believes that human beings universally acquire metacognitive knowledge about people such as, the concept of a mistake, thinking there is understanding and later finding out there is not, knowing that short-term memory is of limited capacity. He believes that knowing such universal phenomena aids management of our lives.

The second category related to metacognitive knowledge has to do with task variables. Individuals acquire knowledge about the demands, effects, and constraints of cognitive tasks. The nature of the task dictates certain cognitive rules. For example, if the information is difficult, dense, and without much repetition the learner knows "to proceed more carefully, slowly, and to process deeply and self-critically" (Flavell, 1987, p. 22). Individuals learn that different kinds of cognitive tasks require different kinds of processing on their part. Flavell says that people learn which task demands are more rigorous, take this into account, and process accordingly to achieve the task goal. Some people do learn to respond to their knowledge of task variables; however, others do not. Many students are deficient in just this type of skill. I am not at all sure they would ever "acquire" this metacognitive knowledge, without instruction. However, most teachers lack the teacher preparation required to teach these skills. Flavell recommends that metacognition be practiced. "Teachers in schools may sometimes model, as well as teach and encourage, metacognitive activity" (p. 26). The critical word here is *may*. Teachers *must* model metacognitive strategies in a deliberate, informed way before some students will master metacognitive processes that are so essential to classroom learning. It is too important to be left to happenstance. Ann Brown (1987) states that all learning involves cognitive self-regulation (an aspect of metacognition). If all learning involves cognitive self-regulation and teachers are not taught how to foster it, then this may explain why many children become poor students—perhaps drop-outs—and become less than productive, contributing members of society. I am convinced that this is one of the missing educational links that prevents learning success for too many of our youngsters.

The third metacognitive knowledge variable is strategy variables. Strategy variables are the knowledge of how to proceed with a task—how to accomplish the goal. Flavell (1981) distinguishes between cognitive and metacognitive strategies. This distinction has been a source of difficulty in the study of metacognition. Flavell (1987, p. 23) provides the following definitions of cognitive and metacognitive strategies: "A cognitive strategy is one designed simply to get the individual to some cognitive goal or subgoal, such as adding numbers; whereas the metacognitive strategy is for monitoring cognitive progress, such as reading the numbers to check the answer." The term *cognitive monitoring* has been used synonymously with metacognitive strategy variables. More recently the term *strategic knowledge* is used to refer to this same mental process. One third grader defined cognitive monitoring as "spying on your own thinking." Other definitions used by elementary youngsters are as follows: "knowing yourself as a thinker," "getting in touch with your own thinking," and "policing your own head stuff."

In reality, person, task, and strategy variables interact. For example, I may decide to use one strategy rather than another strategy (strategy variable) to solve the complicated word problem (task variable) because I am not as proficient in mathematics as I am in spelling assignments (intraindividual person variable). This metacognitive knowledge enables one to process, study, store, and retrieve information in more productive ways. Adequate metacognitive knowledge provides an explanatory distinction between effective and ineffective learning.

In addition to metacognitive knowledge, Flavell names a second major concept in the taxonomy, (i.e., metacognitive experiences). Metacognitive experiences are defined as conscious realization or awareness of one's own cognition, most frequently a current, ongoing one.

Examples of metacognitive experiences:

1. Reading a whole page and suddenly realizing you are not comprehending a single word. (The realization, when you tell yourself that comprehension is lacking, constitutes the metacognitive experience.)

2. Driving a familiar route and then suddenly realizing you do not remember driving through a certain town. (This is a scary experience: you wonder who was driving and you hope there are not others on the road like you.)

3. Adding a column of numbers and becoming aware that you need to recheck. You think you have made an error. (Frequently, you have correctly analyzed that an error has occurred, without being told from an external source.)

4. Typing and you suddenly know you've made an error. (How do you know an error has occurred when your eyes are not even looking at what you are typing? You know because your mind's eye was checking for accuracy.)

5. Hearing the professor's (or parent's or teacher's) voice and then realizing that you do not know what is being discussed. (I tell college stu-

dents that one of the first skills a college student learns is how to "appear interested." Their minds may be on the weekend but their body language says, "I'm listening." Some elementary teachers corrected me when they pointed out that occasionally elementary students, beginning as early as third grade, have acquired the skill of "appearing to be interested." Perhaps this skill is not unique to college students. In any event, metacognitive processes are required to keep the face and body attentive; while the mind is off in another direction.)

6. Saying a word or answering a question you did not know you knew until the word or answer came from your mouth and realizing that you were unaware of knowing that particular piece of information. (This "sensation" also happens when you are cleaning out old test papers and you reread your answers.)

The realization or cognitive awareness serves as the metacognitive signal. Once individuals have the signal they can ignore it or translate it into self-regulation. Cognitive self-instruction is aimed at teaching students to heed their metacognitive signals and to translate them into self-directed learning techniques. An implicit forerunner to this is teaching students to become adept at cognitive monitoring. One place to begin is to know when metacognitive experiences are likely to occur. To paraphrase Flavell (1987, p. 28), these experiences are most likely when (1) the situation requires them (e.g., someone is asked to give a rationale for his/her lesson plan), (2) the cognitive task is somewhere between totally unfamiliar and totally familiar. "Totally unfamiliar" relates to those times when we say "I didn't even know enough to ask a question" and "totally familiar" situations are when we are so familiar with something that it has become automatic and effortless. An example that comes to mind is when individuals commute for a long period of time and their driving becomes automatic and routinized. This is why we may not recall driving through a particular town on our commute route. We have stopped monitoring our driving. Other situations provoking cognitive monitoring are (3) when it is important to make correct responses (if individuals know that their decisions are crucial they are more likely to monitor them) and (4) when individuals are in disequilibrium. An example is trying to find lost keys and monitoring cognitively every place you have been with your keys. Other examples, fraught with disequilibrium, are following a rather complex recipe, losing your way on the expressway, realizing the test is not what you studied, and trying to find the right words to mend a damaged relationship; (5) attention and motivation are not clouded by overriding physical or emotional states, such as pain, anxiety, grief, panic, or depression. Most of us are keenly aware that cognitive monitoring is diminished if we are dealing with the death of a loved one, or with physical pain such as a ruptured disc. In most cases, our energies are directed toward grief or pain, not toward monitoring our own cognition.

Comprehension Monitoring

Comprehension monitoring is defined as "awareness and regulation of one's own listening and/or reading comprehension." Flavell (1977, p. 178) said "there is a need to engage in comprehension monitoring for reading or for actively trying to comprehend and remember what someone just said . . . In life adults and children are constantly receiving messages of all kinds . . . Children do little or no thinking about the cognitive interpretations the message may stimulate, or about the possible relationship between message and interpretation." Comprehension monitoring has become a well-researched area, although researchers have not always used this term. Indeed some researchers (e.g., Paris, Cross, & Lipson, 1984) list fourteen different comprehension strategies (e.g., locating main ideas) as metacognitive that in some cases seem more cognitive than metacognitive if Flavell's conceptual model is followed.

Cognitive Analysis: Definition of Terms

Cognitive monitoring Awareness and regulation of one's own cognition.

Cognitive strategies Designed to reach cognitive goals or subgoals (e.g., answering a test question).

Comprehension monitoring Used by Ellen Markman in her research with elementary students. The term means the deliberate cognitive processing of information as it is heard or read. This processing requires self-awareness, self-questioning, and self-regulation. The term has been stretched to include reading skills that are questionable, concerning their classification as a metacognitive skill, rather than a cognitive one.

Knowledge-about-one's-own-cognition Awareness, knowing about one's own cognition; stable and statable; within Flavell's construct it involves person, task, and strategy variables and the interactions between and among the three variables. For an example, Flavell and Wellman (1977) suggested that information recalled depends on who learned it (Person x Task), whether studying aloud or whispering is best for him or her (Person *x* Strategy) and the learning tasks (e.g., essay or short-answer) he or she must recite or put into writing (Person *x* Strategy *x* Task).

Metacognition "Knowledge and cognition about cognitive objects, that is, about anything cognitive" (Flavell, 1987, p. 21). Knowledge and cognitions about cognitive, affective, perceptual, or motoric human characteristics.

Metacognitive experience Conscious realization or awareness of one's own cognition, most frequently a current, ongoing one.

Metacognitive knowledge "One's acquired world knowledge that has to do with cognitive matters" (Flavell, 1987, p. 21).

Metacognitive strategies Designed to monitor cognitive progress (e.g., realizing the test question is too difficult).

Person variables Refers to one's metacognitive knowledge about what individuals are like as cognitive organisms. There are three subcategories of person variables: (a) intraindividual—cognitions within yourself, about your own specific cognitive functioning, (b) interindividual—comparison between or among individuals about each person's cognitive abilities, (c) universal—acquired knowledge about the universal "truths" of cognitive functioning (e.g., understanding what it means to make a mistake).

Regulation-of-one's-own-cognition Relatively unstable, not necessarily statable, age independent, task and situation dependent; it is the overseeing and control of one's own learning. Brown called this a "process term" and it involved such skills as planning ahead, monitoring, resource allocation, self-questioning, self-directing, checks, etc.

Statable One of the characteristics of metacognitive knowledge about one's own cognition; it is not considered "knowledge" unless individuals can reflect on their own cognitive processes and be able to articulate these processes to someone else in a meaningful manner. The other characteristic is that this knowledge remains stable (constant and predictable).

Strategy variables Refers to one's metacognitive knowledge of how to proceed to accomplish a goal.

Task variables Refers to one's metacognitive knowledge about the demands, effects, constraints (characteristics) of cognitive tasks.

Cognitive Synthesis: A Summary

John Flavell set the wheels in motion for the growth of the metacognitive domain. When he introduced metacognition, psychologists began to research the ideas Flavell formulated. This body of research was innovative, and resulted in the analysis of metacognition. In this chapter, Flavell's conceptual scheme is described. His taxonomy of the metacognitive domain sets the stage for classroom application. The application promotes development of metacognitive skills. These skills are essential and heretofore have not been required in educational settings. This is not to say that metacognitive skills are not emphasized by teachers. Teachers have been emphasizing careful monitoring of school tasks for as long as there have been teachers. However, it was often happenstance and intuitive. There are two major reasons why teachers need to have knowledge of metacognitive teaching procedures and curriculum. First, these skills are too important to be left to happenstance and intuition. Second, we know so much more now about self-directed teaching and self-regulated learning that it seems unfair not to pass this knowledge on to the many students who need these skills. Our teachers and our students deserve to have information that has the potential to improve teaching and learning. Cognitive monitoring is prerequisite to cognitive self-instruction. The monitoring sets up mental awareness. Subsequent self-instruction is based on this mental awareness.

3

Other-Regulation

Overview

Self-regulation is the focus of this book. However, it is important to note that much learning occurs through the guidance, direction, and support of others. This type guidance is referred to as "other-regulation," which implies transformation from other to self-regulation. The types of intervention categorized in this chapter as "other-regulation" are proleptic/dyadic instruction, cognitive behavior modification, informed training, and reciprocal teaching. These are examples and not a finite list of other-regulation interventions. Each of the other-regulation examples are described in light of CSI in the classroom.

Self-Questions

1. Knowledge. State the definition of cognitive behavior modification.

2. Comprehension. Explain the concept of other-regulation.

3. Application. Provide a classroom, clinic, and/or home example where I would use proleptic or dyadic instruction. Why would this be an effective approach for my particular example? In the literature, find another example of other-regulation, as defined in this chapter.

4. Analysis. Write a lesson plan using all the components of reciprocal teaching. Label the components.

5. Synthesis. Write a proposed research study using informed training as an important thrust.

6. Evaluation. Support the use of cognitive behavior modification with regular education, average learners rather than a clinical population.

Parents, teachers, and knowledgeable peers structure learning tasks (formal and informal) to promote mastery of a task. Bruner (1985) refers to this process of structuring learning for someone else as scaffolding. Wertsch (1978) and others (e.g., Brown & French, 1979) conducted research concerned with the social interactional origins of problem-solving abilities. Wertsch was interested in the origination and development of children's problem-solving abilities. In addition, Wertsch and Stone (1979) provided a social interactional analysis of learning disabilities remediation. They combined Vygotsky's theoretical framework, discussed in chapter 1, with metacognitive development involving the strategy variable of metacognitive knowledge (Flavell, chapter 2).

Inherent within the definition of other-regulation is the progression from other-regulation to self-regulation. The research conducted on "other-regulation" rests within the framework of Vygotsky's (1978) theory of internalization. That is, that all cognitive/psychological processes begin as social exchanges, particularly between child and parent, or child and teacher. This interpersonal aspect of thought development is transferred to a qualitatively different form of thought, to an intrapersonal basis. This transformation from an interpsychological to an intrapsychological plane of functioning is, for Vygotsky, the fundamental process of cognitive development. Thus, this development is contingent upon the quality, the richness, of the linguistic experience between child and parent, child and teacher. It is this dyadic experience that Wertsch researched.

Wertsch (1978, 1979) investigated mother-child dyads. The mothers were viewed as change agents, responsible for questioning and regulating the child's activities. The mother's regulatory/structuring roles of the child's environment promoted the child's internalizations of the regulatory parent processes. This enables the child to gradually assume self-regulation. It follows then that the quality of these interactions are extremely important, because under these systems of guidance from others, the child learns "not only how to get a particular task done independently, but also learns how to set about learning new problems," using similar strategies. "In other words, the child learns how to learn" (Brown, Bransford, Ferrara, & Campione, 1983, p. 124). If the reader who is just beginning to study in this area is saying "These comments also remind me of the notion of the zone of proximal development," you are monitoring your comprehension quite well! Congratulations. The zone is the distance between what the child is able to perform independently and what he or she is able to perform with other-regulation. Therefore, the zone of proximal development is a related concept of other-regulation.

Proleptic/Dyadic Instruction

Wertsch and Stone (1979), during social interactional analysis of learning disabilities remediation, examined other-regulation that occurs on the interpsychological plane. Wertsch and Stone also analyzed independent strategic functioning that occurred later on the intrapsychological plane. They did this by drawing the learning-disabled students into a communicative situation built around a problem-solving task. Initially the actions of the child were regulated by the verbalizations of the clinician with a gradual transfer of regulation to the child (self-regulation). They called this type of interaction "proleptic instruction" (p. 18). Wertsch and Stone (1979) suggested that educators who teach learning-disabled students view learning disabilities as metacognitive in nature, because the learning-disabled child seems to lack many cognitive and linguistic strategies. In addition many children, regardless of exceptionality, lack these same strategies. They are sitting in regular classrooms, often with an educator who assumes (in good faith) that children know much more than they actually do about learning and how to learn, how to study, what it means to concentrate and so forth. These children need "proleptic instruction" as well.

Cognitive Behavior Modification (CBM)

In 1971, Meichenbaum and Goodman developed a training package to teach impulsive children to talk to themselves as a means of developing self-control. This program was extremely successful in reducing impulsivity and promoting reflectivity which in turn fostered self-control. Meichenbaum (1984) sees this program as the joining of those who had studied impulsive children in laboratories (e.g., Kanfer & Zich, 1974; Patterson & Mischel, 1976) with the theoretical framework of social learning theory, verbal mediation, and Soviet psychology. About this same time, behavior management procedures, such as operant conditioning applied to classroom management and known as behavior modification, were failing to promote lasting improvements that would generalize to situations other than the trained ones. Therefore, it was Meichenbaum's hope that adding a cognitive element to behavior modification could provide efficient generalizability and enduring improvements in behavior. Thus his cognitive intervention program became known as cognitive behavior modification

(CBM). CBM means altering the behavior of individuals via their own cognitions. In this case the cognition is speech-to-self. Meichenbaum believes that by teaching self-regulatory cognitive skills, the intervention will have greater influence than shaping the child's environment. According to Meichenbaum (1984) the goal is to instruct children in self-regulatory skills to control their own behavior more effectively in a variety of settings.

The focus of CBM is to teach children how to think, not what to think. The CBM self-instructional strategies were geared toward teaching children to spontaneously produce and use cognitive strategies and self-instructions. Meichenbaum defines self-instruction as verbalizations and images to oneself that initiate, guide, or maintain one's own nonverbal behavior. Said another way, the self-instructional CBM training aims at teaching children to employ verbal mediation responses that represent a general strategy for regulating one's own behavior under various situations. The following procedural steps are included (Meichenbaum, 1977, p. 32):

1. An adult model performs a task while talking to self aloud (cognitive modeling);

2. The child performs the same task under the direction of the model's instructions (overt, external guidance);

3. The child performs the task while instructing self aloud (overt self-guidance);

4. The child whispers the instructions to self as he/she goes through the task (faded, overt self-guidance), and finally

5. The child performs the task while guiding his/her performance via private speech (covert self-instruction).

Inherent within CBM is cognitive performance skill such as (1) problem definition ("what is it I have to do?"); (2) focusing attention and response guidance ("carefully... draw the line down"); (3) self-reinforcement ("good, I'm doing fine"); (4) self-evaluative coping skills and error-correcting options ("That's okay . . . even if I make an error I can go on slowly") (Meichenbaum, 1977, p. 32).

Meichenbaum's cognitive behavior modification approach is an innovative method for altering impulsivity, to help children learn to bring their behavior under their own cognitive control. The CBM approach has been extremely successful in helping various populations learn to think before they act. These individuals then have a cognitive strategy that can bring benefits to them for a lifetime. The individuals are taught and learn to help themselves, rather than having to be dependent upon an external agent.

Informed Training

The term *informed training* was derived from research studies in which subjects were provided information about the reason for, and expected benefits/outcomes of the instructed procedures. The result of informed training was that subjects were more likely to transfer the training benefits to other tasks or settings. Brown, Campione, and Day (1981) define informed training as the intermediate levels of instruction. Examples of studies where subjects have been informed about the significance of the procedures are Burger, Blackmon, Holmes, and Zetlin (1978) with retarded children and Ringel and Springer (1980) with children in regular classes.

Those of us in regular education may be reminded of an educational given: providing our students with "a purpose," the reason for learning certain concepts. Based on the results gained from "informed training" (Brown, Bransford, Ferrara, & Campione, 1983), this educational practice is a sound one.

Other characteristics of informed training may include (1) indirectly informing, or (2) successful strategy use during the time of training, or (3) checking for metacognitive awareness of strategy benefits during the instructional program. Brown et al. (1983) indicate the benefits of informing subjects indirectly about the many uses of a strategy. Therefore, a given strategy is demonstrated across a variety of contexts. It seems that when subjects could see more than one context use they were better able to transfer this skill to an untrained context (Belmont, Butterfield, & Borkowski, 1978). As with other informed training studies, when subjects were required to show mastery of a strategy during training, they were able to use the strategy longer. This practice is closely akin to guided practice sessions in direct instruction approaches. Finally, metacognitive awareness of strategy benefits may be the reason the informed subjects continue to use a strategy after training.

There are multiple components constituting informed training programs. Because of this multidimensionality it is often difficult to know which factor made the difference. Theoretically it is important to know which aspect is contributing the most to the success. However, educationally speaking, if an intervention reaps positive results, multicomponents or not, the intervention is educationally important "in its own right" (Brown et al., 1983, p. 135).

Reciprocal Teaching

Since the early 1980s, Ann Brown and Annemarie Sullivan Palincsar have investigated a strategy they call "reciprocal teaching." Reciprocal teaching is interactive dialogue between teachers and students in the area of reading.

Eventually students serve in the role of "the teacher." Then, peer tutoring with peer modeling of comprehension strategies become the techniques. The procedure is similar to Wertsch's proleptic/dyadic instruction in philosophical/theoretical underpinnings. However, in reciprocal teaching, the verbal exchange is not necessarily one on one and not necessarily in a clinical setting. In fact, reciprocal teaching most often occurs in the context of a reading group in a school setting. The teacher and students are jointly arriving at comprehension of the text via teacher–student and student–student dialogue. The teacher or more capable peer structures the students' learning through four strategies (Palincsar, 1986, p. 119):

1. Summarizing: identifying and paraphrasing the main idea in the text.
2. Question-Generating: self-questioning about the type of information that is generally tapped on tests of comprehension and recall.
3. Clarifying: discerning when there has been a breakdown in comprehension and taking the necessary action to restore meaning (e.g., reading ahead, rereading, asking for assistance).
4. Predicting: hypothesizing what the structure and content of the text suggest will be presented next.

Early research studies on reciprocal teaching have involved junior high students enrolled in remedial reading classes. More recent studies have involved other ages (e.g., first graders). Accounts of the first studies of reciprocal teaching can be found in Brown and Palincsar (1982) and Palincsar and Brown (1984).

Cognitive Analysis: Definition of Terms

Behaviorism Evolved from Pavlov's classical conditioning and Skinner's operant conditioning: what one learns is shaped by the environment; there is no inner rational person.

Clinical intervention Research studies conducted in a laboratory setting, usually involving the researcher and one subject. The laboratory is a place that is not a typical setting for the subject.

Cognitive behavior modification The alteration of one's behavior through a cognitive training program of five steps which moves the trainee from external guidance to covert self-guidance.

Cognitive modeling Modeling one's own cognition to enact for the learner a thinking process by talking aloud to accomplish, to guide, to cope, and to reinforce self. The model serves as one example of how to cognitively perform a task.

Cognitive semanticists Psychologists who focus on the impact of meaningful verbalizations upon behavior, usually spoken by an individual to him or herself. According to Meichenbaum, George Kelley, Albert Ellis, Aaron Beck, and Jerome L. Singer are considered cognitive-semantic therapists.

Dyadic instruction Synonymous with proleptic instruction. Used during Wertsch's research: mothers were viewed as change agents, responsible for questioning and regulating the child's activities. The characteristics of this regulation affected the child's ability to assume self-regulation.

Dyads Two units regarded as one; pair. From a Wertsch perspective it was an adult and child working together on a problem-solving task.

Enduring improvements Improvements from training, treatment, or instruction that last over a period of time; maintenance effects. Meichenbaum checked for maintenance of self-instruction after one month (1971).

Generalizable improvement Transfer of improvements from the trained tasks or setting to a different task(s) or setting(s).

Imagery Visualization of a situation through visual images created in the mind by the learner.

Impulsivity A sudden inclination to act and then acting without conscious thought. Meichenbaum trained impulsive children how to become more reflective.

Informed strategy training This is explicit training whereby teachers inform students what the strategies are, how they are applied, why they are important, and under what conditions (when) to use them. Teachers try directly to convince students that they should implement the strategies.

Interactive teaching Face-to-face communication, usually including both verbal and nonverbal communication involving one to one or one to many. Interactive teaching as related to metacognition has been labeled (e.g., proleptic, dyadic, mediated learning, participant modeling instruction, and expert scaffolding) by a variety of researchers. This approach, in light of metacognition, involves modeling with teacher explanations and teacher support, as the student is urged to move gradually from other-regulation to self-regulation.

Multiple component instructional program A package of instruction that includes a variety of techniques that are distinctly different one from the other.

Therefore, when benefits are realized from such a program it is not known which component contributed the most (or perhaps, all) to this success.

Nonclinical intervention Research studies conducted in a setting that is usually familiar and typical for the subject. The study may involve one to one or one to many.

Other-regulation The guidance and structuring of a learning task by an adult or more capable peer for the learner. This regulation by others appears on the interpsychological plane and fosters the qualitative shift to self-regulation of learning, which occurs on the intrapsychological plane.

Predicative characteristic of private speech A form of abbreviation: namely, omitting the subject of a sentence and all words connected with it, while keeping the predicate.

Proleptic instruction A communicative, verbal exchange built around a problem-solving task between adult and child. Wertsch used this type of instruction with learning-disabled children. Initially the actions of the child were regulated by the verbalization of the clinician with a gradual transfer of regulation to the child.

Psychosocial The branch of psychology dealing with the functional relations between the social history of an individual and that individual's development of the mind.

Reciprocal teaching. A term used by Annemarie Palincsar and Ann Brown to refer to an innovative tutoring strategy whereby teachers and students assume the role of "the teacher." Therefore, peer tutoring is a characteristic of reciprocal teaching. The adult or student "teacher model" aids learners in the internalization of similar comprehension strategies.

Reflectivity The condition of being thoughtful prior to acting. A reflective person is able to create more distance between stimulus and response by the act of reflection, than is an impulsive person who moves quickly from stimulus to response.

Self-statements Statements representing meaningful wholes are spoken to self. Self-statements are one component of self-instructions.

Self-instructions To instruct oneself using statements and questions to self in the areas of problem defining, focusing attention, self-reinforcement, and self-evaluative coping (Meichenbaum, 1977).

Self-instructional strategies Strategies which Meichenbaum used in his CBM training. Clients learned to instruct themselves using self-statements and imagery, following an adult cognitive model.

Self-regulatory skills Skills that impact on one's own learning. Overseeing the development and growth of one's own learning; please also refer to "regulation-of-one's-own-cognition," a synonym. Examples of self-regulatory skills are to plan, select, connect, and monitor effective strategies for learning (Corno & Mandinach, 1983).

Semantic Of meaning, especially meaning in language communication.

Social learning theory Theory that extended traditional learning theory by postulating that social behaviors could also be explained by the principles of learning, including observational learning (Bandura, 1977).

Social origins of intellect Our intelligence develops out of the social interactions characterizing our lives; Vygotsky's explanation of intellectual development.

Strategic reading activities Brown used this term to refer to techniques or procedures taught to learners to increase their ability to understand what they have read. In this context, she was arguing that such strategies had been around and referred to by such people as Dewey (1910) long before the term *metacognition* was available.

Subvocal Inaudible verbalizations.

Syntax The arrangement of words as units in a sentence to express relationship, sentence structure.

Cognitive Synthesis: A Summary

The concept of other-regulation implies a gradual progression from other-regulation to self-regulation. The adult or more experienced learner structures the task verbally and nonverbally for the less experienced learner. This "guided practice" period of time is critical to what the learner will be able to perform independently. The guided practice by others is conducted to insure that the learner is understanding the task accurately and to provide the initial step of mastery. When students are left to self-regulation prematurely, asking too much too soon, the learner often becomes frustrated and/or performs the task incorrectly. Meichenbaum recommends that coping skills be modeled for the student as part of other-regulation to preempt predictable obstacles inherent in the task. Therefore in addition to modeling the cognitive steps in a task, the emotional side is role-played for the learner to teach cognitive and emotional actions and reactions. After the modeling stage, the learner practices overtly and covertly the internal dialogue (both cognitive and emotional aspects) that accompany a specific task. It is important to communicate to the learner the how, why, what, and when certain procedures and thinking processes are beneficial to goal achievement. What a learner is able to accomplish, with help, should be considered as a viable measure of assessment, just as teachers value the measurement of what a learner is able to accomplish independently.

4

Theories Related to Verbal Self-Regulation

Overview

In this chapter, four related theories of cognitive self-instruction are explained. The theories selected are attribution theory, information processing theory, self-efficacy theory, and self-regulated learning theory. Each is discussed separately, although there is overlapping among the theories. These four are seen as examples, rather than the finite group of support theories for cognitive self-instruction. They represent theories that bolster a fuller, richer understanding of cognitive self-instruction for classroom learning and teaching. No attempt to be exhaustive is made.

Self-Questions

1. Knowledge. Name one theory related to cognitive self-instruction.

2. Comprehension. Explain the conditions which hinder or foster self-regulated learning, according to Corno.

3. Application. Show how information-processing theory is related to a classroom theory of self-regulated learning.

4. Analysis. List the three determinants for attributions and give an example for each one.

5. Synthesis. Compare and contrast attribution theory with self-efficacy theory.

6. Evaluation. Judge the merits of using self-regulated learning strategies as a means to reduce the drop-out rates in our schools.

In this chapter, four theories that are important to understanding cognitive self-instruction are reviewed. Other individuals may believe that substitutions or additional theories should be included in this chapter. These four theories are not intended to be a finite, all-inclusive list of support theories for cognitive self-instruction. They do, however, represent four theories I have used to provide my students with a clearer picture of cognitive self-instruction for classroom teaching and learning. Theories such as verbal mediation are not included because they were addressed previously in chapter 1 as an integrated part of the whole theoretical perspective of verbal self-regulation. Therefore, in this sense, such theories are considered a part of the theory of verbal self-regulation for classroom use; not simply a "related theory."

The four related theories are attribution theory, information processing theory, self-efficacy theory, and self-regulated learning theory. Each will be discussed separately, although there is overlapping between and among theories.

Attribution Theory

The underlying premise of both verbal self-regulation and attribution theory is that thought influences behavior. Heider (1958), an early pioneer of attribution theory, argued that knowing an individual's life experiences is necessary to understand how this individual reacts to a specific situation. Subsequent similar situations may be understood by knowing the individual's account of what caused the situation. Fennema (1985) refers to causal-attribution theory and defines it as "that portion which deals with the perceived causes of success and failure experiences in achievement tasks . . . what people believe are the reasons for their past successes or failures will directly affect their future achievement-related behavior." Frieze (1976) cites three determinants for attributions: performance results, performance history, and performance of others. To give an example, a person's explanation for a test grade is affected by how well the person performed on the test, how well the person performed on other, similar tests, and how well other students performed.

Weiner (1979) stated that perceived causes of success and failure on academic tests are affected by ability, effort, and task difficulty. Elig and Frieze (1975) developed a classification scheme for these attributions. Weiner (1979) applied an adaptation of this scheme to a three-faceted categorization of internality (internal or external), stability (fixed or variable), and controllability (controllable or uncontrollable). Within this classification, ability is categorized as internal, fixed, and uncontrollable. Effort is classified as internal, variable, and controllable; while task difficulty is viewed as external, fixed, and uncontrollable.

Consequences of attributions have affected a person's expectancy for future performance (McMahan, 1973; Weiner et al., 1976), persistence (Rest, 1976), learned helplessness (Miller & Norman, 1979), affective reactions (Sarason & Stoops, 1978), task choice (Nicholls, 1984), and study strategy use (Palmer & Goetz, 1988).

Weiner's (1979) classification system has received attention in cognitive intervention studies, where a change in subjects' behavior has been a major goal. For example, Kurtz and Borkowski (1984) reported that learners who believe their efforts will reap success are more likely to use what they have learned in a different context. Borkowski, in Meichenbaum (1977), emphasized the importance of incorporating attention to attribution theory with cognitive strategy training. A subject's attributions are instrumental in situations where a behavior change is sought. Changing behavior without changing unproductive attributions will not result in a lasting, cross-situational change. For example, if young elementary children believe that their teacher is responsible for their behavior at school (externality attribution), they are much less likely to respond to cognitive behavior modification (CBM) strategies. These children need to see themselves as responsible (internality attribution); therefore, a cognitive strategy aimed at teaching responsibility for their own behavior is very important. Borkowski has repeatedly urged the inclusion of attribution retraining in such cognitive strategy studies. Manning (1988) reported success in changing first- and third-graders' locus of control (internality aspect of Weiner's taxonomy), while at the same time producing improved classroom conduct. These benefits were maintained after one and three months and transferred to another classroom context and to home. Manning's study documents the relatedness of attribution theory to cognitive strategy studies. They seem to go hand in hand. Other recent training efforts have combined an attribution training component within strategy training packages (McCombs, 1988).

Information-Processing Theory

Information-processing theory is defined here as a historical root of metacognition, specifically the notion of executive control. Most of the information-processing models designate functional power to a "central processor, interpreter, supervisor, or executive system capable of performing an intelligent evaluation of its own operations" (Brown, 1987, p. 79).

Brown (1978) reports the following basic requirements that comprise information processing of a metacognitive nature: "It must include the ability to (a) predict the system's capacity limitation; (b) be aware of its repertoire of heuristic routines and their appropriate domain of utility; (c) identify and characterize the problem at hand; (d) plan and schedule appropriate problem-solving strategies; (e) monitor and supervise the effectiveness of those routines it calls into service; and (f) dynamically evaluate these operations in the face of success or failure so that termination of activities can be strategically timed." (p. 152). With the increasing interest in computers and synthetic intelligence, information processing theories developed. Since the mid 1960s comparisons between human cognition and the computer have motivated psychological models and monopolized theories of human cognition (Brown, 1987, p. 79). By the early 1970s, the notion of executive control was well established in psychological circles. Developmental psychologists used the computer metaphors to evaluate the emergence of efficient learning for humans.

Brown (1987) provides a complete description of information processing as an approach to the study of thinking. Prior to information processing models, there was a two-process model: automatic and controlled processes. Automatic processing is defined as "a fast, parallel process, not limited by short-term memory, that requires little subject effort, and demands little direct subject control" (p. 80). Automatization of thought may result from a simple task demand that is not viewed as cognitively challenging by the learner. Controlled processing is defined as "a comparatively slow, serial process, limited by short-term memory constraints, requiring subject effort, and providing a large degree of subject control" (Schneider & Shiffrin, 1977) in Brown (1987, p. 80). As with many other terms, automatic and controlled processes have been discussed in the literature, under a variety of names (e.g., conscious strategies vs. automatic activation, Posner & Snyder, 1974; controlled vs. systematic processing, Shiffrin, 1975; deliberate vs. involuntary, Brown, 1975; effortful vs. automatic, Hasher & Zacks, 1979).

Some developmental psychologists explain development in terms of controlled, effortful, and sometimes laborious thinking becoming automated (Brown, 1975). Another developmental premise is that processes that become automatic are more efficient than those in the controlled state.

Brown (1987) provides an account of three computer planning models that aim to portray problem-solving activity. These three are the GPA (General Problem Solver, Newell & Simon, 1972); NOAH (Nets of Action Hierarchies, Sacerdoti, 1974); and Hayes-Roth and her associates' model of planning function (Goldin & Hayes-Roth, 1980; Hayes-Roth & Thorndyke, 1980). For a description of these models, please refer to the Brown (1987) reference, pp. 83–84.

In conclusion Brown (1987) recommends more programmatic research on planning and planning-in-action within a structure that considers task familiarity and processing load. These considerations are necessary when examining children's ability to plan, monitor, and guide their own behavior. Such abilities are integral components of cognitive self-instruction.

Self-Efficacy

Self-efficacy is the degree of confidence individuals possess about their own capabilities. Bandura (1977) and his colleagues (Bandura & Schunk, 1981; Schunk, 1981) reported that people with low self-efficacy tend to give up when presented with a challenging task; often before they have even attempted the task. Borkowski, Johnston, and Reid (1987) referred to a similar situation, which they designated as strategic and nonstrategic learners. The nonstrategic learners are the ones who give up easily. When learners attend to shorter-range subgoals, instead of long-range, overall goals, self-efficacy and cognitive performance are improved (Bandura & Schunk, 1981).

There are instances where individual efficacy expectations are not parallel with performance. One of these is when individuals underestimate their efficacy for a task demand and perform poorly because of their feelings of inadequacy. A different example occurs when students underestimate the task requirements, have expectations of high efficacy, but are unable to perform well on the task. This often happens to young children and learning-disabled students who do not comprehend the task demands because of these deficient metacognitive skills (Wong, 1985). Such learners are surprised when their efficacy estimations do not match the task at hand. They are often confused and frustrated by their grades on such assignments. Among these populations, this metacognitive problem produces a lack of appropriate strategy use. The hope is that these metacognitive strategies are teachable and learnable as documented by a growing body of research studies (e.g., Manning, 1984). Combining self-efficacy theory with verbal self-regulation, pupils may not know when to use metacognitive strategies, especially when they believe the task is too easy or the task is overwhelmingly beyond them. Regardless of which task perception they have, the repeated failures lower their personal self-efficacy.

Beyond young children and learning-disabled students, I have witnessed regular education populations of older students, including college age with no known or diagnosed learning disabilities, experiencing similar failure experiences because of unrealistic efficacy expectations, both positive and negative. For example, when I require article critiques from undergraduates I often receive shocked moans and groans when I return the graded critiques. Some students have had low efficacy expectations, while more have had unrealistic high efficacy expectations. They have underestimated the difficulty of the task. In both cases, poor performance results. Executive planning (including problem defining, focusing, guiding, coping, reinforcing) is often not up to par because the students thought the task was too complicated or too easy. Cognitive self-instruction would be an appropriate intervention with these students. Within the framework of metacognitive strategies such as cognitive self-instruction, students will have greater self-efficacy beliefs "if they perceive that they have the level of ability and effort required for effective use of the strategy, and that the strategy is appropriate for tasks like the one they are required to perform" (Palmer & Goetz, 1988, p. 51). Palmer and Goetz state that individuals' decisions about metacognitive-strategy use is based on their perceived attributional match between self-efficacy and the required task. For example, Fyans and Maehr (1979) found that students who believe their success on achievement tasks was due to their ability, effort, or luck preferred tasks they believe also required the same, corresponding attributes of ability, effort, or luck.

Self-Regulated Learning

Zimmerman (Zimmerman & Schunk, 1989) discusses the emergence of theories of self-regulated learning whereby six theoretical perspectives on self-regulated learning (i.e., operant, phenomenological, social cognitive, volitional, Vygotskian, and cognitive constructivist) are outlined. The relatedness of self-regulated learning to cognitive self-instruction overlaps in Zimmerman's discussion of the Vygotskian views of self-regulated learning (see pages 16–19). While Zimmerman and Schunk place Vygotsky's theory as one of six models of self-regulated learning, I view the emerging self-regulated learning theory as explanatory support for the use of cognitive self-instructional strategies for learners who need such strategies as a means for developing self-regulation of learning and behavior. Zimmerman (1989) differentiates Vygotsky's view from the other five models when he says "... Vygotsky's theory is distinctive from other views of self-regulation ... by its emphasis on linguistically mediated social agents in children's development and in the functional role of inner speech" (p. 17).

Zimmerman provides a definition of self-regulated learning: "students can be described as self-regulated to the degree that they are metacognitively, motivationally, and behaviorally active participants in their own learning process" (p. 4). He states that "more precise definitions than this vary on the basis of a researcher's theoretical perspective" (p. 4). Examples of these perspectives are the six models of self-regulated learning listed above.

One researcher, Lyn Corno (1987, pp. 249–266) characterizes self-regulated learners as (1) enactive, (2) facilitators of their own learning that sustain self-motivation, (3) self-starters, and (4) students who seem to make learning easier for themselves. In addition she points out that self-regulation develops in part via self-instruction, but self-regulated learning underscores the finding that these processes become automatic (and thus not self-instructive in a formal sense) over time. This is the ultimate aim of becoming truly self-regulating (Corno, personal communication, June 1990).

Corno says that the characteristics 1–4 mentioned above separate students who employ self-regulated learning strategies from those who do not, depending on personal and environmental conditions. Self-regulation is used or not used depending on classroom situations. Even students who use a great deal of self-regulation do not always use the strategies. For example, in a particular classroom task, students who often use self-regulated learning may slip in and out of this use during the task and across tasks. Therefore, even students who use self-regulation often can improve in their use when they learn appropriate points of application. In addition, students not learning to use self-regulated learning techniques can be taught to do so (Corno, personal communication, June, 1990).

Self-regulation for classroom functions includes such habits as starting assignments on time, asking relevant questions, persisting with tasks, self-guiding to facilitate learning, and completing work promptly and accurately. In the Corno chapter (1987) being used as a resource here three conditions (that are aspects of the person, not the environment) are motivation, volition, and cognitive competency. These conditions foster or hinder self-regulation. In some cases, these three conditions might be found as separate entities with each being theories related to metacognitive strategy use, and not combined to explicate a larger concept, such as self-regulation. However, Corno has done such an efficient job of putting them in the context of self-regulated learning that her approach is used here instead. She discussed each condition briefly as a precursor to self-regulated learning.

Motivation theory promotes the idea that engagement in academic tasks depends partly on an individual's incentives. What we value varies among individuals and across time within an individual. Therefore, one's motivation to pursue a task is specific and personal. Another dimension of motivation is perception of task assignments. This is based on self-efficacy theory, previously discussed in chapter four. These perceptions include beliefs that a task is easy, difficult, boring, overwhelming, or totally irrelevant to one's life. A person's motivation to learn does or does not set up a condition for self-regulated learning.

A second determiner is what Corno calls *volition* or self-discipline. Volition is distinct from motivation in that it manages motivational processes such as self-percepts and attributions (Corno, personal communication, June

1990). According to theories of volition, motivated individuals may not possess enough self-discipline to selectively avoid unproductive intentions or distractors (Kuhl & Beckmann, 1985). These individuals do not have enough self-management skill to control their own learning. These distractors may come in the form of (1) competing, off-task thoughts, (2) irrelevant distractions such as someone moving about, (3) anxiety about the task at hand, (4) physical conditions such as anemia or other energy-draining ailments, or (5) combinations of above. Students may be capable, motivated, and still lack self-regulatory skills, due to inadequate self-discipline. Such students do not seem to have the adequate, powerful self-management skills required to overcome environmental distraction or competing emotional or physical needs.

The third condition required for self-regulation is *cognitive competency.* When students do not possess productive learning strategies, deficits in cognitive competencies are blamed. Students may be motivated to learn, have enough self-discipline to focus, maintain attention, and finish tasks, but lack cognitive skills required for awareness of effective learning strategies and how and when to use them. Indeed, as Corno points out some psychologists (e.g., Sternberg, 1982) believe that knowing when and how to use cognitive self-instructional strategies is a major aspect of intelligence (p. 252).

The point of this book is that cognitive self-instruction is a teachable and learnable skill. Deficits of this sort cause many students to view school as beyond their capabilities. Destructive thought such as this often causes students to experience lowered expectations for success and a lack of confidence in their own efforts to compensate for their failures in school. Seligman (1975) terms this self-limiting belief "learned helplessness." Often students who hold this belief will refuse to try in school. They give up. They drop out. Corno (1987) states that the most powerful and reliable motivator for school tasks is to teach students how to become self-motivated, by teaching them how to manage and control their own leaning (p. 253).

Corno talks about how teachers are most often told to plan exciting, attention-grabbing lessons that eventually wear the teacher out and really do not help children overcome self-regulation/self-management learning deficits. Research studies such as those of Corno and Mandinach (1983); Corno and Rohrkemper (1985); Novak and Gowin (1984); Palincsar and Brown (1984); and Manning (1988) have documented that teaching self-regulation of learning is possible and "leads to the kinds of success experiences in school that in turn relate to positive feelings about oneself as a learner and a competent person" (Corno, 1987, p. 252). The aim of this book is to provide the rationale, background, and tools to promote successful learning experiences through self-regulation in a classroom setting. Readers who are interested in a comprehensive discussion of self-regulated learning are referred to Zimmerman and Schunk (1989).

Cognitive Analysis: Definition of Terms

Attributions Those things which we think of as belonging to, produced by, or resulting from. Assign or ascribe to. Perceived causes for one's own successes and failures.

Attribution theory The perceived causes of a person's successes and failures on academic tasks are affected by that person's ability, effort, and the task difficulty (Weiner, 1979). Weiner's taxonomy designates ability as internal, fixed, and uncontrollable. Effort is classified as internal, variable, and controllable. Task difficulty is external, fixed, and uncontrollable. Weiner's coding scheme includes a three-dimensional classification of internality (internal or external), stability (fixed or variable), and controllability (controllable or uncontrollable).

Automatic processes "A fast, parallel process not limited by short term memory that requires little human effort, and demands little direct human control" (Brown, 1987, p. 80). A term originating from information processing theory. Synonyms include: *automatic activation, systematic,* and *involuntary.*

Cognitive competency One of the conditions for self-regulated learning. Possessing knowledge of productive learning strategies, how, and when to use them. Some consider this type competency a major aspect of intelligence. Corno (1987) believes that deficits in this area hinder the development of the self-regulated learner.

Controllability One of Weiner's (1979) three coding categories. Controllability is either controllable or uncontrollable. Within this taxonomy effort is controllable, while ability and task difficulty are uncontrollable.

Controlled processes "A comparatively slow, serial process, limited by short-term memory constraints, requiring human effort and providing a large degree of human control" (Brown, 1987, p. 80). A term originating from information processing theory. Synonyms include: *conscious, deliberate,* and *effortful.*

Executive control A term originating from information processing theory that is synonymous with self-monitoring and self-evaluation of one's own mental functioning.

Information-processing theory Involves the notion of executive control or the mental overseeing of one's own cognitive operations. Terms such as *storage and retrieval of information, long term and short term memory* originated in information-processing theory. It is defined here in chapter 4 through the lens of metacognition, using Ann Brown's work as the expert source.

Internality One of Weiner's (1979) three coding categories. Sometimes referred to as internal or external locus of control. The source of one's successes and failures. Internal attributions for successes and failures. Internal attributions for success are credits to one's own ability and efforts; whereas, external attributions credit an outside agent (e.g., the test was too difficult).

Learned helplessness A self-limiting belief named by Seligman (1975). Lowered expectations for success as a result of past failures and a lack of confidence in one's own efforts to compensate for failures in school. In these cases, students have learned helplessness and often will not try, will give up, and often will drop out of school.

Locus of control The place of responsibility for one's own behavior. There exists an internal or external locus of control orientation. Individuals who attribute responsibility for their successes and failures to themselves are acting from an internal locus of control. Those who attribute responsibility for successes and failures to someone or something other than themselves are behaving from an external locus of control perspective.

Motivation theory One of the conditions for self-regulated learning (Corno, 1987). Engagement in academic tasks depends partly on individuals' incentives. Motivation to pursue a task is specific and personal as it varies among individuals and across time within an individual.

Self-efficacy theory Involves the degree of confidence individuals possess about their own capabilities. Low self-efficacy beliefs cause a person to give up when presented with a challenging task. Borkowski, Johnston, and Reid (1987) refer to this learner as a nonstrategic learner.

Self-regulated learners Defined by Corno (1987) as those learners who are self-starters, who are enactive facilitators of their own learning that sustain self-motivation, who seem to make learning easier for themselves.

Self-regulated learning theory The emerging theory (Zimmerman & Schunk, 1989) has an underlying assumption that self-regulated learning is teachable and learnable. Please also see *Self-regulated learners* in this section.

Stability One of Weiner's (1979) three coding categories. Stability is either fixed or variable. Ability and task difficulty are fixed, while effort is variable.

Volition theory One of the conditions for self-regulated learning (Corno, 1987). According to theories of volition, motivated individuals may not possess enough self-discipline to selectively avoid unproductive intentions or distractions. Such learners lack sufficient self-management skills to control their own learning.

Cognitive Synthesis: A Summary

The four theories described in this chapter relate directly to the use of cognitive self-instruction in regular classroom settings. Attribution theory involves students' perceived causes for successes and failures based on past learning experiences which impact on future learning tasks. These perceptions must be considered when planning metacognitive strategies which cause students to assume more responsibility for their own learning. The second theory described was information processing. Comparisons between computer planning models and human problem-solving activities indicate efficient learning patterns for human beings. This theory includes an emphasis on the intelligent overseeing of one's own mental operations. Cognitive self-instruction also includes this emphasis: students must monitor and evaluate their own cognitive behavior during learning. The third theory, referred to as "self-efficacy," is the degree of perceived competence individuals possess about their own learning capabilities. Efficacy expectations, whether unrealistically too high or too low, affect the way learners perform on tasks. When teaching students to use cognitive self-instruction, efficacy expectations must be considered. Finally, self-regulated learning theory, with the determining conditions of motivation, volition, and cognitive competency is intricately tied to cognitive self-instruction for teaching and learning. Skills of self-regulation and self-management of school work habits are major components of cognitive self-instruction.

These four theories, taken together, form a clearer view of the complexity involved in cognitive self-instruction for classroom use. It is not a quick fix-it repair for students who are having difficulty in school. It is not a simple recipe intended for teachers to follow. Teachers have been asked to follow too many recipes. This is insulting to the teaching professional. Cognitive self-instruction offers a process for teaching and learning how to become responsible, self-motivated, self-regulated, self-managed learners. I believe that without such instruction we will continue to lose too many students as drop-outs from our schools, homes, and society.

5

Related Cognitive Psychologies: Cognitive Self-Instruction

Overview

In chapter 5, an affective side of metacognition is presented. This presentation is in the form of cognitive psychology, specifically cognitive semanticism. Cognitive semanticism deals with the impact of one's language upon behavior, feelings, and mental states. Said another way, the meaning of verbal messages to self serves a powerful shaping role upon actions and feelings. Two of the examples, provided in this chapter, have been in vogue for quite some time: Albert Ellis' rational emotive therapy (RET) sometimes referred to as rational emotive thinking was introduced in the 1950s. Eric Berne and Thomas Harris in their 1960s publications brought about an interest in transactional analysis (TA). These two psychologies are described and bridged to cognitive self-instruction in this chapter. Both RET and TA emphasize the importance of the verbal environment. RET deals directly with the effect of internal messages to self, while TA emphasizes the social transaction, using language as the primary delivery system between individuals.

Two contemporary cognitive semanticists are Pamela Butler and Shad Helmstetter. Butler gives credit to the following cognitive pioneers: Karen Horney, Albert Ellis, Eric Berne, Aaron Beck, R. S. Lazarus, Donald Meichenbaum, Bob Goulding, and Mary Goulding. Butler's self-talk judges: the drivers, the stoppers, and the confusers are defined. Butler's steps for learning the language of self-support are listed. Helmstetter's five levels of self-talk and his recommendations for reprogramming our past negative self-talk tapes are briefly outlined. The emphasis from the examples is upon altering self-talk to produce human change, growth, and development. The reason they were chosen over more mainstream approaches (e.g., Aaron Beck) is simply because they seemed to be less clinical in the vocabulary of their publication; more lay person oriented. In my experiences my students, who are not psychology majors, have understood their messages more readily.

These approaches represent an affective component of metacognition and are presented only as examples. There are other cognitive psychologies not mentioned (e.g., William Glasser's, Reality Therapy, 1975) that may also be considered from this perspective.

Self-Questions

1. Knowledge. Name the three maladaptive/irrational beliefs (RET) that foster maladaptive self-talk.

2. Comprehension. Describe the three ego states of adult, parent, and child (TA). Explain how they differ from each other.

3. Application. In the following social transactions decide which state is speaking: adult, critical parent, nurturing parent, natural child, adapted child, or rebellious child. Label each communication with one of the states.

Example 1	TA state?
(a) Teacher: What is the answer to number 6?	(a) ________
(b) Student: Noise pollution is the answer.	(b) ________
Example 2	
(a) Student A: Boy! That was a great field trip. It was so much fun! I loved it! Did you see those whales! Man!	(a) ________
(b) Student B: Wow, I know! I feel so great about this! Those animals were the neatest things I ever saw!	(b) ________
Example 3	
(a) Teacher: I've had it with you. You are such a pest. Either shape up or get out!	(a) ________
(b) Student: Oh you think you're so smart, teach! You just try to make me leave!	(b) ________

Example 4

(a) Student: Oh no! I didn't get my paper signed. I'll be in trouble now. What can I do? (a) ___________

(b) Teacher: It's okay. It will be fine. Don't worry. Everyone forgets sometime. (b) ___________

Example 5

(a) Teacher A: My class is so bad! Kids are not like they used to be. These children are losers. (a) ___________

(b) Teacher B: I know what you mean. You should see my zooey class. Half the kids look like hippies. (b) ___________

Example 6

(a) Student: When do we need to hand in this assignment? (a) ___________

(b) Teacher: Sit down and be quiet right now. (b) ___________

4. Analysis. Diagram the RET sequence which, according to Ellis, can lead to mental illness. Explain how a rational sequence is substituted and how it promotes mental health.

5. Synthesis. Develop an original program of my own in which I choose a habit I want to change. Describe how I can accomplish this through the self-talk solution according to Helmstetter.

6. Evaluation. Judge the strengths and limitations of the cognitive semanticist approach for educational purposes.

Affective Side of Metacognition

Brown et al. (1983) in a section called "Beyond Cold Cognition" emphasize the emotional/affective aspects of learning. The way individuals perceive themselves as learners can promote or hinder learning, depending upon whether these perceptions are positive or negative. For example, some children avoid mathematics tasks because they believe they are not competent in mathematics. Such children may or may not be deficient in metacognitive processing. Their feelings are contributing to the problem, and this affective side of learning must be considered when planning instructional intervention. Brown et al. (1983) say it very well: "It seems clear that the cold cognitive aspects of learning are only part of a much larger system that influences development; indeed the purely cognitive aspects may be less primary than we like to think they are" (p. 147).

Combining cognitive and affective aspects of metacognition is critical to a self-motivated, self-controlled student. An effective instructional program aimed at such (cognitive and affective) metacognitive deficits is essential to a modern-day education. Improving students' intellect can not be separated from the students' social/personal history.

Meichenbaum (1977) in the prologue to his book *Cognitive Behavior Modification* (CBM) describes his work with CBM as a bridge between the clinical concerns of cognitive-semantics therapists (e.g., Ellis, Berne, and Harris) and the technology of behavior therapy. Meichenbaum, as well as others, have seen a need to go beyond behaviorism. Therefore, he joined cognitive/affective factors with behavior modification. When teaching cognitive self-instruction to students, considerations must be given to how they feel about academic tasks, their beliefs and attitudes about learning, as well as how they process information and use cognitive strategies for learning. The affective and the cognitive components of learning no longer match classroom reality if they are treated separately. Therefore, the affective side of self-instruction is included as an integral and a simultaneous part of cognitive self-instruction.

Rational Emotive Therapy (Albert Ellis)

Rational Emotive Therapy began around 1955. The major principle of RET is illustrated in the quotes of Epictetus (1 AD) in *Enchiridion:* "Men feel disturbed not by things, but by the views which they take of them"; and William Shakespeare in Hamlet: "There exists nothing either good or bad but thinking makes it so." RET is based on a humanistic, educative model. The basic premise is that individuals, even in early life, have more choices than they acknowledge. Most conditioning in life is really self-conditioning. Therapists, teachers, parents serve the role of clarifier: helping individuals to see more clearly that they have a range of alternative reactions for any given situation. Their choice of reactions affects their mental health. RET attempts to show individuals how they behave in self-defeating ways and how they can change these ways.

RET does not follow the usual medical model, which holds that emotional problems are alleviated by an outside person telling another person what they must do to get better. RET does however, claim to know what is rational versus irrational for all people, which may be an unrealistic claim

(Meichenbaum, 1989). RET is also not similar to conditioning models that assert that individuals are disturbed by outside influences, and that they must be reconditioned by an outside person who shapes them into new patterns of behaving through schedules of external reinforcement. RET has emerged as a semantic therapy. This is because RET espouses changing and improving oneself by means of "clearly seeing, understanding, disputing, altering, and acting against (detrimental) internal verbalizations" (Ellis & Harper, 1985, x). Individuals in rational-emotive therapy are asked to monitor their "semantic usages so as to concomitantly change their thinking, emoting, and behaving" (p. xi). RET emphasizes a semantic approach to understanding and minimizing human suffering. One of the main tenets of RET is that thinking creates feeling. Vygotsky defined thinking as inner speech; therefore by deduction, inner speech creates feeling. Ellis contends that when individuals talk to themselves rationally it aids in ridding them of disorganizing panic and rage. On the other hand, Meichenbaum believes in the reciprocity between thought and behavior/feelings. Meichenbaum (1989) stated that posing an unidirectional impact of thought upon behavior/feelings is an oversimplification and is problematic. In sum, Meichenbaum agrees with some of the basic premises set forth by Ellis and others; however, he cautions against believing that changing behavior is always as simple as merely changing our thought.

RET labels as "rational thinking" that kind of thinking that helps you to survive and achieve the goals you choose to make your existence pleasurable and/or worthwhile. Maxie Maultsby in Ellis & Harper (1975, p. 23) lists five characteristics of RET: "(1) It bases itself primarily on objective fact as opposed to subjective opinion. (2) If acted upon, it most likely will result in the preservation of your life . . . ; (3) If acted upon, it produces your personally defined life's goals most quickly; (4) If acted upon, it prevents undesirable personal and/or environmental conflict; (5) It minimizes your inner conflicts and turmoil."

Ellis in RET believes that virtually all "spontaneous" emotional responses arise in the same way (i.e., "At point A, you perceive what goes on around you. At point B, you evaluate how likeable or dislikeable you find this situation at A . . . Then you react emotionally at point C") (Ellis & Harper, 1975, p. 47).

At point B, I believe it is the self-talk of an individual that determines the subsequent response. It can also be viewed in a broader sense than just the emotional responses to which Ellis and Harper were referring. For example, an educational situation at point A could be that a student screams profanity at a teacher. Point C is the teacher's behavioral response. Point B is the self-talk the teacher engages in which promotes the response at point C. The nature of the teacher's response C (e.g., rational, irrational, sane, crazy) is related to how he/she talks about this situation to self at point B. For example, the teacher who says to self at Point B, "Well that little brat, I'll show him/her who's the boss" will most likely react at point C in a recognizably different manner than the teacher who (at Point B) says to self, "What is bothering Melanie today? She usually handles herself much better than this. I'll look into this further."

The self-verbalization at point B mediates between situation A and response C. This is true in the clinical sense as described by Ellis. Furthermore it is true for educational responses and other nonclinical populations. It is a waste to apply rational emotive thinking exclusively to maladjusted populations when it also makes logical sense for adjusted individuals. For those interested in Ellis' terminology, he calls point A, the Activating experience or event; point C, the emotional Consequence; and the mediating point B, your Belief system. The verbal self-regulation comes into play at point B and affects responses at point C.

Ellis believes that individuals often possess maladaptive/irrational beliefs which lead to maladaptive/irrational self-talk, which in turn fosters maladaptive/irrational behaviors. The sequence moves from belief to self-talk to behavior. These maladaptive beliefs are manifested in human beings as maladaptive self-talk. Ellis also believes that much mental illness is attributable to this faulty belief system. Therefore, to improve mental health, the RET position is to help people (1) realize their irrational beliefs, (2) change them to rational beliefs, which in turn (3) leads to rational self-talk, followed by (4) productive, healthy behaviors. Three examples of maladaptive beliefs/self-talk/behavior sequences are described, followed by the corresponding adaptive beliefs/self-talk/behavior sequences. The first maladaptive belief is: "I should not make mistakes and if I do it is awful." This belief causes a person to magnify the importance of never making a mistake. Obviously, this belief can lead to a lot of needless stress when such an unrealistic expectation is placed upon oneself. The self-talk accompanying such a belief goes something like this: "If I don't get this right, it will just be horrible. I can't stand it if I don't do this perfectly!" The behavior that occurs as a result of such catastrophizing and awfulizing (as Ellis calls it), is most likely tension, stress, anxiety, migraine headaches, nervous stomachs, and other such unhealthy behaviors. The more rational belief is: "I will do my best; I don't want to make mistakes, but if I do I can stand it. It might be unfortunate, but it will not be awful." This is putting "mistake making" in its proper perspective. Subsequent examples of self-talk may be "I am a human being which means I am prone to error. I'll do the best I can. If I make a mistake, I can handle it. It will not be the end of the world." Behaviors following such self-talk are much more likely to be relaxed and emotionally healthy.

Another maladaptive/irrational belief is that "everyone should approve of me and if they don't it's awful." The adaptive counterpart is "it is nice to have the approval of others. However, if I do not I will still be okay." The third example of a maladaptive/irrational belief is "people should be the way I want them to be." The adaptive/rational counterpart is "people are the way they are: I cannot change them but I can change the way I react to them." This third belief gave rise to Ellis' book entitled *How to Live with a Neurotic* (1975).

There are additional irrational beliefs that Ellis and his colleagues believe are at the root of mental illness. However, these three examples can be blamed for a large portion of the insane belief—self-talk—behaviors that encourage mental illness.

By now, the reader may be saying, "But this book is about teaching and learning in regular education, not about mentally ill people." Nevertheless, I have found Ellis to be helpful in dealing with mentally healthy individuals, not just those diagnosed as "mentally ill." Even healthy individuals often catastrophize, awfulize, and talk to themselves irrationally. It is more a matter of degree or severity, which explains why a person becomes totally incapacitated (psychotic/mentally ill), or partially incapacitated (neurotic/emotionally disturbed), or occasionally incapacitated (bouts with tension headaches, occasional depression, stress, tension, anxiety). What Ellis has to say, I believe, is just as important to *prevent* irrational behavior, as it is to treat mental illness. I use his ideas frequently when dealing with troubled, anxious student teachers who are learning to teach for the first time. They often are operating from all three of what I term Ellis' *major irrational beliefs:* "I have to be a perfect teacher; everyone must think I'm doing a great job; and my students have to change and behave exactly the way I want." Such student teachers' beliefs cause difficult problems, as you might guess. If their belief system can become more rational (e.g., "No perfect teachers exist; that includes me! Everyone will not approve of everything I do; I'm learning; I'm supposed to receive some constructive criticism. These students are the way they are. They will only change when they see the need to do so. In the meantime, how can I react differently to them?") then these student teachers are much more likely to find student teaching a pleasant, more successful experience.

Transactional Analysis (Eric Berne/Thomas Harris)

As with RET, only that portion of transactional analysis (TA) which supports the understanding of cognitive self-instruction will be included here. Obviously, volumes have been written about both RET and TA. Only a cursory look can be presented here due to space limitations.

TA is a helpful framework for looking at the verbal interactions between teacher and student, parent and child, etc. TA does not deal with self-talk. Indeed its unit of analysis is the social transaction between individuals. Nevertheless because of its major focus on verbalizations and their great impact on others, TA is included in this book. *Inter*transactions are often preceded by *intra*transactions. What one says to self may affect what one then says to another, except in cases such as automaticity, impulsivity, and insanity. Most of us have been guilty of speaking to others impulsively, before speaking to ourselves about the most rational way to respond, often to our later dismay. We can recount times when we have spoken to another harshly, impulsively, without proper inner dialogue first. On the other hand, sometimes we have engaged in internal dialogue and then still spoken harshly and impulsively.

According to TA, there are many different persons within us. TA is closely tied to psychoanalytical theory of Sigmund Freud, specifically that our inner energies consist of three elements: (1) the id, instinctual drives, (2) the superego, restrictive force over these egocentric drives or needs, and (3) the ego, which serves as the mediator, balancing between hedonism and repression. Individuals are in a constant, dynamic state of the interplay among these three constructs, as the ego referees between individual urges and restraint. Eric Berne (1964) in the book *Games People Play* and Thomas Harris (1969) in *I'm OK—You're OK: A Practical Guide to Transactional Analysis* have translated these abstract Freudian concepts into practical application for adults, teachers (Ernst, 1973), children (Freed, 1971), and teens (Freed, 1973).

A major assumption of TA is that the brain is a recorder. It has recorded every experience we have ever had. Bernie S. Siegel (1988) in his controversial book entitled *Love, Medicine and Miracles* documents that the brain records experiences even without our conscious awareness. For example, people under anesthesia record what is being said around them, and this affects the brain. Siegel believes it can affect the recovery of patients. In addition, he believes that individuals can heal themselves through optimism, positive self-talk, and imaging themselves as healthy, disease-free individuals. Siegel, through his work with cancer patients, would agree that the mind is a recorder.

Berne observed overt behavior as individuals played their internal tapes from these stored-up experiences. Stored experience is quite similar to Vygotsky's idea of internalization: that is, children are first regulated by significant others' verbalizations. Then the children internalize these parent verbalizations, which subsequently constitute the childrens' self-language and verbal self-regulation of their own actions. TA proponents are saying the same thing when they talk about replaying the stored-up tapes from our past. This idea of repeating stored-up experiences is also at the heart of understanding why abused children frequently become abusive parents, why parents parent the way they were parented (Friday, 1977), and why teachers teach the way they were taught (Goodlad, 1984).

Berne concluded that all individuals contain three voices or three kinds of tape: a child state (corresponding to the id), a parent state (superego), and an adult state (ego). To explain, our child state is the "little person" in each of us, our stored-up childlike experiences causing us to be impulsive, whining, silly, and creative. The parent state is based on our experience with parents and authority figures. The adult state is the rational, responsible, and objective part of each of us. To explicate, we will take a closer look at each of these voices.

Child

This aspect comes from our recordings which deal with our feelings and sensory input throughout our lives. There are three different identifiable parts to the child ego state. The "natural child" is the part of us who expresses spontaneous feelings of happiness, love, and joy—the giddy, lighthearted kid in all of us. The "adapted child" is the part of us who collects bad feeling such as anxiety or depression. This part often plays the victim or the persecuted (e.g., "Everyone is always picking on me"). The rebellious child part is the one who is defiant, stubborn.

Parent

This state contains both the good and bad remembrances of our parents and other authority figures. Therefore we have two aspects of this state: the critical parent and the nurturing parent. The critical parent voice is often blaming, criticizing, punishing, hurting others, or being aggressive toward others. Verbal clues to this voice are "never," "always," "should," "must," "have to," "don't," "ought to," "you will." The nurturing parent voice is to soothe, calm, and comfort others (e.g., "Everything will be okay.")

Adult

As children move from being a toddler, they begin to store rational information for use in later events. The adult state itself is rational, emotionless, processing data objectively, solving problems. Verbal clues include the "W" questions: who, what, when, where, and also how. Other examples are "In my *opinion,*" "Let's take a closer look," and "In conclusion."

When viewing the three states, it is important to note that the balance among the three is the important point. For example, too much child can lead to irresponsibility; too little child can lead to a lack of creativity and spontaneity. Too much rebellious child can cause us to lose friends, but too little can cause us to be passive wimps that people run over. Too much nurturing parent causes "smothering," and too little causes "coldness." Too much adult causes us to be boring and nonfeeling, and too little causes us not to know how to solve problems and look after ourselves. Balance among the three is the key to healthy social transactions.

The premise of TA is that all individuals need to feel adequate. If the child state holds the greatest influence of all three states, individuals have an attitude of "I'm not okay, but you are okay." If the parent holds the greatest influence of the three, the individual's attitude is "I'm okay, but you are not okay." If the parent and child are in conflict with very little rational adult intervention, we see an attitude of "I'm not okay and you're not okay."

To apply TA to education see Wolfgang and Glickman (1986). Briefly they say that the teacher first determines which of the three states is speaking by listening to the verbal message and observing the nonverbal signals (e.g., hands-on-hips parent; pouting-lip child). Use complementary messages—termed "stroking" or "warm fuzzies"—instead of cross-transactions—termed "cold pricklies." The teacher tries to appeal to the child's adult state. Teachers also must diagnose the games students play (Ernst, 1973). Teachers should use their own adult state or parallel/like responses (i.e., parent to parent, child to child) in their social transactions with students.

Two contemporary cognitive semanticists, Pamela E. Butler in her book *Talking to Yourself: Learning the Language of Self-Support* (1981) and Shad Helmstetter, in his book *What to Say When You Talk to Yourself* (1986) and *The Self-Talk Solution* (1987) outline specific guidelines for altering unhealthy, inappropriate self-talk to healthy, appropriate, and facilitative self-talk. Neither of these psychologists are educators, nor do they apply their works primarily to classroom teaching and learning. However, both have strong implications for educational practice because talking-to-yourself is not domain or population specific. The way students and teachers talk to themselves have a direct effect upon teaching performance and classroom learning.

The Language of Self-Support (Pamela E. Butler)

Butler says the first step to a happy, fulfilling life is to examine the quality of our day-to-day self-talk—the running dialogue inside our heads. She says in the introduction to her book: "It is through this internal dialogue that you make decisions, set goals for yourself, feel pleased and satisfied, dejected or despondent." This self-talk affects behavior, feelings, attitudes, self-esteem, stress level, interpersonal relationships—in short, every aspect of life.

Butler describes three types of judges that impose too much or ill-directed judgmental structures on our behaviors. The "Judge" internal tapes undermine our adaptive responses to situations in our lives. The judges are known as the "drivers," "stoppers," and "confusers" in our lives.

The drivers are our internal push to "get busy," "do it right," etc. Of course, we need such messages, unless we overdo them and drive ourselves relentlessly. The driver self-talk is not to be confused with the terms *motivated* or *drive*. A motivated person is consciously choosing and wants to pursue certain tasks in specific ways. The driver tape pushes us with commands such as: *You should be writing. You must do it perfectly. Try hard to finish it!* Drivers often prevent us from taking adequate care of ourselves, in the same way that we would nurture a special loved one. They keep us from knowing when we need and deserve to rest, to not accomplish, etc. Driver commands include *be perfect, hurry up, be strong, please others,* and *try hard.* Our "be perfect" tape constantly pushes us to perform at unreasonable levels. It also limits us to 100 percent or nothing, with nothing in-between (e.g., if we can't play a perfect game of tennis we don't play at all). The "hurry up" tape pushes us to do everything quickly. It reminds me of the message in David Elkind's book *The Hurried Child* (1981) whereby, children are even hurried to grow up. The hurry-up driver is one of the major contributors to the Type A behavior, associated with heart disease. The permitter self-talk that can counteract "hurry sickness" is to say: "It's okay to take the time I need. I'll get there when I get there." The "be strong" self-talk regards any need as a weakness to be overcome. Feelings of loneliness, sadness, or hurt are intolerable. This self-talk prevents us from asking for needed help. The permitter is to say to self, "It's okay to have feelings and okay to express them." The "please others" self-talk involves an intense fear of rejection, even when the disapproving person is unimportant to us. Pleasing other people can be rewarding, but it becomes maladaptive when we lose sight of our own feelings in exchange. Some people spend entire lives doing what other people want them to do, rather than pursuing their own goals. Pleasing others should be done because we want to, not because we feel we have no other choice. The permitter is to say, "It's okay to please myself. I will lose who I am if I do not acknowledge my needs." The fifth and last driver is the "try hard." This is the push to take on more and more responsibilities, without considering our own limitations—the inability to say no—impervious to the setting of appropriate limits. The permitter self-talk is "it's okay to recognize my own limits; it's okay to give my responsibilities enough time, backing, and energy to succeed."

The second judge is called "the stopper." The stoppers interfere with our self-expression and therefore limit us. These are the internal messages that tell us "no," "don't," "only if," etc. The stoppers keep us from asserting ourselves. They include: catastrophizing, negative self-labeling, setting rigid requirements, and witch messages. Catastrophizing is the internal dialogue of rehearsing horrible events that might occur if we were to engage in certain behaviors. We exaggerate the risk of engaging in that behavior so much, that we decide to do nothing. The permitter voice is to say, "So what if?" So what if I ask for a favor and my friend turns me down? Is that so awful? Is that a catastrophe? Negative self-labeling is to attach arbitrary judgments to natural, healthy impulses. For example, a student may want to compliment the teacher but restrains him or herself because the student labels self as a "brownnoser." "I'd really like to tell Teacher X that I enjoyed that lesson, but she'd probably think I was trying to get extra points, so I won't." Many good acts towards others are squelched because we talk ourselves out of them, through negative self-labeling. The "setting-rigid-requirements" stopper imposes a set of conditions that must occur before an action can take place. These conditions often limit alternatives and block our own feelings and behaviors. We can recognize this kind of self-talk because it usually begins with the word, *if*. Examples are "if everyone will approve of this, I'll say it"; "if this won't hurt anyone, I'll try it." The final stopper is what Butler calls "witch-messages." These messages always begin with "don't!" Some examples are "don't change," "don't be yourself," "don't grow up," "don't be different." The best antidote to a witch-message is the assertion of your right to listen to and honor all aspects of yourself.

The third kind of judge in our self-talk is referred to as the "confuser." The confusers distort our reality. Butler categorizes confusers as *arbitrary inferences, misattributions, cognitive deficiency, overgeneralizations, either/or thinking, vague language,* and *magnification.* Definitions for each of these "confusers" can be found in the definition section (under "confuser self-talk tape") at the end of this chapter. The important point to keep in mind with all three of the judges (i.e., drivers, stoppers, and confusers) is that they are maladaptive self-statements and questions spoken to oneself. They are not a part of social interaction; they are a contributing factor to intrapsychological functioning.

Butler provides steps to move from self-criticism to self-support: (1) become aware of self-criticism and the way others are talking poorly to themselves. Become aware of this nonfacilitative self-talk through careful monitoring/listening to your own and others' self-talk; (2) try to keep an accurate record of just how often negative self-talk occurs. Use counters, notebooks, tape-record, list, etc., to quantify the presence of unhelpful self-talk; (3) interrupt self-critical tirades with the firm statement to self, "STOP!" This is a thought-stopping procedure. This helps to rid ourselves of unhelpful self-talk. However, we are left with a vacuum which will quickly be filled with the old, familiar, self-defeating self-talk if we do not take steps to learn a self-language that supports, rather than diminishes us. Butler says that learning a new, more helpful way to talk to ourselves is like learning a foreign language. Both require time, competence, patience, and energy. However, if we will replace the usual nonsupportive self-talk with supportive self-talk, benefits are realized in the areas of feelings, behavior, interpersonal relationships, self-esteem, and level of stress.

Butler provides five basic steps for learning the language of self-support: (1) be aware; listen to your own self-talk; ask yourself the following question: What am I telling myself?; (2) evaluate by deciding if the inner dialogue is supportive or destructive; ask yourself the following question: Is my self-talk helping?; (3) identify whether you are using a driver, stopper, and/or confuser to maintain inner speech. Ask yourself the following question: What driver, stopper, or confuser is maintaining my inner speech?; (4) support yourself by replacing your negative self-talk with permission and self-affirmation. Ask yourself: What permission and self-affirmation will I give myself?; (5) develop a guide for yourself by deciding what action to take consonant with your new support position. Ask yourself: What action will I take based on my new supportive position? (Butler, 1981, pp. 71–72).

Self-Talk (Shad Helmstetter)

Helmstetter believes that what we say to ourselves is the greatest determiner of how successful we are at anything we choose to do. However, based on his clinical practice, he states that 77 percent of everything we say to ourselves is counterproductive and works against us. This counterproductive self-talk originates from our past negative programming, contributed by social interactions. This is the same concept as Vygotsky's internalization, the three inner constructs of transactional analysis, and the three judges described by Butler.

Helmstetter continues by saying that it is not surprising that three-fourths of our self-talk is negative. By the time we are eighteen if we grew up in fairly average, reasonably positive home environments we were told "No" or what we could not do, more than 148,000 times (Helmstetter, 1986, p. 8). Helmstetter, like Siegel (1988) and Butler (1981), believes that there is a portion of the brain that believes whatever it is told. In time, we become whatever it is we have been told we are, even if it would not have been true of us otherwise. Eventually, we believe what others tell us and what we most often tell ourselves. We live out our negative programming. If the programming is more positive, then our lives, which follow the programming, are correspondingly more positive. Teachers and parents need to be extremely careful about the verbal environments they are creating for their children. The children's feelings, attitudes, and behaviors reflect what they have heard about themselves. It is exactly the process Vygotsky proposed: social interactions are the cornerstones of individual human development.

Helmstetter is strong in his message that the brain creates whatever you tell it because he believes that there is a portion of the brain that has no choice, no evaluation, and makes no counterarguments. This portion of the brain accepts without evaluation whatever it is told. Then the mind regulates health, personal relationships, careers, and futures according to these messages. Helmstetter's perspective reminds one of information-processing theory, in the sense that whatever is put into the mind (input) will affect output: garbage in, garbage out.

Helmstetter (1986) defines self-talk in the following way: "self-talk is a way to override our past negative programming by erasing or replacing it with conscious, positive new-directions" (p. 59). Helmstetter names five levels of self-talk starting with the least beneficial and moving up to the most beneficial:

Level I Self-Talk	Negative Acceptance "I can't" "If only I could"
Level II Self-Talk	Recognition of the need to change "I need to" "I should"
Level III Self-Talk	Decision to change "I never" "I no longer"
Level IV Self-Talk	The Better You "I am"
Level V Self-Talk	Universal Affirmation "It is"

Self-Talk Levels I and II have not worked to help anyone grow, change, or get better. Replace Levels I and II with Levels III and IV self-talk. On the surface, Level II self-talk may appear helpful, "I need to lose some weight;" however, Helmstetter says the unspoken, but still-programmed remainder of such statements is "but I won't" or "but I just can't right now," etc. Level II self-talk does not promote accomplishment, instead it promotes excuses, then "guilt, disappointment, and an acceptance of our own self-imagined inadequacies" (p. 62). To remove frustrating roadblocks, Levels III, IV, and V are the ones to use for helpful self-talk. Helmstetter continues by describing a step-by-step procedure for ridding oneself of negative self-talk and replacing it with a new positive program. Interested readers are urged to consult his procedures.

In addition to Butler and Helmstetter, Mahoney and Mahoney (1976) investigated negative monologues versus appropriate monologues for losing weight, which they referred to as "cognitive ecology," what you say to yourself; Novaco (1975) used self-statements rehearsed in stress inoculation training for controlling anger; and Turk (1975) used self-statements rehearsed in stress inoculation training for controlling pain. These researchers represent the focus of cognitive semanticism (e.g., altering self-talk to foster human changes, growth, and development).

Cognitive Analysis: Definition of Terms

Affective side of metacognition Ann Brown calls this "hot cognition." It is the affective component of metacognition: attitudes, values, beliefs, motivations, fears, etc. that must be considered if we are to match the reality of the classroom.

Adult state (TA) Similar to the ego state in Freud's psychoanalytical theory. The rational, problem-solving, reasoning, computerlike aspect of ourselves.

Awfulizing Ellis uses this term to describe the distortion of reality by increasing the intensity of situations or events. For example, thinking it would be awful if everyone did not approve of you merits the label of "awfulizing."

Cognitive ecology Mahoney and Mahoney (1975) used this term to refer to their work which focused on using appropriate versus negative self-talk monologue for weight loss.

Catastrophizing Ellis uses this term to describe the distortion of reality by overmagnifying events and situations. For example, thinking it would be a catastrope if you make a mistake is usually considered catastrophizing.

Child state (TA) Similar to the id state in Freud's psychoanalytical theory. The child state is subdivided into the natural, adapted, and rebellious child. The natural child represents the uninhibited, spontaneous creativity aspect; the adapted child is the whining, persecuted victim; and the rebellious child represents stubborn defiance.

Cognitive psychology The study of human behavior from the perspective of the intellectual activity of the mind.

Cognitive semanticists Psychologists who are interested in human behavior, focusing on our own language as a determiner of this behavior.

Cold cognition Implies the omission of person's feelings, beliefs, perceptions, attitudes, and values about one's own cognition. These words (e.g., attitudes) describe what is sometimes referred to as the affective aspect of cognition. Examples of cold cognition are the storage and retrieval of information without consideration of an individual's feelings, beliefs, etc., about their abilities to store and retrieve information.

Cold pricklies (TA) The opposite of complementary messages. Verbal or nonverbal communication that the sender and/or receiver perceive as unpleasant, rude, negative, harsh, and/or cruel.

Complementary messages (TA) Messages that the sender and/or receiver perceive as pleasant, affirming, positive reinforcement. The messages may be verbal or nonverbal.

Conditioning models A behavioristic model whereby an individual's behavior is shaped by external reinforcement or extinction.

Confuser self-talk tape The confusers distort reality. Butler (1981) refers to these as *arbitrary inferences, misattributions, cognitive deficiency, overgeneralizations, either/or thinking, vague language,* and *magnification.* A brief definition is presented for each of these since they are not defined within the chapter.

1. arbitrary inference: conclusion that is drawn without careful consideration of all the facts involved.

2. misattribution: the direction of blame or responsibility is moved away from the real causative agent onto something or someone else (similar to external locus of control) (e.g., she made me angry).

3. cognitive deficiency: the failure to be aware of the complete picture; tunnel vision.

4. overgeneralization: to recognize only the similarities between people or between events and to ignore the differences. Racial, cultural, and gender prejudices are based on this confuser (e.g., all women belong in the kitchen).

5. either/or thinking: *dichotomous thinking* is a synonym; seeing everything as black or white, agree or disagree; no consideration is given for degrees, continuum, or in-between ground.

6. vague language: the use of words that have not been defined clearly by ourselves (e.g., *success, accomplishment, unhappiness,* etc.)

7. magnification: overestimation of the importance of an event or a situation; blowing something out of reasonable proportions.

Driver self-talk tape Our internal driver that pushes us unrealistically. The drivers prevent us from taking adequate care of ourselves, keep us from knowing when we need and deserve to rest, to not accomplish, etc. The drivers include *be perfect, hurry up, be strong, please others,* and *try hard.* These are defined in this chapter. All definitions are according to Butler, 1981.

Educative model Diagnostic. Teaching individuals ways to help themselves by using their own trained capacities. Teaching others how to help themselves, usually from within themselves.

Empty (mental) apartment The description Helmstetter gives to the brain when we have stopped using negative self-talk. Describes the brain which has used positive thinking self-help techniques. A vacuum or void is left when negative self-talk is removed and no replacement of positive self-talk occurs.

External reinforcement Receiving attention that increases the likelihood of more incidences of a certain behavior. This acknowledgement is provided by someone or something other than oneself.

Hot cognition The affective aspect of cognition; taking into account the individuals' feelings, beliefs, perceptions, attitudes, and values as they interact with the mechanical processing and use of knowledge.

Internal tapes (TA) The sum total of accumulated, stored-up experiences since birth (see *Dianetics,* Hubbard, 1985 for discussion of internal tapes beginning at conception, rather than birth). The experiences are recorded in the mind and are played out in our lives (similar to Vygotsky's idea of the internalized parent messages).

Internal tapes Our inner speech which many believe originated from our stored up, past experiences. These past experiences have become stored in our memories, and upon certain stimulus are played out in our minds as running dialogue within ourselves.

Judge tapes Impose too much or ill-directed judgmental self-talk, which has an effect on our behavior, feelings, and state of mind. There are three judges according to Butler (i.e., drivers, stoppers, and confusers).

Language of self-support Language spoken to self which fosters caring and support of self. Supporting self verbally in the same way that a loved one is supported by us. Nurturing oneself through helpful self-talk.

Maladaptive beliefs Sometimes referred to as irrational beliefs. Beliefs that distort reality and challenge reason. Such beliefs cause an individual to live inharmoniously with him/herself and/or others.

Medical model Prescriptive. Imposing an outside, external remedy for human needs and ailments.

Negative programming That set of messages we have stored as internal tapes that tell us "no" and what we can not do, rather than telling us what is permitted. The negative programming sounds like the critical parent voice in transactional analysis.

Parent state (TA) Similar to the superego state in Freud's psychoanalytical theory. The parent state is subdivided into the critical and nurturing parent. The critical parent represents restraint, while the nurturing parent represents comforting care.

Permitter self-talk Giving oneself permission or affirmation to talk to self in a healthy, facilitative, appropriate, and/or positive manner (e.g., I am permitted to make mistakes).

Rational emotive therapy (RET) Also called rational emotive thinking (RET). RET is based on the premise that thinking shapes behavior. Individuals with a rational belief system talk sanely to themselves and this leads to healthy, rational behavior.

Self-conditioning RET premise that we condition ourselves by our choice of reactions to various situations. Individuals shape their own behaviors not because of an external event, but because of our reaction to the external event.

Self-defeating Thinking, talk-to-self, feeling, believing, and behaving in ways that may have a negative result for an individual. For example, Ellis would say that catastrophizing is a self-defeating behavior.

Self-talk Helmstetter's definition of self-talk (1986, p. 59): a way to override our past negative programming by erasing or replacing it with conscious, positive new directions.

Self-talk tapes Refers to audiorecording of fifteen to eighteen self-talk phrases supplied initially by Helmstetter (1987). Individuals make their own tapes by repeating each self-talk phrase three times with pauses in between, using self-talk Levels III or IV, then repeating the self-talk phrases one last time, substituting "you" for "I."

Semantic therapy The modification of maladaptive behavior by having individuals see, understand, dispute, alter, and act against self-defeating, negative internal verbalizations.

Social transaction (TA) Receiving and sending verbal and nonverbal messages from and to another individual.

Stopper self-talk tape The stoppers interfere with our self-expression and therefore limit us. They keep us from asserting ourselves. There are four types of stoppers: *catastrophizing, negative self-labeling, setting rigid requirements,* and *witch-messages.* These are defined in chapter 5; all definitions are according to Butler (1981).

Stroking (TA) The act of sending complementary messages to another individual. (Please see "complementary messages" in this section.)

Transactional analysis (TA) Based on Freud's psychoanalytical theory. Social transactions are affected by whether individuals are acting from their adult (ego), child (id), or parent (superego) voices. These three states originate from all the stored experiences from our past (similar to Vygotksy's idea of internalization).

Warm fuzzies (TA) Complementary messages. (Please refer to the definition of complementary messages in this section.)

Cognitive Synthesis: A Summary

In this chapter, the affective considerations for a metacognitive instructional program are illustrated via four cognitive semantic approaches. Rational emotive therapy (or thinking) (RET) and transactional analysis (TA) are related to and support the idea of teaching students to become more responsible for their learning and behavior at school. This can only be accomplished through attention to how we talk to students and how they learn to talk to themselves to focus, define, guide, cope with, and reinforce their own school tasks. The other two approaches (i.e., Butler and Helmstetter) acknowledge the existence of a great deal of nonfacilitative self-talk, and believe procedures exist to change negative self-talk to positive self-talk. The first step for changing self-talk is to become aware of negative self-talk in ourselves and those around us. Next individuals become familiar with their negative self-talk: Butler advocates counting the occurrences and Helmstetter advocates writing self-talk and then converting the negative into positive. Butler provides some important insights into the development of a language of self-support. She does not provide actual self-talk phrases for specific habits (e.g., getting to sleep); however, she does describe permitter self-talk that counters the self-defeating judge tapes within us. On the other hand, Helmstetter provides his readers with the levels of self-talk, why positive thinking alone will not be effective, and fifteen to eighteen self-talk phrases for approximately sixty habits, situations, and attitudes that individuals may wish to use.

Summary of Part One: Theoretical and Conceptual Framework of CSI

Theory makes at least two contributions to the study of teaching and learning: (1) it guides research and (2) it organizes and provides new perspectives and meanings. It is commonly said that "theory informs practice." I like to think instead that theory informs educational study, and research findings from these studies guide educational practice. Because educational practice is not an end result but is a process—an ever-evolving process—practice then informs theory and the process begins again.

The theoretical and conceptual underpinnings of cognitive self-instruction have contributed meaning to cognitive self-instruction. In short, without them, cognitive self-instruction would be a haphazard recipe, lacking professional sophistication. Classroom teachers and their students deserve methods and curriculum steeped heavily in theoretical and conceptual reasoning, soundness, feasibility, and importance.

Cognitive self-instruction, as I define it, grew out of combining a cognitive and affective emphasis on metacognition. Vygotsky's theory and concepts represent the seminal work for understanding how cognitive self-instruction impacts on learning behaviors via verbal self-regulation. Some individuals after Vygotsky incorporated his ideas as springboards. From their work, new perspectives and meanings enriched the idea of cognitive self-instruction. Cognitive self-instruction (ala Meichenbaum) for classroom use evolved from a cognitive emphasis, metacognition itself, and an affective emphasis. The meaning of cognitive self-instruction is tied intricately to understanding all three emphases. Thus, an instructional program called "cognitive self-instruction" (to be presented in Part Three) is defined in the following manner: putting students in charge of their own learning through a systematic program based on a progression from other-regulation to self-regulation. Students' motivation, volition, cognitive competency, attributional styles and feelings are assessed as prerequisites to students' abilities to transfer responsibility from teacher to student. The expected outcomes and benefits of this program are also cognitive and affective in nature. Cognitive self-instruction should improve students' motivation, attributions, and cognitive competencies, as well as self-awareness, self-acceptance, self-esteem, self-confidence, and self-control. The ultimate goals of cognitive self-instruction are to produce (1) students capable of self-regulation, (2) students who eagerly assume responsibility for their own learning, and (3) students who acquire lifelong skills for taking control of their own cognition, behavior, feelings, intrapersonal and interpersonal relationships.

Part Two

Related Research in Cognitive Self-Instruction

Overview of Part Two

Part Two is not intended as an exhaustive, all-inclusive discussion of the research studies which impinge on cognitive self-instruction (CSI) for classroom practice. The amount of research activity since Flavell introduced the term *metacognition* has been staggering. Some studies have been very worthwhile, while others have latched onto the terminology, "metacognition," without sound reason. The area became a dumping group for many cognitive studies that were not really metacognitive in nature, except in the title of the article. Therefore, some research studies have not related directly to cognitive self-instruction as it was defined theoretically and conceptually in Part One. These studies are not reported in Part Two.

In addition, recently there has been an abundance of research studies in a large variety of areas related to CSI (e.g., spelling, reading, handwriting, behavior control, problem-solving, stress, etc.). It has been very difficult to read them all thoroughly. Therefore, the reader should know that I am providing examples of studies conducted in various areas. I am attempting to create "a large picture," "a gestalt." I am unable to say the studies I write about in Part Two represent the complete picture of all research studies conducted in this area. I hope to mention many of the classic, landmark studies; however, my perception of the important works may not coincide directly with that of other readers. Nevertheless, the studies I mention in Part Two do help to document the effectiveness of a CSI-type training and instruction for various populations (e.g., children and adults), for various cognitive areas (e.g., memory, problem solving), for various academic areas (e.g., reading, spelling), and in various settings (e.g., clinical, classroom).

6

Cognitive Self-Instruction Research by Grade Levels/Domains

Overview

In chapter 6 an attempt is made to present samples of metacognitive strategy research by grade levels and/or age groups. The categories are preschoolers, early elementary, middle school, high school/college, and adults. The five age groups are discussed using the research studies from the cognitive domain areas of metamemory, comprehension monitoring, dyadic problem solving, and cognitive self-control as the framework for each age group presentation.

No attempt is made to present an exhaustive review of literature in each of the domain areas. In some cases a specific research study could be categorized into more than one domain or age group. However a decision, based on the primary focus of the article, is made; and therefore, studies are categorized into one area only. Please remember that only a few examples of studies are provided due to space limitations that have been imposed on the author.

In addition to the age divisions and cognitive domains, a brief look at metacognitive research in some academic subject areas (e.g., mathematics) is provided. The final section of the chapter includes the definitions of terminology found often in the literature, as a means of clarification (i.e., general metacognitive strategies, cognitive monitoring, cognitive behavior modification, cognitive self-instruction, self-regulated learning, and self-directed learning).

Self-Questions

1. Knowledge. Provide examples of researchers in the areas of metamemory, metacomprehension, dyadic problem solving, and cognitive self-control.

2. Comprehension. Explain why the majority of metacognitive research studies has focused on children and not adults.

3. Application. Describe a reading group's activities using Brown and Palincsar's notion of reciprocal teaching.

4. Analysis. List the major metacognitive findings for preschoolers' abilities to problem solve.

5. Synthesis. Consider the findings of the metacognitive research studies in any two age categories. Compare and contrast these two sets of findings.

6. Evaluation. What are the major strengths and weaknesses of the overall metacognitive research program presented in all four cognitive domains (i.e., metamemory, comprehension monitoring, dyadic problem solving, and cognitive self-control)?

Before discussions by grade/age groups are provided, an introduction to the four domain areas of metamemory, comprehension monitoring, dyadic problem solving, and cognitive self-control are offered, as these apply generally to classroom application. The specifics of these applications are provided in Part Three.

Metamemory

The idea of metacognitive strategic organization was investigated initially in the area of memory. These first metamemorial studies (Flavell, Beach, & Chinsky, 1966; Keeny, Cannizzo, & Flavell, 1967; Corsini, Pick, & Flavell, 1968; Flavell, Fredrichs, & Hoyt, 1970) comprise the classics of metacognition because they stirred great interest in a new psychological concept. This research consistently showed that children often fail to use cognitive procedures that could in fact improve their performance. It was shown that verbal rehearsal aids retention; however, young children often do not spontaneously organize their cognitive efforts in such a way that they produce these learning aids. With brief training to rehearse, the six and seven year olds did rehearse and their recall scores improved correspondingly. However, when given an opportunity to rehearse on their own, they tended to not employ the rehearsal strategies. Therefore, Flavell and his colleagues attributed the cause to a production deficiency, and not mediation deficiency (Reese, 1962). The results of the metamemory studies and those of others some years later (Brown, Campione, & Barclay, 1978; Brown & DeLoache, 1978; Flavell & Wellman, 1977; Keniston & Flavell, 1979; Kreutzer, Leonard, & Flavell, 1975) suggest that younger children are far less attuned than older children to their own cognitive processes and knowledge. However, the reasons the younger children did not spontaneously rehearse in these studies may have been the meaningless of the task (Istomina, 1975) or insufficient training to remember to rehearse. The implications for education are that young elementary children can learn to verbally rehearse, group, elaborate, etc., and such strategies do improve retention rates. This has implications for school study habits and memorization work (e.g., spelling words, alphabet, mathematics facts, terms, etc.).

Edwards and Middleton (1987) provide discussion and future recommendations for research on remembering. Using F. C. Barlett's 1932 book entitled *Remembering: A Study in Experimental and Social Psychology* as their foundation, they argue for studying memory in terms of its social and personal functions. Bartlett's premises are hauntingly similar to Vygotsky's ideas on the social origins of intellectual functioning. These authors, based on Bartlett's work, criticize the study of memory in isolation, apart from its social communication origins. They cite three neglected themes in metamemory research: "(1) the role of feeling and attitude in remembering, (2) the nature of cross-modal symbolic remembering (e.g, written accounts of spoken conversation), and (3) remembering as a function of conversational discourse, where remembering occurs in the context of communicative purposes that often override simple notions of reproductive accuracy, and where the social dimensions of symbolic remembering is most accessible to examination" (p. 9).

Metamemory research that includes motivational, affective dimensions (e.g., fatigue, moods, personality, social discourse) still remain scarce. Perhaps this will be a trend for this particular cognitive domain for the '90s decade.

Even though metamemory research continues to be rather slow to include the affective dimension of mental functioning, it has experienced a change in focus from the study of nonsense syllables and rote serial recall to the study of memory for meaningful words and more complex structures used in natural, everyday language (Gick, 1986).

Comprehension Monitoring

Markman's studies (1977, 1978, 1979, 1981) were ground-breaking studies in the area of metacognitive research for comprehension. She referred to her focus as "comprehension monitoring." She dealt specifically with elementary children's ability to monitor their own listening comprehension as directions for a game and a magic trick (1977) were read aloud to them. She also read inconsistent essays (1979) to subjects. Markman (1978) related the importance of her research for an educational setting: "The ability to monitor one's comprehension is necessary for academic excellence. In order to study effectively one must be able to differentiate what is understood from what still needs clarification. One must be sensitive to the level of one's comprehension to know what to reread, when to ask questions, what additional information is needed, etc. . . . " (pp. 30–31). The ability of elementary school children to monitor their comprehension (according to Markman's studies) develops slowly, and at the sixth-grade level total comprehension monitoring is still not complete. When first and third graders were given instructions for playing a game, with the omission of a critical step, only one out of the twelve first graders recognized the omission before the game was played (Markman, 1977). Ten out of the twelve third graders commented on the omission before playing. Markman concludes that the first graders were receiving the directions without mentally processing as they listened, while the third graders seemed to mentally play the game as a way of evaluating the information.

In another study, Markman (1979) investigated the abilities of third and sixth graders to recognize inconsistencies in short nonfiction essays. There were explicit and implicit inconsistencies. Between 40 and 50 percent of the children did not notice the explicit inconsistencies. Almost 100 percent failed to notice the implicit ones. There was no significant difference between the performance of the third and sixth graders. Interestingly however, the sixth graders improved a great deal and the third graders' performance remained the same when all were told ahead of time that an inconsistency might be present. The sixth graders seemed to have the cognitive strategies available to use when the need was explicitly indicated. The third graders did not seem to have this skill available. Both age groups seemed not to have an awareness for the need of conscious mental processing of material they hear.

Although the task difficulty remained the same for all ages in Markman's studies, I believe she highlights an important point for teachers and parents (i.e., we must not assume that children have not listened when they fail to understand oral directions). Often adults present directions to children and when the directions are not followed we say, "You weren't listening!" In some cases, we may be correct. However, Markman's research emphasizes that children may have listened to every word we said, but did not have the necessary processing skills to realize they did not understand. This realization often comes about as a result of "enactment." When children attempt to perform the task for which we have provided our exact, often multistep directions, they suddenly realize that they have not understood what to do. A strategy to eliminate some of this "not-realizing-that-you-don't-understand" until enactment, is to try an example of the task, under adult supervision, before children (students) are asked to perform independently. This is what happens in the "guided-practice" step of direct instruction (Rosenshine, 1987). The teacher monitors the initial work assignments before students engage in independent practice. This guided practice phase is in direct congruence with Markman's findings.

Haller, Child, and Walberg (1988) conducted what they called a "quantitative synthesis" (p. 5) of twenty studies to assess the impact of strategy thinking on reading comprehension. Of the 115 effect sizes for a total student population of 1,553, or contrasts between experimental and control subjects, the mean effect size was .71. These authors state that the "average effect size of .71 is among the larger ones that have been uncovered in educational research." Other findings were (1) that later studies had larger effect sizes than earlier studies, (2) studies with few subjects produced larger effects, (3) urban students benefitted more from metacomprehension instruction than rural or suburban students, (4) various types of measures, including nationally standardized tests, were used without statistically significant outcomes among them, documenting that all were effective measures of the benefits of the metacognitive interventions, (5) effects were largest for the seventh and eighth grades, (6) metacomprehension instruction had the least effect on students in the fourth, fifth, or sixth grade, (7) ten minutes or less of instruction per lesson proved insufficient, (8) strategies involving textual-dissonance, self-questioning, and backward-forward seemed more effective than others, (9) reinforcement was the most effective teaching method, and (10) several, varied instructional approaches were better than a few for improving comprehension. In summary, this metanalysis clearly documents an impressive average effect size for metacognitive instruction on reading comprehension.

Annemarie Palincsar has researched extensively in the area of comprehension monitoring. The concept she is most noted for is reciprocal teaching. Reciprocal teaching is a "dialogue between teachers and students for the purpose of jointly constructing the meaning of text. There are four activities or strategies which are used to structure the dialogue: summarizing, questioning, clarifying, and predicting" (Palincsar, 1986, p. 119). The teacher and reading group together review strategies, importance of strategies, and the context where the strategies are useful. Teachers are responsible for selecting and matching the most useful strategies that will enhance a particular group of students. Research studies have revealed that the students must be kept well informed about strategy use. Specifically they should know the value of metacognitive skills, where the skills are most helpful, how they can acquire the skills, and the need to review skills every day. The key to reciprocal teaching is that the skills gradually transfer to the students so that they become independent in their use of the skills. Palincsar (1986, p. 119–121) describes the reciprocal teaching process by mentally traveling through a daily reading lesson in which reciprocal teaching is being incorporated. Because of the length and great detail, interested readers are referred to her description.

The majority of research on reciprocal teaching was conducted with junior high students enrolled in Chapter I remedial reading classes. These students were performing at least two years below grade level in reading comprehension. In the earlier research studies (Brown and Palincsar, 1982; Palincsar and Brown, 1984) reciprocal teaching was employed for twenty consecutive school days. The intervention was deemed successful by measures of transcript dialogues, daily measures of reading comprehension, generalized tasks of reading in social studies and science classes, percentile ranking on comprehension tests (moved from the twentieth percentile to the fiftieth percentile). In addition Palincsar (1985) compared three other instructional conditions to the traditional reciprocal teaching. She found that the guided, interactive reciprocal teaching resulted in the most impressive benefits on comprehension measures. This type of guided, interactive instruction (relying heavily on dialogue) has also been called "scaffolded instruction (Wood, Bruner, & Ross, 1976), "proleptic instruction" (Wertsch, 1978), "instrumental enrichment" (Feuerstein, 1979), and "Socratic dialogue" (Schallert & Kleiman, 1979).

Since the initial reciprocal teaching studies completed by Palincsar and Brown, additions to reciprocal training have been noted (i.e., peer tutoring, reciprocal teaching in the content areas, specifically science texts, and with nonreaders, specifically at-risk first graders, [Palincsar, 1989]). Current research is aimed at investigating the means by which teacher-student dialogues can encourage the transfer of strategy control from the teacher to the student. Also, these investigators are examining the benefits of reciprocal instruction as collaborative problem solving (Palincsar & Brown, 1988).

Wittrock (1988) has a very interesting section on the teaching of reading comprehension. His discussion came about after he attempted to teach enlisted men at the Army Research Institute how to read with better comprehension. These men had one thing in common: they had failed reading comprehension tests. Therefore, Wittrock attempted to teach them learning strategies similar to the ones we have just highlighted (e.g., summarizing). In some cases he was successful and in others the strategies did not help. Wittrock says the reason the learning strategies were sometimes not facilitative was because the learner was not interested (e.g., "some topics we thought they would be interested in reading did not interest them," p. 293). Therefore, he reminds us how crucial it is to know the learners' interests, backgrounds, motivations, and aspirations. He brings us back to the need for affective consideration in any type of instruction. I found this consideration to be lacking in many of the comprehension monitoring studies mentioned previously. What learners and teachers bring to the instructional setting, including interests, attitudes, feelings, beliefs, and values, as well as what the learning context communicates (e.g., supportive, threatening, uncomfortable) are important variables that need to be incorporated into the future research on comprehension monitoring. Another future direction in this area of research may include a more pronounced blending among the four cognitive processing areas. The distinctions between comprehension and problem solving, for example, are blurring as Palincsar and Brown (1988) embark on the study of comprehension as collaborative problem solving. Other trends may include more attention to what the learner brings to comprehension, the comprehension/learning context, what the teacher believes to be a model of comprehension, and comprehension in the subject matter areas (e.g., science).

Dyadic Problem Solving

The third cognitive processing area is designated as "problem solving." Problem solving is an important facet of comprehension and self-control. The overlapping is obvious and makes it difficult to study and write about this cognitive domain in isolation. However, there are some interesting factors to consider if we view this area as general problem solving in the broad sense (Brown, 1978; Brown & DeLoache, 1978; Flavell, 1976). Brown (1978) expressed it this way:

> . . . we believe that many skills currently being studied as skills of metacognition are trans-situational (i.e., they apply to all forms of problem-solving activity rather than being restricted to a certain process area. Self-interrogation concerning the current state of one's own knowledge during problem solving is an essential skill in a wide variety of situations, those of the laboratory, the school, the everyday life. (p.61)

Brown (1987) described metacognitive activities that are used to oversee problem solving: "These processes include planning activities (predicting outcomes, scheduling strategies, and various forms of vicarious trial and error, etc.); monitoring activities (monitoring, testing, revising, and rescheduling one's strategies for learning) during learning; and checking outcomes (evaluating the outcome of any strategic actions again criteria of efficiency and effectiveness)" (p. 68).

Flavell (1976) suggested imperatives and questions that a metacognitively oriented individual might produce and respond to when solving problems:

> Examine task features carefully. Is there a problem here that needs solving? Is the problem I just solved the one I initially intended to solve, or is it only a subproblem of the main problem or even an irrelevant problem? Keep track of past solution efforts, their outcomes, and the problem-relevant information they yielded. Remember to retrieve and apply this information when needed. (p. 54)

Initially most of the research on the development of strategic activity for problem solving was concerned with how children function as independent problem solvers (Egeland, 1974; Goulet & Hoyer, 1969; Ridberg, Park, & Hetherington, 1971). An interesting deviation from this was seen in the works of James V. Wertsch (1978, 1980) in which he advocated examining how adults and children function together in problem-solving tasks. Wertsch's studies provided a social interactional model for learning disabilities remediation and a schema for adult-child dyadic interactions during problem solving thus the name *dyadic problem solving*. These models were proven effective for increasing the problem-solving abilities of learning-disabled elementary children and very young children (ages $2^{1/2}$ to $4^{1/2}$ years old).

Research studies, such as mentioned earlier, dealt primarily with general problem solving to improve cognition alone. Another cluster of studies focused on direct training of verbal strategies to improve social problem solving (Goodwin & Mahoney, 1976; Pitkanen, 1974). More recently Lowenthal (1986) proposed a metacognitive plan of action to help learning-disabled students (preschool through adolescence) to solve everyday problems: (1) reflect on prior knowledge, (2) develop a plan for attacking the problem, (3) monitor one's own progress, and (4) evaluate the outcome of the plan. These steps are very similar to those proposed by Ann Brown. Lowenthal also recommended the use of Meichenbaum's self-instructional training and categories of self-communication: (1) problem definition—What did the teacher say to do? (2) focusing attention and response monitoring—First, I will draw a straight line, (3) self-reinforcement—Yay! I got it right the first try! (4) self-evaluation and error correction—I better try this again and use a ruler this time. In addition, Goldman's (1982) "Goal Story Interview" is suggested as a means of using a structured interview format to lead learning-disabled students to monitor their problem-solving processes. This story-form interview proceeds from the student first making a plan of how to reach an imaginary goal, explaining why the goal is desired, brainstorming the specific means for reaching the goal, and mentally planning a hypothetical way of coping if the goal cannot be reached. In addition to the Goal Story Interview, goal-oriented planning is fostered through alternative thinking in early childhood, means-end thinking in elementary, and consequential thinking in adolescence.

Along these same lines, the Shure and Spivack studies (1974, 1978) with preschool and kindergarten children are important to the area of verbal training for social problem solving. They developed "a social problem-solving training program that produced a positive effect on children's ability to verbalize alternative plans, solutions, and consequences when faced with social problems" (Camp & Bash, 1985, p. 10).

Camp and Bash (1985) developed the Think Aloud program. This program combined Meichenbaum and Goodman's self-instructional training (1971) for cognitive problem solving and Shure and Spivack training (1974, 1978) to improve communication of social problem solving. The major appeal of combining these programs was the emphasis on training children to "cope" with problems on their own after receiving a systematic approach to handling their own social and academic challenges. The Think Aloud program was evaluated and found to be effective for cognitive and social problem-solving outcomes. It should be noted however that initial evaluation studies (e.g., Camp, 1977; Camp & Bash, 1981) were conducted by the authors of the program. Nevertheless, Hughes (1985) in a recent study reported positive results from two case studies when parents served as cotherapists in a social/cognitive problem solving Think Aloud program. This program involving parents as cotrainers was a modified version of the Think Aloud, twenty-three lessons covering problem definition, generation of alternative solutions, predicting and evaluating consequences, monitoring plan implementations, and self-evaluation. Readers who are interested in cognitive interventions to improve children's problem-solving abilities should consult an excellent review by Urbaine and Kendall (1980).

A recent direction in metacognitive strategic problem-solving activities has involved the use of the computer (e.g., Cohen, 1989; Derry, Hawkes, & Zeigler, 1989; Kunz, Drewniak, & Schott, 1989). The computer programs developed by psychologists and educators lend themselves well to assessing and training metacognitive strategies for general problem solving.

Cognitive Self-Control

Meichenbaum did a great deal of pioneering and focusing of the work in this area. Meichenbaum and Goodman (1971/1979) concluded that teaching individuals how to talk to themselves, how to alter the content of speech-to-self in terms of both the self-statements and images, resulted in behavior changes. Their self-instructional paradigm for change was presented earlier. Teachers are seeing the need for discipline systems that teach autonomy, self-directedness, and self-management. For much too long teachers have been provided with primarily behaviorism and behavior modification techniques which shape children externally. Everywhere I go for educational conferences and in all my classes, teachers are asking for ways to foster directly the self-controlled learner.

Since the area of cognitive self-control is quite large, three conclusive reviews will be used to facilitate some manageability of this research area, in a historical sense (i.e., Pressley, 1979; Rosenbaum & Drabman, 1979; Fish & Pervan, 1986). The Pressley and Rosenbaum/Drabman articles are used to portray cognitive self-control in the 1960s, and primarily in the 1970s; Pressley, because of his emphasis on cognitive intervention; Rosenbaum/Drabman, because of their emphasis on the classroom setting. Fish and Pervan bring us into the 1980s and deal directly with self-instructional training, the focus of this book. Please note that there are many important studies in this area which will not be named, as an exhaustive discussion is beyond the space limitations of this chapter. Readers who are interested in a discussion of the history of self-control are referred to Karoly (1977) and Mischel (1974).

Various theories have differed in their explanations of self-control. Nevertheless, there is general consensus that young children do not possess the same degree of self-control that adults possess (Pressley, 1979). Children often do not respond well to demands for self-control. In the last two decades, cognitive psychologists have attempted to develop strategies to promote self-control in children. A self-control situation is defined here as "a situation that requires both the omission of inappropriate responding and the substitution of appropriate responses" (Pressley, 1979, p. 320).

Pressley's review meets two important parameters for purposes of this text: (1) cognitive self-intervention to (2) promote a change in behavior. He does not address spontaneously occurring speech-to-self to modify behavior. The focus of his paper was on studies designed to modify self-control by modifying cognitions. Two types of manipulations were applied (i.e., instruction to use a cognitive strategy and experimenter manipulation of the environment). For purposes of this book only the former (cognitive strategy application) is considered. Pressley, in his impressive, scholarly review divides cognitive self-control into three areas of discussion: (1) young children's verbal control of their motor behaviors, (2) children's use of cognitive strategies in resistance-to-temptation studies, and (3) cognitive modification of impulsive responding. Problem area #1 is a thorough discussion of the Soviet position, primarily Luria's bulb press experiments. Pressley does an excellent job of continuing Luria's line of research through American studies (e.g., Birch, 1976; Masters & Binger, 1976; Meacham, 1973). Pressley states that there is evidence from some studies that verbalizations can increase children's motor control.

Problem area #2 is the discussion of cognitive interventions to effect children's delay of gratification (e.g., Mischel & Baker, 1975) and resistance-to-temptation (e.g., Fry, 1975). Pressley provides a thorough discussion of this group of studies broken down into preschoolers and elementary school age categories. He recommends that much more research needs to be conducted in classrooms to investigate children's self-control in an ecologically valid and meaningful setting.

The third problem area Pressley addresses is the effect of cognitive strategies to modify impulsive behaviors. This area has more direct application to classroom processes because a goal of modern-day education is to foster reflective thinking as opposed to impulsivity. Researchers have often used visual discrimination tasks as the dependent variable. The Matching Familiar Figures Test (MFF [Kagen, Rosman, Day, Albert, & Phillips, 1964]) is often used. On such tests, impulsive children often spend less time and make more errors. Quite a few researchers have investigated the results of teaching impulsive children self-verbalizations to bring behavior under their own control (e.g., Palkes, Stewart, & Kahana, 1968; Meichenbaum & Goodman, 1969/1971). When the data from these studies were combined conceptually, Pressley's major concern was the lack of generalization to intellectual functioning and to settings other than the training setting.

In summary, Pressley's careful review revealed that children who were taught a cognitive strategy acted in a more controlled way than those who were not. This finding documents that children are capable of learning such strategies and are able to use them to improve self-control. In many of the studies, self-verbalizations were used as the cognitive intervention technique. While Pressley applauds the accomplishments of the studies in his review, he calls for "many longer term experiments in naturalistic settings" (p. 363).

Rosenbaum and Drabman (1979) reviewed self-control training in the classroom. The training referred to by these authors is broader in scope and definition than cognitive interventions for self-control. The components reviewed were self-recording, self-evaluation, self-determination of contingencies, and self-instruction in the classroom setting. If Pressley's emphasis on cognitive intervention for self-control and Rosenbaum and Drabman's emphasis on classroom self-control are blended and modified conceptually, implications for cognitive self-instruction for classroom use emerge. Definitions of terms seem appropriate here to explain such implications. Self-observational procedures "involve individuals monitoring their own behavior and subsequently recording that behavior" (Rosenbaum & Drabman, 1979, p. 468). This is not the same as monitoring one's own cognition to investigate what one is thinking about his/her own cognitive enterprises. That procedure is referred to as cognitive monitoring. However, both procedures involve the ability of individuals to oversee their own human activity: self-observation deals with overseeing overt behaviors; while cognitive monitoring deals with overseeing one's own covert thinking. Self-observation has the capacity to function as a behavior-change agent (e.g., Kanfer, 1970;

Kazdin, 1974; Nelson, 1977), due to the reactive effect on the behavior an individual is self-observing. Self-recording is where "behavior is monitored and recorded with a minimum amount of judgement" (p. 468). Self-evaluation involves follow-up evaluation on a subjective level, often with a rating scale of 1–10. Both self-recording and self-evaluation are types of self-observational procedures. Some examples of studies that have documented the benefits of self-recording in classrooms are: Broden, Hall, and Mitts (1971), Gottman and McFall (1972), and Lovitt (1973). Benefits have included appropriate behaviors increasing and inappropriate behaviors decreasing. However Rosenbaum and Drabman reiterate that these changes have been modest ones and short term.

The self-evaluation studies have generally yielded poor results (e.g., Turkewitz, O'Leary, & Ironsmith, 1975). In most of these studies an external evaluation was needed to produce a significant decrease in disruptive behavior. The self-evaluation procedure did not seem to bolster the effectiveness of self-recording. The authors, Rosenbaum and Drabman, also provide an extensive summary of self-determined contingencies studies, where students decide their own reinforcement and provide this reinforcement for self (self-reinforcement). One of their conclusions was that "self-determined contingencies can be as effective as or more effective than externally determined contingencies during periods of reinforcement" (p. 472). Drabman, Spitalnik, and Spitalnik (1973) conducted a self-control study for the maintenance of appropriate classroom behavior. They used successive steps to gradually transfer evaluation and reinforcement from the teacher to the students. (Prior studies had revealed that abrupt transfer of control from the teacher to the student resulted in an increase in undesirable behaviors.) These transfer steps are very important for classroom functioning as often classroom teachers eager to promote self-control may learn some self-control strategies and apply them without the necessary gradual transfer from other- to self-regulation. Therefore, these steps (found on page 473 of the Rosenbaum and Drabman review) will be paraphrased here: (1) students recorded the points provided by the teacher, (2) students earned extra points if their self-evaluation matched that of the teacher rating, (3) matching was faded out in four phases with successively fewer students being required to match the teacher's criterion, (4) students rated their own behavior and determined their own reinforcement, independent of the teachers' matching criterion. Other factors contributing to the success of this self-control program were: (1) teachers continued to praise appropriate student behavior, (2) peer reinforcement increased, (3) accurate self-evaluation was acknowledged by the teacher. Other classroom studies of self-control programs (e.g., Glynn, Thomas, & Shee, 1973; Glynn & Thomas, 1974) for elementary students produced impressive increases of on-task behaviors.

The final set of studies, reviewed by Rosenbaum and Drabman, was those dealing with self-instructional training. This group has the most direct application to cognitive self-instruction. In fact even though not emphasized by Rosenbaum and Drabman, self-verbalization is the crucial ingredient in self-instruction. These authors define self-instruction as "training in which individuals are taught to make suggestions to themselves to guide their own behavior in a manner similar to being guided by another individual" (p. 476). The role of talking to oneself to regulate behavior was beneficial in laboratory settings (Bem, 1967; Hartig & Kanfer, 1973; Meichenbaum & Goodman, 1969; Monohan & O'Leary, 1971). Examples of classroom studies using self-verbalizations for self-instruction are: Bornstein and Quevillon (1976), Friedling and O'Leary (1979), Manning (1988), and Robin, Armel, and O'Leary (1975).

In summary, Rosenbaum and Drabman (1979) believe that the purpose of continued self-control research is to promote students "who can manage as much of their own education as possible to enable the teacher to devote time to teaching . . . without having to control disruptive behavior and to provide incentives constantly for academic performance" (p. 479). I believe that every educator I know would agree with that goal for education. The statement represents perhaps the major crisis and major need in our school systems nationwide, today. The Rosenbaum and Drabman review provides educationally exciting recommendations for future research in this area. Their review documented "that students can be taught to observe and record their own behavior, determine and administer their own contingencies and provide instructions to guide their own behavior" (p. 480). They believe that much research is still needed to clarify thinking and improve generalization effects to real-life situations.

A look at a published self-control article in 1985, six years after reviews by Pressley and Rosenbaum/Drabman, reveals many of the same studies being cited. Very few have been added if we limit our search to cognitive self-instruction for self-control. Fish and Pervan (1985) name the self-control strategies of self-observation, self-recording, self-instruction, self-reinforcement, and problem solving. Their paper deals only with self-instruction which they define as "teaching children to talk to themselves" as a verbal coping strategy to control overt behavior. The studies that overlap with the previous two reviews will not be described again. Fish and Pervan have a comprehensive discussion of self-instruction training in school settings. They begin as most reviews do with Meichenbaum and Goodman's 1971 seminal work. The studies they cite between 1971 and 1979 are the same ones mentioned previously. Between 1980–1986, these authors highlight only five additional studies related to self-instruction in the classroom. They are: Burgio, Whitman, and Johnson, (1980) (ages nine to eleven to increase attending behaviors in the classroom); Bryant and Budd (1982) (impulsive preschoolers' accuracy and completion of worksheets); Kendall and Zupan (1981) (third to fifth graders compared training contexts and conditions on self-control and perspective taking); Genshaft and Hirt (1980) (seventh-grade girls to increase math achievement); Schleser, Meyers, and Cohen (1981) (generalization of self-instruction and comparison of task-specific self-instruction training to generalized self-instruction training).

Results from the vast majority of studies mentioned by Fish and Pervan document significant effects of self-instruction training on their dependent variables. In addition, Schleser et al. (1981) found that children taught general content self-instructions performed better on a transfer task than did those given content-specific self-instructions. This finding is in agreement with Ann Brown's recommendation that general cognitive strategies (that cut across content areas) should be taught. Other findings, revealing benefits of cognitive self-instruction were evident for decreasing distractibility, aggressiveness, and restlessness (Kendall, 1982; Kendall & Zupan, 1981). Fox and Kendall (1983) and Roberts and Dick (1982) suggest that self-instruction training may be more facilitative for approaching familiar tasks than for acquiring new task behaviors. Also Roberts and Dick (1982) and Shepp and Jensen (1983) suggest combining operant conditioning techniques (behavior modification) to self-instruction to increase the benefits of self-instruction techniques used alone. The idea is to fade the external contingencies as soon as possible. Several researchers (Kendall & Finch, 1978; Kendall & Zupan, 1981) concluded that combining self-instruction training with contingency management enhances effectiveness.

The fourth domain, cognitive self-control provides support for educational programs that involve a balance of adult control and student self-control. The goal of the adult is to help children to help themselves: to help children build their own self-guidance. We now have some tools based on the diligent work of the many researchers named in this section. We also have a great deal of work left to do and answers to find. Future research in this area will dig deeper into ecologically valid contexts (e.g., the classroom) using more meaningful tasks. More indepth qualitative studies, such as the case study approach are needed to study the intricacies involved in teaching self-control. Hopefully self-control instruction will come to be viewed as instruction, not something separate from instruction. Instead of the term *self-control,* perhaps we will use terms like *self-guidance* for this sort of socializing instruction (see Brophy, 1984), to foster school and social responsibility (see Anderson & Prawat, 1983).

Next, a discussion of metamemory, comprehension monitoring, dyadic problem solving, and cognitive self-control are structured within grade/age group.

Preschoolers (birth to age five)

Metamemory. Since the early 1970s, a great deal of attention has been focused on children's awareness, organization, and direction of their own memory processes. These functions have been referred to as metamemory by John Flavell (1971).

Within the area of metamemory research, there is great complexity, pertaining to the types of studies being conducted. Schneider (1985) has an excellent review of metamemory by types by grade levels. Readers interested in an indepth discussion of the developmental trends of metamemory research by grade level should not miss this scholarly piece. The types of studies (described by grade levels) are memory monitoring (rote memory), memory monitoring (prose materials), organizational strategies (clustering), organizational strategies (paired associate), and training studies (organizational strategies). For studies involving preschoolers as participants, Schneider designates only in the area of memory monitoring (rote memory). The correlations between metamemory and memory behavior-performance for preschoolers are documented: Posansky (1978) = .64, Wellman (1977) = .19, Wippich (1981) = .45, Worden and Sladewski, Awig (1982) = .29, (see Schneider, 1985, pp. 103–104).

In one of the early classical studies of memory span prediction task, Flavell, Friedrichs, and Hoyt (1970) asked preschool children, kindergartners, second, and fourth graders to predict their memory ability. Participants in this study were shown increasingly longer series of familiar objects, via pictures. Participants predicted whether they could recall them in the correct sequence. When the participants determined that the sequence of illustration could not be recalled because of their length or when a series of ten illustrations had been shown, the prediction process ended. Then, the participants actual memory recall was evaluated, repeating this procedure. In general, the two youngest groups (i.e., preschool and kindergarten) overestimated their memory capacity. More of the older children (i.e., second and fourth grade) did not. Over half of the younger children erroneously predicted they could recall ten items. Fewer than one-fourth of the older participants erred in their predictions. According to these findings, children younger than seven years may not be able to evaluate their memory abilities realistically. It should be pointed out, however, that some of the younger children (more than one-fourth of them) were able to accurately predict their memory abilities. Many investigations following the one just noted were conducted in an attempt to explain why young preschoolers have difficulty with memory prediction. For a complete review of these studies, please refer to Schneider (1985). Schneider summarizes these findings by saying that "preschooler's metamemory concerning the prediction of serial recall is generally not well developed" (p. 65).

In another metamemory study, young children judged the merits of certain memory strategies that would be helpful in a sort-recall task. Justice (1981) required preschoolers, kindergartners, and second graders to determine the value of four different memory strategies: (1) grouping, (2) repeating, (3) naming, and (4) looking for a sort-recall assignment. The strategies named as best by the children were compared with the memory strategies the children actually used on the task. This comparison was made to evaluate the metamemory-memory connection. Findings indicated that only 20 percent of the preschoolers and 15 percent of the kindergartners implemented the memory strategy they had designated earlier as best. Fifty percent of the second graders used their chosen strategy. Second graders also selected the more advanced strategies of grouping and rehearsal, both in selection and use of the strategy, than the young participants (Schneider, 1985, p. 83).

Istomina (1975) conducted memory research with children three to seven years old. He compared children's memory for lists of rote, meaningless words versus their memory for comparable lists embedded in a meaningful activity. Recall was clearly superior in the meaningful task. Istomina noted a qualitative shift between the age of four and five. At this time, older subjects seemed to actively rehearse by moving lips, and repeating the words read to them. The older subjects (five to seven years) seemed to make active attempts to remember by monitoring their own memory states and self-checking to determine how well they remembered. The younger group (three to four) did not actively rehearse, self-monitor, or self-check. Ledger's research (1985) indicated that preschoolers are capable of acquiring strategies taught directly to them to improve their recall abilities. DeLoache (1985) with very young subjects one and one half to two years old, described what she called strategy-like behaviors in a memory-for-location task. She believed these results were evidence of an early natural propensity to keep alive what must be recalled. This was thought to be a rudimentary version of what will later become more elaborate mnemonic strategies. The four year olds remembered more items when they sorted the items, rather than just playing with them (Sodian, 1986). Five year olds, after rehearsal strategy training, were able to use overt and covert rehearsal equally well for a serial order recall task (Johnston, Johnson, & Gray, 1987).

Hayes, Scott, Chemelski, and Johnson (1987) tested Flavell's cognitive monitoring model and metamnemonic development with 120 three and five year olds. Their research documented the importance of mental states (e.g., happy/sad; fatigue/alert) upon preschoolers assessment of the ease or difficulty of studying and their actual study habits.

In general, memory studies with preschoolers have illustrated that they do not spontaneously use metamemory strategies to aid recall; however Schneider (1985) makes it clear that such generalizations are dependent upon certain factors (e.g., whether the task was a sort-recall task or a memory monitoring task). In the memory monitoring tasks, preschoolers and kindergartners occasionally demonstrated an efficient relationship between metamemory and memory behavior. Specifically when the memory task "required recall or recognition of either single items or small item sets" (p. 99), a positive relationship was noticeable between metamemory and memory performance for young children. In addition, this age group was able to use rehearsal strategies overtly and covertly when a training program was implemented. They seem to possess some natural rudimentary versions of mnemonic strategies from which to work. These were identified by DeLoache when she studied eighteen- to twenty-four-month-old children during a memory for location task. Along these same lines, Wellman (1977) stated that preschoolers have some knowledge about what makes a memory task hard or easy (e.g., number of items, distractions, study time, help from others, cues). Finally, there is documentation that mental state and fatigue are important considerations when studying the memory abilities of preschoolers.

Comprehension monitoring. Most of the reading comprehension monitoring studies have occurred with older age groups due to the rather obvious reason: most preschoolers are unable to read. On the other hand, some listening comprehension studies have involved preschoolers. For example, Revelle, Karabenick, and Wellman (1981) investigated comprehension monitoring with $2^{1/2}$ to $4^{1/2}$ year olds. The overall results of this study were counter to other studies which indicated that young children have little ability or disposition to monitor their listening comprehension. Evidence from Revelle et al. indicated for at least some types of comprehension even $2^{1/2}$ to $3^{1/2}$ year olds can employ appropriate and efficient strategies for resolving comprehension problems. The older subjects ($4^{1/2}$) demonstrated monitoring for the comprehension problems.

Dyadic problem solving. Preschoolers have been the target age group for many studies aimed at general problem solving (e.g., solving puzzles). The theme of these studies has been to investigate Vygotsky's notion that young children learn through the verbal dyadic interaction between adult and child. Pellegrini (1984) reviewed the development of preschoolers' private speech in a Piaget versus Vygotsky framework. Putting the Piagetian/Vygotskian discussion aside, some of the interesting findings about preschoolers' private speech as a result of the adult-child interaction are: children's acquisition of syntax may originate from adult-infant exchanges, private speech becomes more covert as children age during the preschool years, and children engage in more private speech in a more social context than in a less social one (Pellegrini, 1984). This last finding indicates that the private speech of the preschooler still has some semblance of social characteristics remaining from the social origins of private speech, which when internalized later serves in the role of the cognitive guide. Kohlberg, Yaeger, and Hjertholms' research (1968) revealed that as children age from five to eight years their private speech becomes less intelligible. The reason the private speech of the older children may appear less intelligible to a researcher may be due to the fact that the private speech of the older children is shedding its social characteristics, as the cognitive function of speech is assumed.

James Wertsch (1980) and his colleagues (1980, 1984) studied the adult-child unit directly as they verbally and nonverbally interacted during problem solving. These dyadic models were effective for increasing the problem-solving abilities of very young children (ages $2^{1/2}$ to $4^{1/2}$ years old). Specifically, the mother-child dyads were involved in a puzzle-making task in which the final product was to be identical with a model provided to the subjects. The older preschoolers were likely to carry out the entire sequence of actions necessary to select a piece and place it correctly in the copy puzzle; whereas younger children usually required additional help from the adult. Their results supported the notion of an ontogenetic transition from other regulation to self-regulation during a problem-solving task. This study was among the first of many in which the adult-child dyad was studied as a problem solving unit (e.g., Renshaw & Gardner, 1987).

A growing body of literature exists that is based on the idea that preschoolers gradually internalize the verbal and nonverbal strategies employed by their parents during joint activities such as games, simple problem solving, and household work. These parental teaching practices and their effect on preschoolers' development have been studied by Moss (1985), Reeve (1987), and others. Researchers have used both proximal and distal outcomes as criteria under investigation. Proximal measures are collected while the adult is working with the child, usually when the child is attempting a task independently, for which the adult had provided aid previously. The distal measures have traditionally been measures removed from the problem-solving task itself (e.g., standardized intelligence tests, school achievement). Regardless of measures, a consistent finding is that an optimal balance between adult guidance and child initiative is required to foster children's learning. Too much help and too little help are barriers to learning. Hasn't this been the case forever in education? Master teachers offer guidance without assuming the responsibility for the task. Parents are teachers. Word and Middleton (1975) found that the effective teachers were mothers who offered less help if their children were successful, and more help if their children failed. Skillful parents offer help without taking over the completion of the task. When children's development is viewed from Vygotsky's notion as the movement from other-regulation to self-regulation, teaching by parents and teachers becomes even more central as it relates to the cognitive growth and development of the child. The interaction then between teacher and child or parent and child becomes the context for learning. This relationship then should be informed, rich, balanced, and encouraged.

Another focus of the problem-solving studies for preschoolers is the direct instruction of cognitive training strategies to improve social problem solving. Lowenthal (1986) proposed a metacognitive plan of action to help learning-disabled children from preschool to adolescence solve everyday problems. Shure and Spivack (1974, 1978) developed a training program for preschoolers and kindergartners that was effective. The program improved young children's ability to verbalize alternative plans, solutions, and consequences for social situations.

Cognitive self-control. Vygotsky (1962) believed that language-to-self could regulate behavior by the end of the preschool period. At this time private speech was internalized and was believed to merge with thought. Inner speech is thought, in the Vygotskian sense, to guide and control human behavior by the end of the preschool period. Therefore, this indicates that most young children come to school fully capable of self-control. However, their self-control capabilities are not nurtured by teachers because teachers are not introduced to and well-trained in cognitive intervention strategies to promote self-control. Instead teachers are taught behavior modification techniques for externally shaping children's behavior, when in reality many children are fully capable of guiding their own behavior in socially appropriate ways. With innovative teacher preparation programs in cognitive self-instruction, this developmentally inappropriate teaching practice can be changed.

Pellegrini (1981) found that preschoolers (ages three to five) regardless of age, used their private speech to encode ongoing activity. His analysis of preschoolers' verbal self-regulation was in contrast to the developmental trend described by Vygotsky (i.e., private speech initially follows actions, then accompanies action, and finally precedes action). It is only in the last instance that speech-to-self serves a regulatory effect upon behavior. Therefore, Pellegrini's research suggests that this trend does not follow as outlined by Vygotsky. Instead it indicates "that children across the preschool period use the lower form of self-regulating private speech" (p. 67). It is important to remember that Pellegrini was analyzing the naturally occurring spontaneous private speech of three to five year olds in a puzzle-solving context. His research did not address the capabilities of preschoolers to learn to use their speech-to-self to purposely guide behavior if they are taught to do so. Meichenbaum and Goodman (1971) documented the capability of five year olds to learn self-regulatory speech-to-self to modify impulsive behaviors. Also, for some motor tasks, preschoolers were able to regulate their own motor behaviors when they used a self-verbalization strategy, (Bem, 1967; Wozniak, 1972). These studies document that it is possible to teach verbal self-control to preschoolers. Other researchers, investigating along these same lines, found that the semantic (meaning) aspect of the self-verbalization affected the actions of preschoolers (Lovaas, 1964; Meacham, 1973). It is important that preschoolers learn situationally meaningful self-talk to control their own behavior. Combining these two sets of studies we see the impact of the motoric and semantic aspects of speech-to-self for the self-control of preschoolers.

Patterson and Mischel (1975, 1976) and Mischel and Patterson (1976, 1978) studied preschooler's ability to use self-verbalization to exhibit self-control during resistance-to-temptation tasks. They found that the preschool children who had been told what to say to themselves during resistance tasks (e.g., resist Mr. Clown Box to prevent being distracted) worked longer and with more persistence. Pressley (1979) described these studies in detail and commented that "they clearly demonstrated that even preschoolers can use a verbal strategy to control their own behavior in a situation where children often 'misbehave'" (p. 331). An important point to remember is that the preschoolers required the exact, imposed verbal message. They did not control behavior when directed to generate a self-controlling verbalization of their own. In other words, the adult had to put self-controlling words in the child's mouth. In this way, the adult served as a role model for specific verbalizations to control behaviors. As discussed throughout the book, the other-regulation is a prerequisite to self-regulation. Self-regulation is facilitated when the other-regulation experience makes explicit the means for guiding self. Self-control can be taught directly to preschoolers via adult and peer modeling, student practicing, and cueing, as was implemented by Manning (1988) for first and third graders.

Meichenbaum and Goodman's self-instructional training (1971) was applied with preschoolers in other studies with beneficial results: Bornstein and Quevillon (1976) with three preschool "overactive" boys, and Bryant and Budd (1982) with three impulsive preschool children in an outpatient clinic. It is very important that research studies aimed at self-control in the naturalistic settings of home and school continue to be conceptualized and formulated. There still remains a severe paucity of ecologically valid studies with all ages in the area of cognitive self-instruction.

Early Elementary: Kindergarten (five to six year olds) to Third Grade (eight to nine year olds)

Metamemory. Flavell and his colleagues (e.g., Keeney, Cannizzo, & Flavell, 1967) conducted most of the original metamemorial studies with primary school age children. For example, the Kenney et al. study was investigated with 89 six and seven year olds serving as the subjects. Flavell, Beach, and Chinsky (1966) had kindergarten, second graders, and fifth graders as their subjects. The focus of these studies was the verbal mediation characteristics of young children during serial-recall tasks. Their studies provided evidence more supportive of the production deficiency hypothesis for the younger subjects.

In addition, Kreutzer, Leonard, and Flavell (1975) asked children in kindergarten and grades one, three, and five to report what they knew about remembering. From these interviews, they found that even kindergarten children knew that short-term memory information is forgotten quickly, that relearning forgotten information is easier than learning new information, that studying improved retrieval of information, and that the amount of required learning affected retention. The third and fifth graders seemed to know more about how the variables mentioned above interact. Also, they appeared to know their memory characteristics better and generated more strategies for aiding recall. All ages tended to be more dependent upon external mnemonic resources (e.g., notes) rather than to rely on their own memory capabilities (internal resources). Nevertheless, since the early interview studies (such as the one just mentioned), there have been many documentations (e.g., see Brown, Bradford, Ferrara, & Campione, 1983, p. 108) that older children have greater knowledge about memory than younger children.

Asarnow and Meichenbaum (1979) demonstrated the effectiveness of a training program on kindergartners' ability to remember the names of objects. Their study supported the contention that children possess the cognitive processes needed for carrying out a task, when an instructional training program is implemented. Other findings that documented the memory enhancement of early elementary children when they were taught to employ cognitive verbal strategies are verified in the studies of Barclay (1980), Miller and Weiss (1982), and Paris, Newman, and McVey (1982). In general, the research conducted and the effects of cognitive intervention to foster memory skills of early elementary children have proven the effectiveness of such rehearsal strategies for this age group.

Borkowski et al. (1983) found that cognitive tempo (i.e., impulsive vs. reflective) and metamemory were correlated during this age period. In addition, significant correlations were evident between metamemory and strategy use. When the variables of tempo and metamemory were partialled out, the correlation between tempo and strategy transfer became nonsignificant, while the correlation between metamemory and strategy transfer remained significant. According to Pressley, Borkowski, and O'Sullivan (1985) these findings support the contention that "metamemorial processes in impulsive and reflective children serve as a mediational base during strategy maintenance and generalization" (p. 123).

Three very active researchers in the area of metamemory and children's learning are John Borkowski (e.g., see Borkowski & Krause, 1985), Michael Pressley (e.g., see Pressley, Borkowski, & O'Sullivan, 1985) and Wolfgang Schneider (1985). Their works have been comprehensive and extensive. In Schneider's review (1985) of the developmental trends in metamemory and memory-behavior relationships he cites the following studies for this age group by type of study (pp. 103–104).

Memory Monitoring (Rote Memory)

Bisanz, Vesonder, and Voss (1978)
Levin, Yussen, DeRose, and Pressley (1977)
Posansky (1978)
Wellman (1977)
Worden and Sladowski-Awig (1982)
Yussen and Berman (1981)

Organizational Strategies (Clustering)

Best and Ornstein (1979)
Salatas and Flavell (1976)

Training Studies (Organizational Strategies)

Cavanaugh and Borkowski (1979)
Kendall, Borkowski, and Cavanaugh (1980)
Kurtz, Reid, Borkowski, and Cavanaugh (1982)
Paris, Newman, and McVey (1982)
Kramer and Engle (1981)

Pressley et al. (1985) emphasize the importance of training procedural knowledge, using such components as self-testing to evaluate the helpfulness of a strategy and memory monitoring to compare the effects of using different strategies. They refer to these procedures as Metamemory Acquisition Procedures (MAPS). Results of MAPS have revealed that children as young as seven to eight years can use MAPS effectively to foster strategy knowledge and strategy usage. Teaching MAPS may improve generalization to tasks that are very different from the training tasks used with this age group and older.

Comprehension monitoring. In Ellen Markman's comprehension monitoring studies (1977), she found that first graders are often unaware that they do not understand oral directions. As a result, Markman believes that first graders often do not mentally process as they listen, while the third graders seem to mentally play through oral directions as a way of evaluating the information prior to actual implementation. It often requires that younger children (e.g., first graders) attempt an assigned activity before they are aware that they do not understand the oral directions. Most classroom teachers can identify with the frustration of (1) giving a set of directions, (2) asking for questions, and (3) having students agree that they understand when in reality they do not. When the teacher turns the task over to the children to work independently, often many of them are unable to perform without further instructions. The key here for elementary teachers of primary grades is to try activities together and monitor for understanding (guided practice) before assigning independent work. Asking children of this age if they understand may be a waste of time when we consider that they often do not realize they do not understand, to use Markman's phrase.

In the area of reading comprehension, Palincsar's reciprocal teaching concept was applied successfully with first graders (Palincsar et al., 1989). However, most of the reading comprehension monitoring studies have been conducted beyond the early elementary grades. Palincsar's work may change such a focus because she is documenting that even at-risk first graders can be taught reading comprehension skills (e.g., summarizing, predicting) via an other-regulation to self-regulation verbalization approach.

Dyadic Problem Solving

Camp and Bash (1985) define verbal mediation as talking to oneself to guide problem solving (Jensen, 1971) or other behavior (Meichenbaum, 1977). Camp and Bash believe that verbal mediation is a major characteristic of the cognitive processing necessary for problem solving. They believe children become capable of this sort of verbal mediation somewhere between five and seven years of age. When this shift occurs, children are able to inhibit impulse, problem solve, reason, and apply logic. Of course, others cited in this chapter believe this shift can happen earlier if cognitive interventions are taught directly. Camp and Bash have developed "Think Aloud" programs for the elementary grades, to encourage and nurture social and cognitive problem solving. These are available commercially through the Research Press.

Metacognitive problem-solving instruction for this age group has been applied, using the dependent variable of error analysis (DeCorte & Vershaffel, 1981), oral directions (Manning, 1984), academic accuracy (Rooney, 1985), neatness (Anderson-Inman, 1984), and social/cognitive problem solving (Camp, Blom, Hebert. & von Doorninck, 1977).

Cognitive self-control. Pressley (1979) reviewed self-verbalization effects upon elementary school-age children's resistance to temptation. O'Leary (1968) found that first-grade boys who were taught to verbally self-instruct about the rules of a game cheated less than first graders who did not verbalize. However, Monahan and O'Leary (1971) in their replication study found that the results cited in O'Leary (1968) were true for rural children but not urban children. The Hartig and Kanfer (1973) study also included seven year olds. As with the preschoolers, the seven-year-old children who told themselves not to look at prohibited toys obeyed themselves better than those who did not verbalize, or verbalized irrelevant information.

Findings generally reflect that verbal self-instructions do not reduce inappropriate classroom behaviors, (Ellis, 1976; Smith, 1975). Interestingly, Toner, Moore, and Ashley (1978) received benefits from self-verbalized prohibitions when age-mates modeled the strategy use. Manning (1988) used adult/peer modeling as well as direct practicing of cognitive self-instruction to improve the behavior of 30 first graders and 25 third graders referred by their classroom teachers for mild conduct problems. The Manning model also included cueing to remind subjects to use their on-task self-talk. Immediate and delayed benefits were obtained from the Manning Model of cognitive self-instruction to improve on-task classroom behaviors.

Meichenbaum and Goodman's (1971) study is a classic metacognition study, applied for the purpose of behavior change and improvement. In Study I hyperactive second graders were used as subjects. They trained these youngsters to use self-instruction to perform tasks while coping with errors and appropriately reinforcing themselves. The self-instruction group demonstrated significant gains on three psychometric instruments (i.e., Porteus Maze, Prorated WISC Performance I.Q., and the Kagan Matching Familiar Figure Test (MFFT); however no improvements were noted from teacher ratings or in classroom behavior. In Study II, reported in the same article, subjects included kindergarten and first-grade children. In this study cognitive modeling alone was compared to a self-instructional program. The self-instructional subjects exhibited a significant decrease in errors. The self-instructional training developed by Meichenbaum and Goodman has been the core of a great deal of subsequent research. The five-step procedure comprising cognitive self-instruction is described in chapter 3 of this book. Other studies, documenting the beneficial effects of cognitive self-instruction (CSI) for the early elementary age group are: Robin, Armel, and O'Leary (1975) used CSI with kindergarten children to improve handwriting deficiencies; Bender (1976), impulsive first graders showed increased response latency and a decrease of errors on the MFFT after verbal self-instruction and strategy training. As a contrast, Friedling and O'Leary's results (1979) yielded no significant improvement of on-task behavior or reading or math performance after self-instruction training. Their subjects were seven- and eight-year-old hyperactive children.

In general, the self-instructional procedures have resulted in consistent benefits for on-task behavior ratings, and standardized psychometric instruments. However, there is very limited evidence that verbal self-instruction improves intellectual functioning and academic achievement.

Middle School: Fourth (nine to ten year olds) to Eighth Grade (thirteen to fourteen year olds)

Metamemory. Before a few examples for this age group are presented, let us turn once again to Schneider's developmental trends review (1985) for an overview of types of metamemory studies by grade levels. For this age group Schneider classifies the following studies:

Memory Monitoring (Rote Memory)

Bisanz et al. (1978)
Levin et al. (1977)
Worden and Sladeuski-Awig (1982)
Yussen and Berman (1981)

Memory Monitoring (Prose Materials)

Brown and Smiley (1978)
Elliott (1980)
Yussen, Matthews, Buss, and Kane (1980)

Organizational Strategies (Clustering)

Best and Ornstein (1979)
Bjorklund and Zeman (1982)

Organizational Strategies (Paired Associate)

Waters (1982)
Pressley and Levin (1977)

An interesting approach to metamemory for this age group was used by Brown and her colleagues (Baker & Brown, 1981; Brown & Smiley, 1977). The metamemory was defined as "reading for remembering" instead of the comprehension monitoring related to "reading for meaning." The reading-to-remember focus subsumed comprehension monitoring and also promoted study-monitoring skills such as focusing on the main ideas of passages and prose organization.

Brown and Smiley (1977) found that metamemory, which they defined as "sensitivity to importance units," was characterized by a developmental progression from third grade to college students. When provided with four levels of increasing importance their findings revealed that third graders did not differentiate among levels of importance; fifth graders chose only the top most important units but did not distinguish difference among the remaining three lower categories; seventh graders differentiated between the two upper and the two lower levels but not between the secondary levels. On the other hand, college students were able to differentiate among every level of importance. The ability to distinguish importance levels was a contributing factor to recall. In another study Brown and Smiley (1978) investigated whether mature readers would use their strategic knowledge about components of texts when extra study time was provided. The results demonstrated that fifth-grade children did not improve recall when extra study time was provided, while children in seventh grade and above benefitted. Brown and Smiley (1978) concluded that fifth graders did not use the extra time well because they were less aware of the important units of the story. Therefore these younger students did not know what passages to focus on, in order to recall them. The older students spent the extra time paying more attention to the main ideas because they knew what the main ideas were.

Lovitt and Curtiss (1968) investigated the effect of verbalizing a mathematics problem aloud before making a written response for an eleven-year-old boy versus simply writing the answer to the problem. It was found that this middle schooler, who had previously experienced difficulty in mathematics, scored more correct answers, with a decrease in error rate, as a result of verbalizing the problem aloud before making a written response. The improvement was stable over time and supports rehearsing aloud as a helpful learning aid for some middle school students experiencing difficulty with school tasks. Students' self-verbalizations seem to activate the mind to remember and reinforce correct problem-solving strategies, which in turn increase accuracy.

Gettinger (1985) worked with nine poor spellers, ages eight to thirteen years. The subjects received four alternating experimental treatments of teacher directed, with and without cues and student directed, with and without cues. The student-directed instructional procedure, incorporating both visual and verbal cues, produced the highest recall accuracy on spelling posttests.

Pressley and Levin (1977) asked children to report the strategy they used in a paired-associate task. This awareness was considered an indicator of metamemory. The participants were categorized as rehearsers, elaborators, or mixed-strategy. As children moved into adolescence between grades five and nine, the proportion of rehearsers diminished. An interesting finding was that elaborators recalled the most, while rehearsers recalled the least at all age levels. The fifth-grade elaborators performed better than the ninth-grade rehearsers. Water's (1982) study corroborated this finding (i.e., verbal or visual elaboration fostered more recall).

Kurtz and Borkowski (1987) investigated the relationship between metamemory and strategic behavior of 130 impulsive and reflective children. Participants were fourth, fifth, and sixth graders. Over half of these children (i.e., 77) were evaluated three years earlier. Therefore, the authors were able to study development of metamemory relationships across time. Participants were instructed in either summarization instruction, summarization instruction plus metacognitive training, or no instructions. The dependent measures were tempo, summarization skills, and teacher ratings of impulsivity. Children receiving the combined summarization and metacognitive training exhibited superior performance. Causal modeling analyses revealed that previous metamemory characteristics were antecedents of later strategy acquisition. Kurtz and Borkowski's research adds to the documentation that metacognition can be taught, can be learned, and provides benefits for children's learning.

Comprehension monitoring. In the area of metacognitive strategies for reading comprehension, middle school students (grades four to eight) have served as subjects more than any other age group. Markman (1979) compared third- and sixth-graders' abilities to recognize inconsistencies in short nonfiction essays. Sixth graders improved in comprehension monitoring when they were told ahead of time that an inconsistency might be present; third-graders' performance remained the same. The sixth graders seemed to have the cognitive strategies available when the need was explicitly indicated.

Metacognitive interventions to improve reading comprehension on a metanalysis level (Haller, Child, & Walberg, 1988) utilizing twenty studies, revealed that effects were largest for seventh and eighth grades. Metacomprehension instruction had the least effect on students in the fourth, fifth, or sixth grades. Most likely, the majority of the twenty studies cited by Haller et al. (1988) involved subjects who were beyond a third-grade level, due to the cognitive demands of reading comprehension when a metacognitive strategy is required. However, recently younger students are being trained and assessed in this area (Palincsar et al., 1989).

To date, the majority of research on reciprocal teaching has been conducted with junior high students (referred to here as middle school students). For the most part, consistent improvement in reading comprehension has been found for middle schoolers when reciprocal teaching methods are applied (Brown & Palincsar, 1982; Palincsar & Brown, 1984). Other studies, with a component of self-instruction for reading comprehension, have documented beneficial effects for middle school students: Miller (1985); Paris and Oka (1986); Cross and Paris (1988).

Dyadic problem solving. There were not very many studies found for this area: cognitive self-instructional strategy training applied to middle schoolers to improve problem solving. Leon and Pepe (1983) investigated the effectiveness of self-instructional strategies designed to teach mathematics to learning-disabled students, ages nine through twelve. The students in the self-instructional group received math instruction based on Meichenbaum and Goodman's self-instructional model. First, the teacher modeled the computation while verbalizing the steps aloud. Second, the teacher verbally guided as the student performed the computation. Third, as the student verbalized aloud and performed the mathematics task, the teacher monitored the task. Fourth, the student whispered self-instructions as the teacher observed the students' computation. Fifth, the student used covert self-guidance to perform the computation as the teacher monitored. The students receiving self-instruction were more successful than those receiving only didactic instruction. In addition, the self-instruction group was able to generalize the self-instructional skills to other problem-solving tasks more effectively than the control group.

Another example of a study in this category is Schunk (1981) who worked with fifty-six children, ranging in age from nine to eleven. Subjects were randomly assigned to a cognitive-modeling group, a didactic-instruction group, or a no-treatment group. A mathematics test and a self-efficacy rating served as the dependent measures, administered in a pre- and post-design. The cognitive-modeling group had significantly greater academic gains than either of the other two groups. In addition, the cognitive-modeling and the didactic groups experienced a significantly increased sense of self-efficacy.

Cognitive self-control. All ages including adults demonstrate weaknesses in self-control in degrees for various situations. Therefore, a need exists for more self-control research for middle school children, as well as ages typically researched. It is reasonable to assume that cognitive self-control strategies would be beneficial for middle schoolers exhibiting deficiencies in this area.

To say that there has been a paucity of research for this age group is not to say that there have been no research studies conducted. Some examples are as follows: Ellis (1976) taught eight- to twelve-year-old boys to self-verbalize with predetermined messages provided to them: "When I don't fight, people are nicer to me . . . Wait. Don't strike out with your fists" (p. 31). Results of Ellis' self-verbalization training indicated no improvement in aggressive behavior. The Bugenthal, Whalen, and Henker study (1977) in which verbal self-instructional training was applied to hyperactive seven- to twelve-year-old boys, revealed the importance of locus of control. Benefits were yielded only for those boys who believed they were responsible for controlling their behavior. Burgio, Whitman, and Johnson (1980) successfully trained verbal self-instruction to two distractible retarded children (ages nine and eleven) to decrease off-task classroom behaviors during mathematics and printing tasks. They were also rated as less hyperactive by their teacher, although no academic gains were realized. On the other hand, academic gains from self-instruction training, paired with direct tutoring, were reported by Genshaft and Hirt (1980). They implemented 16 forty-minute sessions to investigate self-instruction training (joined with direct tutoring) to improve mathematics achievement in 12 seventh-grade girls. Results indicated that the self-instruction-plus-tutoring group improved in mathematics computation skills as well as mathematics attitudes when contrasted with a tutoring-only group and a no-treatment group.

Hughes and Hendrickson (1987) taught fourth, fifth, and sixth graders at risk for academic failure and school maladjustment to monitor their attention to an independent school task by using a self-recording procedure. Their results indicated that self-monitoring, without external reinforcement was effective for improving on-task behavior.

Ten fourth-grade classrooms with a total of 240 children, were studied by Stefanek, Ollendick, Baldock, Francis, and Yaeger (1987). The children were categorized as withdrawn, aggressive, or popular. Inhibiting and facilitating self-statements were investigated for resolving conflicts and initiating social interactions with friends and strangers. The popular children made significantly more facilitating than inhibiting responses when compared to the aggressive or withdrawn children.

Finally, Neilans and Israel (1981) compared self-regulation to a conventional token economy, using seven 13-year-old delinquent children. Both programs produced improvement in disruptive behavior and on-task behaviors. The authors note that the self-regulatory strategies produced greater improvements and even maintained when external controls were removed.

Secondary/College Students: Ninth grade to Twelfth Grade and College Students

High school students and college students were combined here because the number of studies using cognitive interventions for this age group to modify memory, comprehension, problem solving, and self-control is more limited than some of the other age groups. Examples of studies for each of these areas are presented and designations of either high school or college will be made in the text.

Metamemory. Four studies used college age students as participants to investigate various aspects of memory performance (i.e., awareness of memory capacity, verbal rehearsal to aid recall, self-monitoring, and a comparison of ages for memory capacity). These four studies are presented as examples for this category.

In the first example, Leal (1987) collected metamemory questionnaires from sixty-four university students enrolled in an introductory psychology course in order to assess their preparation for examinations. The students' predictions of their "recall readiness" for the examinations were also collected. Results indicated a positive relation between test performance and their recommended use of metamemory strategies for planned study. Students were accurate at assessing their exam readiness.

In the second example, Muth, Glynn, Britton, and Graves (1988) found that verbal rehearsal of key ideas in text were correlated significantly with recall. Furthermore, these authors found that rehearsal and recall were greater with objectives than without objectives for reading. Subjects were thirty-two undergraduates enrolled in an introductory psychology course.

In the third example, Morgan (1987) used college students (n=180) enrolled in a psychology course in order to investigate self-monitoring and goal setting. The dependent variable was the score on a final examination, requiring recall. It was hypothesized that self-monitoring combined with goal setting should improve students' learning (recall for an examination). Three experimental groups (i.e., self-monitoring alone, goal setting alone, and a combined self-monitoring and goal setting condition) and two control groups were established. All three experimental groups scored significantly better on their final exam than did either of the two control groups. It should be noted that combining self-monitoring and goal setting did not produce greater benefits than either of these conditions taught independently.

In the fourth example (Miller & Weiss, 1982) a college group served as a comparison group along with kindergartners, second, and fifth graders. The investigation was aimed at determining children's and adults' knowledge about variables that impact on attention. All subjects indicated how many animals a person would remember under easy and difficult levels. They found that the greatest increase in understanding of memory capabilities came between kindergarten and second grade.

In summary, college students often serve as a comparison group when children's metamemory skills are being compared with adult's metamemory skills (e.g., Levin, Yussen, DeRose, & Pressley, 1977; Masur, McIntyre, & Flavell, 1973; Miller & Weiss, 1982).

Comprehension monitoring. As stated previously the majority of reading comprehension studies (involving cognitive interventions) has centered on elementary and middle schoolers up through the eighth grade. Since reading is usually not taught as a subject per se, apart from content reading in high schools and colleges, fewer opportunities exist to study and apply strategies in naturalistic settings, such as the classroom. Two examples whereby attempts at metacognitive strategy instruction for reading comprehension are presented (i.e., Lindquist-Sandmann, 1987; Wong & Jones, 1982). Both authors discussed comprehension-monitoring steps for understanding text while reading. Wong and Jones (1982) conducted a comprehension-monitoring training study with LD students from grades six, eight, and nine. The training increased reading awareness and comprehension.

The Lindquist-Sandmann article is not an account of a research study; rather it is an account of a high school teacher's experience using metacognition to promote independent learners "who could decide for themselves the relative worth of material from reading text" (p. 326). In this teacher's estimation, this strategy was effective for her students.

Dyadic problem solving. Again, a scarcity of studies are realized when the focus is narrowed to cognitive interventions for general problem solving for high school/college students. One example in this category is Sarason and Sarason (1981). Perhaps this study can lead interested readers to other studies. Sarason and Sarason studied the effects of cognitive/social interventions on 127 drop-out-prone high school students' abilities to cope with and perform in difficult problem-solving situations. They were defined as potential drop outs on the basis of low academic scores, poor school attendance, and low SES. Subjects were randomly assigned to one of three groups. Treatment conditions were (1) live modeling of cognitive and social coping, (2) videotaped modeling of cognitive and social coping, and (3) control. Examples of the problem situations are: interviewing for a job, resisting peer pressure, and cutting class. Problems were selected based on the kinds of problems students were likely to encounter in their daily lives. Post measures consisted of a problem-solving measure, an alternative test (developed to assess the students' abilities to generate alternative responses to the problem scenarios), interview, records of tardiness and absenteeism, and behavioral referrals for the next year. There were significant differences between the control group and the treatment group on the problem-solving measure and on the alternative responses assessment, with the experimental group performing better on both. The live modeling treatment group performed better in the interview than either the video modeling or control groups. Both treatment groups had significantly fewer numbers of absences, tardiness, and behavioral referrals when compared to the control group.

Cognitive self-control. Blick and Test (1987) investigated the effects of self-monitoring and self-recording procedures on mildly handicapped high school students' ability to increase on-task behaviors. The training had very beneficial effects: academic achievement increased as well as on-task behavior. In addition, subjects continued to use these procedures without prompting from the teacher.

Meichenbaum (1975), in a widely cited study on metacognition and creativity, improved the creative abilities of a group of volunteer college students. Briefly, he trained the students to mentally note their negative self-statements and to modify what they said to themselves to reflect positive statements about their creativity abilities. This self-instructional training group showed an increase in both their perceptions of creative ability and performance on creativity measures. Both of these studies document the effectiveness of self-instruction for modifying behavior in this age group.

Adults

Metamemory. When college students are categorized in a group separate from adults, few examples of cognitive self-instruction to improve the memory skills of adults have been found to date. This may indicate an omission or gap in the metacognitive research efforts. It is highly likely that many more isolated studies do exist; however, the fact that my search revealed so few may be indicative of a lack of concentrated effort in this category. Another explanation may be that metamemory studies focusing on adults, as subjects, have been conducted in noneducational settings (e.g., business, home) of which I am unfamiliar.

Three examples of metamemory research using adults as subjects are Cox and Paris (1979); Lawson and Fuelop (1980); and Pressley, Levin, and Ghatala (1984). Cox and Paris (1979) found that young adults and elderly participants depended on categorization for memory skills. The majority of fourth graders, included in the study, continued to use rehearsal and rank it higher than other strategies. The production deficiencies of the children and elderly adults appeared to be similar on the surface; a closer look revealed different causes for their deficiencies (i.e., the elderly lacked self-testing strategies and task familiarity, while the fourth graders were unaware of the categorization strategy as an aid to recall).

Lawson and Fuelop (1980) worked with retarded adults with a mean I.Q. of 55. The strategy task demand was cumulative rehearsal for serial recall when provided. Benefits included one week maintenance of strategy use.

In a study by Pressley et al. (1984) adults were required to attempt two learning strategies for vocabulary learning: (1) rehearsal—repeating the words and their meanings over and over—and (2) keyword (see Pressley, Levin, & DeLaney, 1982). The keyword strategy "involves using part of the vocabulary words that sounds like a known English word as a keyword, with the keyword placed in an interactive image with the word's meaning" (p. 127). During the testing part of this experiment, the adult subjects volunteered remarks about the benefits of using the keyword method. Pressley et al. (1984) designated the test as a metacognitive experience which in turn affected the subjects' knowledge of effective memory strategies (metamemory per se). Pressley believes that this occurrence was a documentation of Flavell's metacognitive model, in which "metacognitive experiences produce metacognitive knowledge" (p. 130).

Comprehension monitoring. Wittrock (1988) discusses metacognitive strategies (although he does not refer to the strategies as metacognitive) for teaching adults (enlisted in the army) who had failed reading comprehension tests. He points out that the success of such strategies for adult readers is dependent upon knowing the learner's interests, backgrounds, motivation, and aspirations. In all probability, this is true for all ages, even though this consideration has been lacking too often in the comprehension monitoring studies, in general.

In a rather unique study, Spring (1985) describes a metacognitive approach in which an adult (i.e., the teacher) cognitively models aloud her own thought processes to teach children how to comprehend while reading. The modeled strategies consisted of planning, formulating strategies, monitoring, and evaluating. The teacher primarily used self-questioning to model reading-comprehension monitoring for students.

Dyadic problem solving. The use of cognitive-monitoring strategies to improve problem solving of adults has been demonstrated with teachers (Gallimore, Dalton, & Tharpe, 1986; Neely, 1986; Riley, 1981). Rogers (1983) recommends the use of metacognition instruction in teacher education. Beyond this, the category of cognitive self-instruction for adult general problem solving reflects another area in need of research efforts.

Cognitive self-control. Meichenbaum and his colleagues (e.g., Meichenbaum & Cameron, 1973) used cognitive self-instruction as a mechanism to improve adult control of various behaviors: schizophrenia, anxiety, anger, pain, and coping with aging. The interested reader should consult Meichenbaum (1977) for specific descriptions of each of these self-instruction programs. In general, the programs consisted of modifying self-talk to modify behavior. These programs have been extremely effective in teaching adults a means for helping themselves.

In an educational area, Szykula and Hector (1978) successfully taught a teacher to implement behavioral self-control strategies to increase certain student target behaviors while decreasing other behaviors. As a result of the teacher's self-modification a positive change in the students' behavior was noted.

Payne and Manning (1988) taught preservice teachers to use cognitive monitoring to increase awareness of negative self-talk and to substitute positive, more helpful self-talk. Sixty-seven female preservice teachers were randomly assigned to either experimental, attention, or assessment control. The experimental group received six hours of classroom instruction on the theory, rationale, and use of cognitive self-instruction for planning, instructing, and managing. The attention control met for the same number of hours, but did not practice cognitive self-instruction. The assessment control received only pre- and post-assessments. The preservice teachers receiving cognitive self-instruction developed a greater internal locus of control as measured by the Rotter Internal-External Locus of Control Scale (Rotter, 1966) than did either of the control groups. A description of a CSI model for teacher education is available in Manning and Payne (1989a). An analysis of teachers' internal dialogue, comparing preservice to inservice teachers is also found in Manning and Payne (1989b).

Forman (1982) evaluated the effectiveness of a cognitive behavioral training program designed to reduce teacher stress. The subjects were twenty-four high school and middle school teachers. They were randomly assigned to experimental and a waiting list control group. The experimental subjects were instructed in coping skills, self-statements to control emotions, imagery, scriptwriting of stressful incidents, and role-playing of alternative responses. The experimental group reported a significant reduction in stress; whereas, the control group reported no change in stress level. These changes maintained for six weeks following the cognitive behavioral intervention. In addition, there was a significant decrease in physical manifestations of anxiety for the experimental group.

Metacognitive Instruction for Academic Subjects

Besides memory, comprehension, problem solving, and self control, metacogni-tion has also been applied to a variety of academic subjects. The area of reading was discussed earlier in the section on comprehension. In addition, Haggard (1985) recently wrote about using a metacognitive, interactive strategic approach for content reading. More specifically a metacognitive approach, using a transition from other-regulation to self-regulation, was implemented to foster self-correction strategies that will enhance science learning (Fisher & Lipson, 1986), and promote self-regulation in science learning (Hawkins & Pea, 1987). Bereiter and Bird (1984) used the think-aloud approach to foster comprehension of science text, demonstrations, hands-on activities, and experiments in the science classroom. Other science-oriented, metacognitive articles are by Dempter (1984), Gwynn (1987), and Middleton (1985).

Employing self-instruction to teach mathematics skills is evident in the research of Grimm, Bijou, and Parson (1973), Lovitt and Curtiss (1968), and Smith and Lovitt (1975). One of the findings highlighted the importance of simply requiring that math problems be read aloud before writing a response. Cognitive self-instruction benefits for mathematics computations were documented by Leon and Pepe (1983) and Barling (1980). Barling found that children who received both self-monitoring and self-reinforcement were superior on assessments of accuracy and persistence. Johnston (1983) found that self-instruction produced more accurate mathematics problem solving than didactic instruction. Thrackway, Meyers, Schleser, and Cohen (1985), stated that specific strategy training yielded improvements on a specific math task; whereas the general strategy training aided generalization tasks. To obtain specific skill improvement and generalized improvements to other mathematics tasks, both specific and generalized self-instructional strategies should be used. Finally Schunk and Cox (1986) have studied the effects of self-instruction on learning-disabled (LD) children's mathematics skills. Their findings revealed that continuous self-verbalization aids math performance and produces higher self-efficacy in LD children than discontinuous or no self-verbalizations.

Other content areas for which self-instruction led to benefits are handwriting (Blandford & Lloyd, 1987); creative writing (Trimbur, 1987); and general creativity (Meichenbaum, 1975).

The final discussion in this chapter will center around the definitions of widely used terminology in recent metacognitive literature. Specifically the concepts of general metacognitive strategies, cognitive monitoring, cognitive behavior modification, cognitive self-instruction, self-regulated learning, and self-directed learning are defined.

Metacognitive strategies is the overall umbrella under which all the other terms mentioned above may fit. Metacognitive strategies help us know what we know and what we don't know (Costa, 1984). Such strategies are defined by Costa as "our ability to plan a strategy for producing what information is needed, to be conscious of our own steps and strategies during the act of problem solving, and to reflect on and evaluate the productivity of our own thinking" (Costa, 1984, p. 57). General metacognitive classroom strategies listed by Costa are as follows: planning strategy, generating questions, choosing consciously, evaluating with multiple criteria, taking credit, outlawing "I can't," paraphrasing or reflecting, labeling students' behaviors, clarifying students' terminology, role-playing and simulations, journal keeping and modeling.

Cognitive monitoring is a concept first introduced and defined by John Flavell, (1979). Flavell presents a model of cognitive monitoring which includes metacognitive knowledge, experiences, goals (or tasks), and actions (or strategies). This model was defined earlier, in chapter 2 of this book. This skill can be applied for both behavior control and academic performance. Cognitive monitoring is the students' use of specific monitoring strategies to achieve a cognitive goal (Brezin, 1980).

Cognitive behavior modification refers to techniques used to promote self-control (Meichenbaum & Asarnow, 1979). Characteristics of cognitive behavior modification include self-treatment, verbalization, strategy, modeling, and evaluation of alternative choices (Lloyd, 1980). Meichenbaum (1977) describes the concept of cognitive behavior modification. I tell students to read the term backwards for a definition: modification of one's own behavior via one's own cognitions; usually the cognition is in the form of self-talk.

Cognitive self-instruction is a procedure for applying cognitive behavior modification methods in educational contexts (Meichenbaum & Asarnow, 1979). Ryan, Short, and Weed (1986) refer to the goal of self-instruction as a self-feedback in a manner similar to external guidance. Learners are taught to use their own statements and questions to either guide learning or control actions (Corno, 1986). Characteristics of the technique include self-treatment, verbalization, a strategy, and modeling (Lloyd, 1980). Modeling has been the traditional mode of instructing, and consists of successive steps: cognitive-modeling phase, an overt-guidance phase, a faded self-guidance phase, and a covert self-instruction phase (Schunk, 1986). When students learn in such a systematic and progressive manner, results are feelings of self-efficacy (Corno, 1987). Manning (1988) used cognitive self-instruction to teach classroom self-control. The components of modeling, student practicing, and self-cueing were instrumental in producing improved classroom conduct.

Self-regulated learning is defined as "individuals manage their cognitive abilities and motivational effort so that learning is effective, economical, and satisfying" (Paris & Oka, 1986). Schunk (1986) defines self-regulated learning as a "process whereby students' cognitions manifest themselves in planful behaviors oriented toward learning" (p. 347). A self-regulated learner self-activates, alters, and sustains learning through specific procedures (Zimmerman, 1986). Some of the processes used in self-regulation are planning, organizing, self-instructing, self-monitoring, and self-evaluating. A by-product of using self-regulation is a positive feeling of self-efficacy; its use is motivating (Corno, 1987). Such success builds confidence, therefore individuals are less reluctant to take risks and to attempt difficult tasks (Paris & Oka, 1986). Self-regulation of learning can promote student independence and lifelong learning (Bondy, 1984).

Self-directed learning is a close relative of self-regulated learning, without the emphasis on self-motivation and self-efficacy. Self-directed learning activities are those that are completely or partially under the control of the learner (Thomas, Strage, & Curley, 1988). These activities consist of student-elective thought and behavior to direct, manage, or monitor a learning task. Consideration of the impact of verbal self-regulation is not necessarily present in the concept of self-directed learning. Dimensions of self-direction are as follows (Durkes, 1985): "following directions, asking for help, making choices, asking concept questions, asking for learning aids, producing idea lists, stating problems and tasks, using a creative problem-solving process; metacognition: making executive decisions, regulating mental abilities, and acting from commitment" (p. 96).

Although these terms differ in emphasis, they all refer to techniques that focus on an awareness of and/or regulation of one's own thoughts to produce a desired behavior change. Cognitive behavior procedures focus on an internal process, giving individuals the power to control their thinking, actions, and successes. Metacognitive strategies have been implemented with subjects of varying ages and in both clinical and school settings. Additionally, cognitive behavior interventions have been applied successfully in dealing with situations related to cognitive deficits and self-control. It has been shown throughout the studies listed in this chapter that successful performance is a powerful mechanism for creating desired changes and fostering feelings of self-efficacy.

Cognitive Analysis: Definition of Terms

Metamemory

Conversational discourse Meaningful social talk between and among individuals. This type of discourse to facilitate remembering is considered a neglected theme in metamemory research.

Cross-modal symbolic remembering Remembering that is expressed in a mode other than the mode the information to be remembered was received (e.g., written accounts of spoken conversations). This kind of remembering has received little attention in metamemory research.

Cued recall Recall of information that is prompted by something or someone other than the subjects participating in a study.

Elaboration group In metamemory studies this group is given more information. In most cases subjects in an elaborated group receive the rationale for using the strategies.

Faded instructions The transition between instructions modeled by another to self-instructions. Often the instructions are whispered by the self-regulating agent as the process from other-regulation to self-regulation is occurring.

Free-recall task A task that requires an individual to remember without prompting.

Isolated-memory task A task that requires memory functioning apart from meaningful contexts.

Mediation deficiency Such a deficiency occurs when a message is produced but this message does not mediate between stimulus and response.

Metamemory Knowledge and awareness of one's own memory abilities, state, and capacities.

Memory encoding The process of internalizing what is to be remembered (recognized or recalled).

Personal dimensions Affective variables such as mood, fatigue levels, motivation, and personality characteristics.

Production deficiency Such a deficiency occurs when an individual does not develop messages which could, if produced, mediate between stimulus and response.

Rehearsal strategy training Teaching individuals to repeat information aloud in order to remember/recall that information.

Retention rate The rate of keeping information stored in such a way that it is retrievable for recall.

Rote memory Memory of information without a meaningful context.

Self-instructional training Meichenbaum and Asarnow used this type of training in their memory research. Cognitive modeling and verbal self-regulation are components of self-instructional training.

Serial recall A rote-memory task used often as the dependent variable in metamemory research. Recalling a list of information in which each unit is not related to the other members of the list (e.g., telephone numbers; a, b, c's; digit span).

Transfer of strategy use The ability to apply the trained strategy in another setting and/or for another task, other than the training context.

Verbal rehearsal Repeating a verbalization aloud to oneself. Flavell and colleagues documented that verbal rehearsal aids remembering. When rehearsing aloud reafference occurs; the word(s) leave the mouth (efferent) and are received back into one's ear (afferent). The process of reafference stimulates recall.

Comprehension Monitoring

Attribution training Based on Weiner's attribution theory whereby individuals are trained to focus on causal inferences made about success and failure experiences. Students' self-attributions are associated with improved academic performance and self-esteem.

Basal reader instruction Reading instruction in the classroom where the published basal reader series is used as the central mode of reading instruction delivery.

Comprehension monitoring Awareness of ongoing comprehension processes, including the detection of obstacles to effective comprehension.

Conscious mental processing Being fully aware and cognizant of the fact that one is thinking about the information as it is being heard and read. Passing this information through a self-detection screen of self-questions, (e.g., Am I understanding this? What should I be learning here? What's the important point? etc).

Enactment Physically carrying out the directions for a task or assignment. In the case of deficient comprehension-monitoring skills, the enactment is often the activity which brings one to the full realization that comprehension has not occurred (e.g., hearing directions, thinking that understanding has occurred, trying to perform the task "enactment," and then realizing that understanding has or has not occurred).

General self-instructions Instructions used by individuals for monitoring a wider range of conceptual information. In many studies, when students are taught general self-instructions, as opposed to task-specific self-instruction, transfer of these strategies to other tasks and settings has occurred.

Guided practice Adult supervised practice of an assigned task to insure accurate understanding and successful completion of the task. Guided practice is a strategy to catch comprehension-monitoring deficits that occur and may go unnoticed in a classroom.

Inconsistent essays Essays originally developed by Markman that contain information that does not conceptually belong together. These were read to subjects to see if the inconsistency would be noticed and under what conditions it would be detected. There were explicit and implicit inconsistencies.

Inferential questions Questions that do not have explicit answers in the text. Answers are derived indirectly from a synthesis of the material.

Informed Strategies of Learning (ISL) The purpose of ISL is to teach students when, how, what, and why to use strategies to facilitate reading comprehension.

Learning context The environmental parameters of the learning situation (e.g., climate in the classroom).

Look-back A measurement of the regulation of comprehension when subjects go back to previously read passages.

Memory overload Requiring an individual to remember more items than the capacity of the mind can handle easily. This was a comprehension problem used in the Revelle, Karabenick, and Wellman study (1981).

Metanalysis A quantitative synthesis of a large group of representative studies for a definitive topic in the literature. A metanalysis on the impact of metacognitive strategies on reading comprehension was conducted by Haller, Child, and Walberg (1988).

Metacomprehension Awareness of one's state of listening and/or reading comprehension. Knowing that one does or does not understand is a component of metacomprehension. Some add that applying strategies independently that promote learning and remembering is also a component.

Reciprocal teaching Dialogue between teachers and students, and between students and students for the purpose of jointly constructing the meaning of text. The four strategies are summarizing, question generating, clarifying, and predicting (Palincsar, 1986). Related concepts are *scaffolded instruction, proleptic instruction, dyadic instruction, instrumental enrichment, mediated learning, Socratic dialogue,* and *collaborative problem solving.*

Referential ambiguity Confusion over which person, place, or thing is being referred to. It is a dilemma in comprehension studies when more than one example is present which will satisfy a verbal direction, and only one example is required. Revelle, Karabenick, and Wellman (1981) used this comprehension problem in their study.

Story grammar strategy A strategy taught to readers for which they use the story schemata to aid comprehension of new material.

Task-specific self-instructions Limited to self-instructions for a particular academic task. Research studies have generally revealed that task-specific self-instructions are very effective for the specific academic task they are intended; however, they rarely have transferred to other tasks, other than the training task.

Unintelligibility When a message is not understood because it does not make sense to the listener or reader. This was a comprehension problem used in the Revelle, Karabenick, and Wellman (1981) study, accomplished when the experimenter yawned while naming items.

Dyadic Problem Solving

Adult-child dyads Used in Wertsch's social interactional model for the facilitation of problem solving. The dyads moved gradually from other regulation to self-regulation for solving laboratory problems.

Alternative thinking A variety of means and approaches considered as viable solutions to a problem.

Alternative plans Term often used in social/cognitive problem-solving studies (e.g., Shure and Spivack) in which children are asked to verbalize another way or ways to solve a social problem. The alternative plans usually are more positive, helpful ways to cope with social dilemmas.

Categories of self-communication The content of self-communication (i.e., problem definition, self-reinforcement, self-evaluation, and error correction) used for problem solving.

Consequential thinking For any alternative (as a possible means to reach a desired goal) what are the predictable consequences? This question-to-self represents "consequential thinking."

Distal outcome measures These measures are collected apart from the adult-child joint activities. They are measures such as skill acquisition, standardized intelligence tests, and achievement in school.

Goal-oriented planning A characteristic of a problem-solving process, whereby procedures are planned based on a desired goal.

Goal Story Interview A structured story-form interview to lead learning disabled students to monitor their problem-solving processes.

Means-end thinking Based on a desired goal, the plausible ways to reach the goal. The emphasis here is on process, rather than product.

Parental teaching practices Joint activities between a parent and a child such as performing household chores together, playing games together, solving puzzles and simple problems together. These practices are thought to be important contexts for learning because the child internalizes the parents' verbal and nonverbal messages during these joint activities which constitute the child's internalized self-guiding speech used later to regulate behavior.

Proximal outcome measures These measures are collected during parent-child interactions, usually when the child is working independently, after having been helped by the adult through modeling or direct instruction.

Self-interrogation Asking questions to self about the current state of one's own knowledge during general problem solving.

Self-monitoring checklist A written check sheet with questions to self about the evaluation of one's own work or problem solving.

Social problem solving Problem solving aimed at everyday socially oriented situations, as opposed to the laboratory tasks of solving a problem in isolation from the social context.

Think Aloud program Developed by Camp and Bash. Combined self-instructional training for cognitive problem solving and social problem-solving training to improve social communication. The emphasis is on coping skills after receiving a systematic approach to solving social and academic challenges.

Trans-situational Cuts across situations. Applying to all forms of problem solving activity, rather than being restricted to a specific area.

Cognitive Self-Control

At-risk students Students who have been identified as high risks for academic failure and/or school maladjustment and/or school drop-outs.

Attention deficit disorder A recognized school problem that involves a lack of concentration and attention to intended tasks.

Attributional retraining Borkowski and his colleagues used this training to modify causal inferences made about success and failure experiences in academic settings.

Cognitive behavior modification A term used by Donald Meichenbaum to describe the modification of one's own behavior through the alteration of what is said to self. Behavior is modified by self-verbalization in a manner similar to being shaped externally by someone else.

Cognitive-behavioral self-control therapy A term used by Philip C. Kendall. He defines it as a therapy for teaching children self-control through an amalgamation of cognitive and behavioral procedures. He says that self-instructional training is the most typical type, but that the therapy also may include social cognitive problem-solving training and social perspective-taking training. The therapy is an attempt to alter cognitive patterns with the aim of changing behavior, regardless of the term used.

Cognitive self-control The cessation of inappropriate behavior and the development of appropriate behavior by means of one's own control, using one's own cognition (usually self-regulating speech-to-self) to accomplish this.

Cognitive self-intervention A strategy that is applied to one's own repertoire of skills, using one's own cognitive engagement for the purpose of change and improvement in behavior.

Distractibility A student's attention is easily transferred from the intended task to a competing object or situation.

Ecologically valid setting An investigative setting which is or has a counterpart in real-life situations that are encountered in daily living.

External monitoring Overt behaviors are monitored by someone other than the individual engaged in the behavior.

Far generalization test A transfer test for cognitive strategy use in a dissimilar (to training) setting or for a dissimilar task.

Generalization effects A synonym of transfer effects. The trained strategy is used in a setting or for a task that differs with the training setting or task.

Goal-orienting self-guidance The purposeful, planned behavior of an individual that is under the individual's self-direction and is aimed at a certain goal, known to the individual.

High-risk students A synonym of at-risk students.

Impulsive responding Responding without thought, especially reflective, meaningful thought.

Interpersonal cognitive problem-solving skills Problem-solving skills aimed at altering cognitions to improve interpersonal conflicts.

Maintenance effects The durability of strategy use; follow-up investigations of strategy use to determine how long the strategy will remain useful to the subjects.

Near generalization test A transfer test for cognitive strategy use in a similar setting or for a similar task as compared to the training setting/task.

Perspective-taking tasks Tasks in which subjects are asked to respond from someone else's orientation toward a situation, rather than responding from their own perspective.

Reactive effect A process whereby self-observation of a target behavior then produces a modifying effect upon that same target behavior.

Resistance-to-temptation studies A cluster of studies reviewed by Michael Pressley related to self-control through cognitive interventions. In resistance-to-temptation tasks, children are usually left with tempting stimuli and are instructed to resist the temptation. The effects of manipulations (e.g., self-verbalization, external verbalization) are investigated.

Self-controlling verbalization A self-verbalization utterance used for the purpose of inhibiting one's own inappropriate behavior and initiating one's own appropriate behavior.

Self-directedness Directing one's own behavior. Realizing that many happenings in one's life can be directed by conscious choice.

Self-directed learners The learners who assume responsibility for their behavior in a learning context (i.e., focusing attention, following through on tasks, and finishing academic tasks as required); self-initiation, self-persistence, and accomplishment of academic assignments.

Self-determined contingencies Students deciding their own reinforcement and providing this reinforcement for self (self-reinforcement).

Self-evaluation Follow-up assessment of self-recording on a subjective level, often with a rating scale of one to ten. Self-recording and self-evaluation are types of self-observational procedures. Neither implies any cognitive monitoring processes.

Self-generate To produce a self-verbalization spontaneously to aid self-control without adult suggestions/prompting. Findings have consistently revealed that young children are unable to self-generate self-controlling verbalizations even when told to do so by an adult. They are able to benefit from self-messages for self-control if adults tell them what to say (e.g., wait my turn).

Self-instructional training Meichenbaum in his cognitive behavior modification program used a Vygotskian approach from other-regulation, progressing in successive steps, to self-regulation. He called this approach self-instructional training.

Self-management As opposed to being managed by other(s). An individual assumes responsibility for the organization and direction of his or her own behavior and choices in life.

Self-modification Changing or altering one's own behavior through a change in self-verbalizations.

Self-monitoring Overt behaviors are monitored by the individual engaged in the behavior.

Self-observational procedures Includes self-recording and self-evaluation. Overseeing one's own overt behaviors.

Self-recording Monitoring one's own behavior to record the occurrences of a target behavior, with a minimum amount of judgment.

Self-reinforcement Self-acknowledgement when appropriate behaviors are exhibited. Reinforcement for self is thought to have similar benefits to those experienced when someone else externally reinforces target behaviors. The great advantage is that self-reinforcement promotes autonomy, while external reinforcement promotes dependency.

Self-statements Messages spoken to self either overtly or covertly.

Self-verbalizations Statements or questions spoken to self overtly or covertly. The crucial ingredient in self-instructional training.

Situationally meaningful self-talk Self-talk that relates to the context of the everyday, typical environment of an individual. A certain set of self-talk statements and/or questions that promote self-control in various real-life situations.

Task-irrelevant self-talk Self-talk collected in an academic setting that is unrelated to the assigned task.

Task-relevant self-talk Self-talk that is used to guide academic tasks; the self-talk utterances are neutral, related to the task at hand. The categories are defining, guiding, coping, correcting, and reinforcing.

General Terms

Adult age group Defined in this chapter as people over nineteen who are not necessarily enrolled in a college or university.

College age group Defined in this chapter as students enrolled as undergraduate or graduate studies in a college or university.

Didactic instruction Direct instruction. When an adult straightforwardly instructs the child. Giving directions for clearly informing. Purposefully providing information directly from the adult to the receiving child.

Direct tutoring A synonym of didactic instruction. External information and external shaping of behaviors are provided by the tutor to the tutee.

Drop-out prone At-risk for dropping out of school, usually high school. Indicators of a potential drop-out are low academic scores, poor school attendance, and low SES.

Early elementary age group Defined in this chapter as children enrolled in kindergarten through third grade, with ages ranging from five to nine years old.

High school age group Defined in this chapter as students enrolled in grades nine through twelve, with ages ranging from fourteen to nineteen years old.

Middle school age group Defined in this chapter as children enrolled in grades four through eight, with ages ranging from nine to fourteen years.

Naturalistic research settings The location or place where an investigation is conducted that is a typical, usual place (e.g., classroom, home) for the participants in the study.

Predetermined messages Verbal messages that are decided upon in advance before they are presented to others. Usually an exact wording is semantically important to effect modification.

Preschool age group Defined in this chapter as children from birth to age five.

Target age group The age under investigation in educational studies. A synonym is *target population.* Certain age group studied, usually for the purpose of understanding growth and development as it relates to a certain phenomenon or procedure.

Token economy A term derived from behaviorism. An exchange system whereby individuals earn rewards that are meaningless per se until they are exchanged for something desired or needed by the recipient. Tokens are used to shape children's behavior via external reinforcement.

Cognitive Synthesis: A Summary

While studying memory in children, Flavell and his colleagues, in the early 1970s, coined the term *metamemory.* This term was followed by other terms (e.g., *metacognition, metacomprehension*). Flavell's concept of metacognition brought about a flurry of research activities. An attempt was made in this chapter to provide a cross section of that activity.

Recognition of the importance of cognitive/mental activities precipitated this cognitive approach in the research literature. This cognitive focus in research has begun to replace behaviorism of the 1940s, 1950s, and 1960s. Behaviorism alone has proven insufficient to promote lifelong, intrinsically motivated learners and self-controlled individuals. Hopefully, the benefits of cognitive instruction documented in the literature will find its way into classroom practice. If this does not occur, the research efforts mentioned in this chapter have been for nothing. Our classroom teachers, students, parents, and administrators deserve to know about these powerful cognitive tools to aid learning. Wittrock (1988) makes an important point: other professions are beginning to reconceptualize their roles (e.g., medical) to include teaching their patients strategies to change their behaviors to control their own health. He comments that he has a variety of professionals enrolled in his learning and cognition class because they are realizing a teaching responsibility. This trend is likely to grow and to continue.

When considering this body of research studies, many disparities are found among them and only a few similarities. The one commonality I wish to highlight is that language leads thought. Of course the relationship between thought and language is recursive and has been argued before. I just wish to point out once more to the reader the important role language plays as it guides and shapes behavior. Some examples are: Palincsar's notion of *discourse* brings about comprehension; Wertsch's dyadic instruction is the idea of adults directing problem solving through *language;* Meichenbaum taught subjects to modify their *language,* which then brought about a change in behavior. In all cases, the language per se was the mechanism of change. Perhaps this may seem old news and it is, I agree. But somehow this piece of news is not reaching the daily lives of students, teachers, parents, etc. Language is crucial to remembering and understanding, and to problem solving and self-guidance. Language is the key; it shapes all these processes. To present an example: the other day I was in a college meeting with five other people for the purpose of making some decisions that would affect many others. A few committee members wanted to dash off something from the top of our heads. Others of us felt the task was important and required more time, thought, and effort. The essential ingredient promoting the committee members' productivity was not however limited to time, thought, or effort. The most important ingredient was "talk." We talked and we talked, we argued, and we compromised, and finally we had representative decisions that were worthwhile and fair. The group's discourse led to information. Language led the group's behavior and its product. Language directs process and product.

Many of the research studies cited in chapter 6 are in concert with the notion that "language-as-instruction" should precede the developmental levels of children. Children's potential for learning can be activated by a quality program of rich verbal interaction. A large portion of Vygotsky's work was related to this idea (i.e., zone of proximal development; role of verbal self-regulation). Vygotsky's study and intellectual reasoning led him to a theory. He thought that language between individuals played an instrumental role in an individual's cognitive development. Now, we have a beginning research base that more or less has confirmed many of Vygotsky and his colleagues' claims. The task now is to convince practitioners to adopt cognitive approaches that have repeatedly reflected benefits. Too often the results of research and the needs of a practitioner never find one another. Miles (1986) has a wonderful two-page discussion of this dilemma (pp. 339–341). He makes some valid, but sad points. In short, his message is that our educational practices are destined to remain unchanged, even in the face of knowing better cognitive strategies (based on research findings) that could greatly improve classroom practice. Miles states (p. 340): "There is a marked lack of translators who are capable of and interested in revising research findings so that they are understandable to classroom instructors. There are few rewards but many possible penalties within the educational process for researchers who actively seek to influence educational practice or for practitioners who seek to apply research findings. The time to change this is now—it is essential to the continued growth of our educational system."

Summary of Part Two: Related Research to CSI

Consistent patterns in research findings of sound research studies should guide the conceptualization and formulation of educational practice. In this part of the book, a review of research on metacognitive processes was outlined. The research literature was viewed from two perspectives. First, metacognitive research was categorized, even though interdependence and overlapping were noted, into four cognitive processing areas (i.e., metamemory, comprehension monitoring, dyadic problem solving, and cognitive self-control). The second perspective was to divide this research literature by age/grade level categories (i.e., preschoolers, early elementary, middle school, high school/college, and adults).

Collectively, this part of the book represents a picture of where we have been and where we are now in our knowledge about metacognitive strategies for classroom use based on research documentation, from many metacognitive studies in cognitive domains and for a variety of populations and ages. As never before, the uniting of cognitive psychology with education is occurring. The wedding itself might be termed "metacognition." Metacognitive experiences have been shown to be instrumental in fostering benefits for students' memory, comprehension, problem-solving, and self-control abilities. Education in general has as one of its major goals to foster these same cognitive abilities. Therefore, metacognitive experiences should be implemented deliberately by teachers into virtually every learning activity with students of every age. This does not mean developing a whole new curriculum called "metacognition instruction." In fact this would be counterproductive. The metacognitive processes of self-planning, self-monitoring, self-questioning, self-coping, self-checking, and self-regulating are critical components of learning activities in every content. Metacognition is not only trans-situational, it is trans-subject matter/content areas. For example, it is unrealistic to think that a student needs to verbally rehearse spelling words to aid recall but does not need to rehearse mathematics facts to aid recall. Another example is that students need to generate self-questions for reading and also for social studies or science. Metacognitive strategies should be tied to a content area (e.g., mathematics) but ways of transferring these same strategies should be clearly articulated and demonstrated for the students. Therefore, metacognition should not be taught in isolation—away from content—but at the same time it is not content specific, either. This means that teachers should become knowledgeable about how to promote metacognitive experiences that will lead to metacognitive knowledge for each of the content areas, and where applicable, should help children transfer these specific-to-a-subject skills to other subject matter where the same metacognitive strategy would facilitate learning.

Some of the researchers in Part Two documented that young children do not possess metacognitive knowledge until around fourth or fifth grade (ages ten to eleven); however the consistent pattern is that younger children can learn to use metacognitive strategies when explicitly taught to do so. Therefore teachers should begin early to model metacognitive skills (e.g., self-checking: "Did I finish all the problems? Did I skip anything?") in order to foster metacognitive knowledge for all students. Research clearly documented that an individual's cognitive abilities can be severely limited when metacognitive ability is not developed. Therefore, many of our students that appear to be limited in cognitive abilities may be reflecting metacognitive deficits (inabilities to focus attention, follow through, and finish tasks via appropriate and helpful self-talk). The student who fails every spelling test may not have limited cognitive spelling ability, he/she may not know how to verbally rehearse to aid retention. Such metacognitive skills are often overlooked, due to the fact that subject matter specialists sometimes discourage attention to general metacognitive processes because they believe such processes are too general. If Part Two is read carefully, a strong case is made for including metacognitive strategies for a variety of school subjects and with every age learner.

Part Three

Classroom Application of Cognitive Self-Instruction

Overview of Part Three

Part Three consists of some essential ideas, approaches, and strategies for including metacognition as a focus within subject-matter instruction. These activities are to serve only as stimuli, to encourage a starting place for teachers. The most productive ideas will come when teachers develop their own approaches based on the needs of their own students, within a given context, and for a specific content. Part Three is included to stimulate teacher thought; to motivate teachers to action. It is written in the hope that teachers will use it as a starting place to translate into classroom use the theory in Part One and the research in Part Two.When I teach CSI, providing underlying theory and research, I am often asked the following questions: "But how do I get started? Where do I begin? How can I keep the activities going?" Part Three is dedicated to the classroom teachers who asked these questions out of a real desire to implement CSI and a real frustration over not knowing exactly how. I have provided only examples, not everything that teachers might do to help children think, learn, and behave responsibly using their own cognitions for awareness and regulation.

7

Manning Cognitive Self-Instruction Model

Overview

Manning's (1988) classroom approach to cognitive self-instruction (CSI) is outlined in this chapter. The components of CSI are modeling, practicing, and cueing. Each of the components is discussed separately with examples of activities, approaches, and suggestions. Three sample lesson plans, following the Manning model, are included. Additional strategies and information about the use of CSI to foster self-management of school work habits (e.g., finishing promptly and accurately) and social responsibility (e.g., waiting turns) are presented. The final discussion is how CSI might fit best into the existing school curriculum.

Self-Questions

1. Knowledge. Describe the four school uses of cognitive self-instruction. Name the purpose for teaching the four school uses of CSI.

2. Comprehension. Explain Manning's classroom approach for teaching cognitive self-instruction.

3. Application. Write a lesson plan in which all three components of the Manning model are used. Label the components in the plan.

4. Analysis. Referring to Meichenbaum and Goodman's (1971) five

steps for teaching CSI, show how these steps were absorbed into the Manning model. How do these two approaches overlap. How did Manning extend the Meichenbaum (CSI) program?

5. Synthesis. Using all three components of the Manning model (e.g., modeling, practicing, and cueing) develop an original plan to help a student experiencing concentration problems at school. Name specific strategies to be used for each component.

6. Evaluation. Debate the pros and cons of (1) integrating CSI as part of the existing curriculum, or (2) as a separate new curriculum, focusing on metacognitive skill development.

In this chapter, Manning's (1988) cognitive self-instruction model for regular classroom use is described and explained. Sufficient examples are provided in the hope that teacher educators and classroom teachers are familiar enough with the concepts to develop their own ideas within the framework presented here. There are at least three components when applying CSI to instruction. These components are modeling, practicing, and cueing. They were derived from teaching fifty-five elementary students to use CSI to manage their own classroom behaviors. Therefore, these components are related to regular education, classroom management to promote self-control and social responsibility in students (Manning, 1988). Readers may see ways to transfer these CSI strategies to other areas of learning (e.g., memory, comprehension, and problem solving); however, the primary emphasis here is classroom organization and management. Each of the components (i.e., modeling, practicing, and cueing) is discussed separately. After explaining the components, sample teacher lesson plans are provided. These plans were developed and field-tested by teachers. Then, additional strategies and activities developed by the author to foster a metacognitive classroom approach are presented. The final discussion in this chapter centers around how CSI fits in the curriculum and methodology as we presently know classroom practice.

Before the discussion of each of the three components of Manning's CSI, the overall picture of this model may be helpful. Please refer to Figure 1 for a total view of CSI for classroom use. We will begin on the left with the area of modeling.

Modeling

Modeling of CSI is essential because of the abstractness of thought processes. It is much easier to teach overt behaviors than to teach metacognitive thinking strategies to regulate overt behaviors. Students need to hear first hand

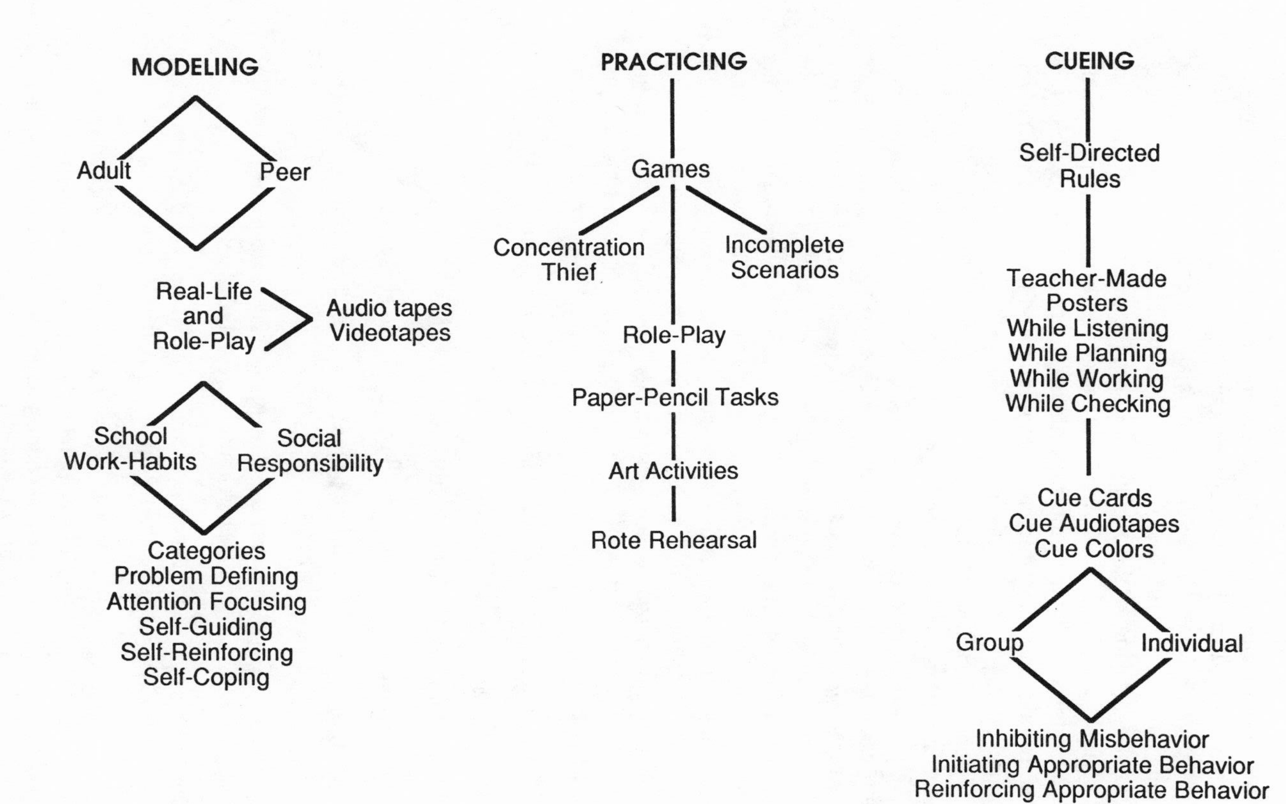

Figure 1 Manning's classroom approach to cognitive self-instruction

how teachers and productive peers guide themselves verbally to regulate behavior. Do not assume students understand and can spontaneously use CSI since it appears to occur very naturally and easily for some individuals.

To overview first, the CSI modeling can be presented spontaneously by adult or peer models, or presented as audiotaped modeling, or videotaped modeling. Students should hear CSI models during school work habits (e.g., concentrating, staying on task) and during social responsibility (e.g., waiting turns, sharing materials). The CSI self-talk categories that need to be explicitly modeled for students are problem defining, attention focusing, self-guiding, self-coping, and self-reinforcing. Please refer to Figure 1 for the modeling component.

Teacher modeling is a viable way for students to learn. Optimally, teachers' modeling needs to occur on four levels within the Manning approach. These four levels are as follows: (1) Spontaneous teacher use of CSI for teacher need (e.g., self-guiding speech to correct the situation when the overhead projector will not work); (2) Role-play CSI for teacher need (e.g., staying calm while being observed by the principal); (3) Spontaneous teacher use of CSI for student need (e.g., teacher sees some students looking on other students' tests and he/she models on the spot the choice between cheating and not cheating), and (4) Role-play CSI for student need (e.g., after several days of pushing in the line for water the teacher subsequently sets up a role-playing situation in which he/she models self-talk for waiting in line for water even when thirst is great). Examples of each of these types are presented below:

1) SPONTANEOUS TEACHER USE OF CSI FOR TEACHER NEED

Categories	CSI
Problem defining	Why won't this overhead turn on?
Attention focusing	Let me see. I'll try all the switches again.
Self-guiding	This arrow points to the right. Did I turn left or right. Try again.
Self-coping	It is easy to get frustrated. Take a deep breath and relax. There must be a solution.
Self-reinforcing	Success: Hey! I stuck with it and found the outlet is faulty. I'll try this other outlet. Yay! It works.
	No Success: I've tried all I know. I'll either show you this information by putting in on the board or call the media specialist to help fix the machine. Which would be the fastest?

2) <u>ROLE-PLAY CSI FOR TEACHER NEED</u>

Categories	CSI
Problem defining	Why am I getting so uptight about being observed?
Attention focusing	Now put a lid on this. Stop panicking myself.Calm down.
Self-guiding	Count slowly. Concentrate on the students. Forget the principal is here.
Self-coping	I may make a few mistakes. It won't be the end of the world even if I do! Things will be fine.
Self-reinforcing	Success: I knew I could get through this observation calmly.
	No Success: My heart never stopped pounding and I didn't teach my very best. Next time I'll be better prepared so I can stay calmer. Learn something from this.

3) <u>SPONTANEOUS TEACHER USE OF CSI FOR STUDENT NEED</u>

Categories	CSI
Problem defining	I forgot to study for my test. Should I look at my friend's test?
Attention Focusing	I can see her paper easily. But, is that right?
Self-guiding	Just do my best. I'll feel better about myself if I don't look.
Self-coping	This is hard. I know my answers are wrong. That's okay. I've done the best I can. Next time I won't leave my book at school.
Self-reinforcing	Success: I'm glad I didn't take answers that didn't belong to me. I feel good about that!
	No Success: I looked at someone else's answer. I feel terrible. I'll just turn in my paper and tell the teacher. I hate this feeling. I'm too important to treat myself this way. Make better choices next time.

4) <u>ROLE-PLAY CSI FOR STUDENT NEED</u>

Categories	CSI
Problem defining	What if I push in line or jump in front of someone?

	How can I follow the rule to wait my turn when I'm so thirsty?
Attention focusing	Look, everyone else is thirsty too. They don't want to wait either.
Self-guiding	Just think about something else. There are just three more people and Mrs. Dollard is moving people along quickly.
Self-coping	I don't like to wait. But who does? I can do it.
Self-reinforcement	I'm proud of myself. I didn't push and I didn't jump up in line. I can wait my turn. I like that about me.

After spontaneous teacher or other adult modeling, review with the students "what," "why," "how," and "when" CSI needs to be employed. Ask students questions such as: "Did anyone notice what I was doing when the overhead would not work? Why was I talking to myself? Sometimes I do this aloud and sometimes I do it inside my head. Either way, it helps me to plan what I need to do." Ask students if they ever talk to themselves? "When? What kinds of things do you say to yourself?" List these on the board or poster. "Why do you use this self-talk? When I was talking to myself about cheating, what did I say to myself? Who remembers something I said?" Continue and prompt if necessary until they have named most or all of the teachers' self-talk and have discussed benefits of guiding themselves verbally. Since the self-talk occurred spontaneously and was used as a teaching tool after the fact, this modeling will most likely not be available on audio or videotape.

Role-playing sessions of CSI can be used for instruction just as any role-play situation can. Prepare the students. Describe the scenario and the self-talk script they will hear. Tape the session. Show the self-talk sessions and teach directly the CSI categories of problem defining, attention focusing, self-guiding, self-coping, and self-reinforcing if the teacher deems that this type of direct instruction is appropriate for his/her group of learners. For example I would not teach categories to most kindergarten groups that I know. Use teacher judgment.

Peer modeling of CSI logically follows teacher modeling. It is important for students to experience how their productive classmates verbally guide themselves at school. There are numerous ways that teachers have used peer models of CSI.

In my research I was impressed with the students' positive and fascinated reaction to a videotape of elementary school children their age or older using self-instruction to guide on-task classroom behaviors during seatwork. The students participating in my research studies internalized and used similar CSI after seeing the tapes for only two weeks, twice per week for fifty minutes. Teachers can easily make their own videotapes. First, you film your class during independent seatwork time, or for older children, during study sessions. Write a script of self-talk (after interviewing students about what they were saying to themselves) and audiotape the self-talk script using a male and female reader to coincide with male and female students on the screen. Dub the self-talk over the original audio soundtrack. Here are some examples of self-talk from the videotape I used:

Problem-defining CSI

What am I supposed to be doing?
Was I supposed to be sitting in my seat paying attention?
Let's see, what was I going to put there?

Attention-focusing CSI

Mrs. Bowersett is telling me what to do. I need to listen carefully.
I better get back to this writing if I want to finish.

Self-guiding CSI

Let's turn back and see if I can get some help from the directions.
I need to be careful while cutting this.

Self-coping CSI

This is a lot of work today, but I'm going to go slowly.
Oops, I made a mistake, but that's okay. I need to slow down.

Self-reinforcing CSI

Yeah! I think I'm getting it.
I did that problem well. No one had to help me.

As students become proficient at identifying categories of self-guiding speech, they become more enabled to supply their own self-talk needs in each of the categories (e.g., student identifies frustration over a task and then identifies the need to use self-coping statements, "I'm having trouble here, but I can figure this out if I take my time."). One exercise is provided below to aid familiarity and identification of CSI categories (i.e., problem defining [pd]), attention focusing [af], self-guiding [g], self-coping [c], and self-reinforcement [r].

CSI Categories Exercise

Directions: Read each self-talk statement or question and decide if it is "pd," "af," "g," "c," or "r" as designated above. In the blank beside each self-talk entry write one of the category letters (e.g, "r" for self-reinforcement). Students may work alone, in dyads, or small groups.

CSI self-talk

_______ 1. Look at this paper in my desk.

_______ 2. And here's another one.

_______ 3. I did it all!

_______ 4. Ooh, I need to quit looking around this room.

_______ 5. I need to get back to work.

_______ 6. Let's see.

_______ 7. Yes, that makes sense. Now I have it.

_______ 8. Read it again. It makes more sense.

_______ 9. Mrs. Lovell said to do 5 of these.

_______ 10. I'm really working hard today.

_______ 11. Boy, watch that! I'm cutting this as carefully as I can.

_______ 12. This looks nice.

_______ 13. This is easy. I'm getting the right answer.

_______ 14. I think I'll number all of these before I turn this page.

_______ 15. Let's see, there's 1, 2, 3, 4, 5, 6.

_______ 16. I'm doing a neat job.

_______ 17. I'll turn the page now.

_______ 18. I'm tired of working, but I think I'm still getting the right answers.

_______ 19. I am busy working.

_______ 20. Am I copying this correctly?

_______ 21. Perhaps I am looking around too much.

_______ 22. Does this make sense to me?

_______ 23. Am I understanding?

_______ 24. Oops, that wasn't correct.

_______ 25. Where is my pencil?

_______ 26. Here it is.

_______ 27. I'm really proud of this work today.

_______ 28. I may not get every one of these right, but I'm trying my best.

_______ 29. My head hurts. I need to stretch before I try another one.

_______ 30. I put the 7 here.

Answer Key

1. af	7. r	13. r	19. r	25. pd
2. g	8. af	14. g	20. pd	26. g
3. r	9. g	15. g	21. af	27. r
4. af	10. r	16. r	22. pd	28. c
5. af	11. r	17. g	23. pd	29. c
6. af	12. r	18. c	24. g	30. g

Exercises such as these are categorized as "informed training." The students are taught directly and explicitly about CSI strategies (e.g., using specific categories of CSI for specific classroom needs).

A second strategy is used when teachers overhear a student using a particularly facilitative self-statement or question. Teachers point out this use of CSI to peers (e.g., "Alice just said, 'Did I skip any problems? Better check one more time.' What Alice said will help her catch her own mistakes. Good strategy, Alice."). One teacher keeps a continuing list of helpful self-talk statements for school work. She lists the statements and puts the student's name beside the contribution(s). Teachers use these displays as a teaching poster that year and sometimes the following year to familiarize students with CSI. Children are especially influenced by older peers. Along these same lines a third peer-modeling strategy is to identify a self-starting, persistent worker and ask this student if he or she will tape what he/she says to start on time, remain attentive, and finish work promptly and accurately. If such tapes can be secured, a valuable resource is available. Using a model tape and earphones, the teacher might set up a learning center designated as "Good Workers' Self-Talk for Starting Work on Time," "Good Workers' Self-Talk for Staying With a Task," and "Good Workers' Self-Talk for Finishing Excellent Work on Time." Students learn well from other students, especially if a cooperative atmosphere is established by the teacher. It is conceivable that Student A who starts work promptly may not persist. Nevertheless, Student A's self-guiding speech (to begin promptly) may be an excellent resource for Student B who flounders around instead of beginning work promptly. Once Student B begins work, he or she may be accomplished at persisting and finishing. The self-talk of these two students may be reciprocally used to help each other. Specifically Student A helps Student B learn self-talk to start promptly, while Student B helps Student A learn self-talk for persisting and finishing. Use the students' self-talk strengths. When students cooperatively teach other students in a problem-solving, collaborative atmosphere, benefits result. All of these examples are related to school work habits (e.g., focusing attention). Peers who naturally use facilitative self-talk to promote social responsibility are often represented in classrooms as well. The motivated teacher needs to keep his/her ears open for such spontaneous self-talk (e.g., while sharing materials) and point out this facilitative self-talk to peers. Self-talk tapes may also be made for such social responsibility situations in the classroom (e.g., not disturbing others while they work) to be shared among peers.

Beyond taking advantage of facilitative "self-talkers" in the classroom as peer models, role-play situations with self-talk as the focus may also be enacted, audiorecorded, filmed, analyzed, and with older students (i.e., third/fourth graders and up) classified as problem defining, attention focusing, self-guiding, self-coping, and self-reinforcement. Learning to recognize these classifications helps students strive to use certain self-talk categories, as needed. For example after students become familiar with coping self-statements, they may realize when to verbally cope instead of nonverbally hitting someone. Another example is to learn when to use self-reinforcing self-talk to diminish dependency on external reinforcement (e.g., "This assignment is looking good"). In so doing, students become more intrinsically motivated. The worksheet below has been used by some third-grade teachers and with older students to teach the self-talk categories of CSI.

Students' Categories of Cognitive Self-Instruction

Directions: After class discussion of each of these self-talk categories students in small groups, dyads, or individually develop other examples.

1. Problem definition (e.g., What did the teacher say to do next?)

___

___

2. Focusing attention (e.g., Now get back to work on this math.)

___

___

3. Self-guiding (e.g., Watch carefully here.)

___

___

4. Self-coping (e.g., Even if I do not get all the answers correct, I will do my best.)

___

___

5. Self-reinforcement (e.g., Good! I remembered to raise my hand!)

___

___

Practicing

It is not enough to just model CSI for students, even if a large amount of modeling occurs and creative development of modeling episodes are used in the classroom. Students need to practice CSI themselves in order to internalize the processes. Practice is crucial for transfer and maintenance of such strategies. Students must create their own metacognitive reality. They need to sensorially experience CSI for themselves. Therefore the following practice examples are provided. The best ideas for practice, however, come from individual teachers who know the needs of their students. These examples have worked for me and/or for the teachers who proposed them. They may require some modification if used by other teachers.

Please refer to Figure 1, Practicing (p. 133). The practicing is intended for students. Students must be directly involved and experience enough repetition to incorporate self-guidance into their present way of thinking about school behavior. The practice strategies are classified as games, role-play, paper-pencil tasks, art activities, and rote rehearsal. Each of these will be briefly addressed. It is hoped that these "starter suggestions" will spark teacher creativity and motivation.

Games

Three *games* that have been tried and endorsed by teachers are "Concentration Thief," "Incomplete Scenarios," and "Can We Play." In Concentration Thief, the teacher initially (and later a concentrating student thief) goes about the room attempting to break students' concentration on an academic task. Students often do not understand what it means when the teacher says "Concentrate on your work." After students are given a certain school assignment to complete, they are told to concentrate on the assignment which means "Keep my mind on my work." As the students repeat aloud with or echo after the teacher, "Keep my mind," they point with fingers to either side of their head, "on my work," they point down to their papers. The kinesthetic/tactual experience of moving hands from the head to the work seems important in helping young students understand the concept of "concentration." Students are directed to say to themselves in whisper or silently, "Concentrate on my work." The game itself helps them to understand the role they must assume to insure the quality of their own concentration. The concentration thief carries a pretend container "Concentration Bucket" and tries to take away somebody's concentration. The teacher (thief) walks among the students making noise, rattling papers, tapping students on shoulders, whistling, laughing, dropping books, trying in any acceptable manner to cause a distraction. If a student looks toward the thief or away from the work, or laughs, that student has just lost his/her concentration to the thief. The thief says, "I just stole your concentration; you'll have to ignore me next time which means don't look at me, think about your work." Students still remaining when time is up (time set by teacher) are designated "Great Concentrators" and a new thief is chosen from among them. In the busy classrooms of today, filled with many interruptions, children have to be able to help themselves concentrate on the task at hand and selectively ignore distractions. A game such as Concentration Thief teaches them to do this.

In addition to the game, some teachers report teaching the use of cue cards (to be explained in detail later in this chapter) during Concentration Thief. Teachers give each student a laminated index card that says "Concentrate on my work." Students are instructed to read the cue card to themselves when the "Concentration Thief" is trying to distract them. In this way students learn to remind themselves to concentrate even during distractions.

The second game, the "Incomplete Scenarios" are geared more toward school/social responsibility. The teacher describes a situation such as "Your class has just come in from recess. It is a very hot day and the line for water is long. The teacher has talked to you about waiting your turn, but she is no where in sight. Your best friend is next to get water and she offers to put you up in line, what will you say to yourself?" After children respond to the incomplete scenarios, role-play can be used with an emphasis on the five categories (e.g., self-coping) of self-talk. Focus on self-guidance of appropriate choices. The following self-talk utterances were developed for this scenario:

"I wait patiently in line for my turn at the water foundation."
"I stand quietly at the water fountain."
"I do not push and shove while waiting my turn at the water fountain."
"It's hard when I am so thirsty to wait patiently. But I can do it."
"I am happy with myself when I wait my turn."
"My teacher is proud of me when I stand quietly and wait patiently at the water fountain. Good for me!"

Another example of an incomplete scenario is focused on lunchroom behavior. Billy wants to get Tim's attention. Tim is sitting several spaces down from Billy. Billy says to himself, "I think I'll yell at Tim, or even better, I'll throw my roll at him to get his attention." What can Billy say to himself to help in this situation?

"I need to eat my food while in the lunchroom."
"After I eat my lunch, I talk quietly to those people sitting beside me."
"I eat my food quietly in the lunchroom."
"I do not play with my food."
"When I want to talk, I talk quietly to my neighbors."
"The lunchroom is a nicer place to come to when I eat my food and talk quietly."
"I feel better when I eat my food slowly and don't rush through my lunch."
"I am proud of myself when I eat my lunch quietly."

Water fountain and lunchroom scenarios were taken from Dagley (1988, p. 163).

A third game is called "Can We Play?" This game was adapted from Markman (1977/1979). The teacher instructs the students to ask themselves (self-questioning) three questions: "Does this make sense to me?" "Is there anything missing?" "What else do I need to know?" The teacher writes these questions on the board or poster and displays them as a stimulus/reminder. Sets of complete and incomplete directions for games and activities are given. Students play the game (with incomplete directions) when they can supply the missing instructions. Any usual classroom games (e.g., Dog and the Bone, Five Up) can be used by omitting essential parts of the directions and then asking the students "Can We Play?" Why or why not?" Remind students to ask themselves the three questions on the board.

Role-Play

The focus here has changed from modeling in a role-play situation to practicing CSI in a role-play situation. Any of the incomplete scenarios might be used as a stimulus to practice the use of CSI through role-play. For example, students may role-play walking to the lunchroom appropriately using a silent self-talk statement (e.g., As I go to lunch, I won't disturb others) before they actually go to lunch for the first time in a given school year. Any school procedure (e.g., fire drill) needs practice, *with accompanying CSI*, to facilitate cooperativeness and a healthy school climate.

A form of role-play that is more appropriate for older students is called "soliloquy," a sociodrama technique (Torrance & Myers, 1970). A volunteer subject is asked to speak aloud his/her thoughts about a school-related problem to aid problem resolution via CSI. The setting for this particular soliloquy is as follows: You have a test in social studies tomorrow. You are really uptight about the test. You know when you get like this you don't make very good grades. Talk to us about what you are saying to yourself about this problem. Other students listen for self-talk categories (e.g., self-reinforcing).

Student's soliloquy. "Well, I've been really paying attention in Social Studies but did I go over my questions every day? Sometimes I didn't ask the teacher questions about the things I didn't understand. Why do I do that? I need to ask right then, but the others would think I was a dummy. Well, I better start studying. But I don't know where to start. Do I have in mind what to study? Guess I better call Samantha; she always makes high marks. Maybe she'll tell me what to study. Why do we have stupid old tests anyway? They make my stomach hurt. My mother thinks I'm lazy. I am not very smart in Social Studies. Did I bring my book home? What if I make a zero and everybody finds out. I'm really going to have to think hard tomorrow. I wish my teacher wouldn't call out everybody's grade. Don't worry so much. I can't study if I worry, and I'll make a zero if I don't study. I better call Samantha. I can do this if I will first calm down, stop saying horrible things to myself, get organized and STUDY. I'm just wasting my time. Get with it. Do the best I can—that's all anyone can ask for or do! I feel better. I can do this. I trust myself."

Paper-Pencil Tasks

These tasks include such things as self-talk journals, CSI booklets, cartoon characters, and handwriting. Each is explained separately as follows:

Students are required to keep *self-talk logs* or journals. This assignment can be varied to fit the age level and specific student needs. Students will have a tendency to describe external events instead of describing their internal talk, unless the teacher spends quality time preparing the students. In classrooms where teachers have been using many CSI strategies, promoting metacognitive skills as vital to learning, the students are more apt to find self-talk journals a natural, creative outlet. Students write in first person what they have been saying to themselves during math class or during recess, or during morning work, or any time agreed upon by students and/or teachers. During or after these classes once every day, or at least once per week, the students write down their self-talk. Many follow-up activities can occur at the discretion of the teacher based on "knowing the students." One example is that students classify their self-talk entries for their math lessons after one month in one or more of the following ways: (1) Positive-neutral-negative, (2) helpful-unhelpful, (3) adult-parent-child, (4) problem defining, attention focusing, self-guiding, self-coping, self-reinforcing, and (5) task relevant-task irrelevant, or (6) on task-off task. As a result the students and teachers gain insight into student frustration, apathy, motivation, boredom, etc. Teachers can learn a great deal about students through "self-talk logs" that they may not discover in any other way. Also, students may convert some of their negative self-talk into neutral/positive task-relevant self-talk. In essence, they learn new, more helpful ways to guide their own learning. The greatest challenge to the teacher will be to get the students to externalize internal thoughts into written journal entries. It can be done with persistence and a creative teacher's touch. I even know a wonderful kindergarten teacher who has her students (in the last half of the year) use their invented spellings and drawings to convey their inner thoughts about various assignments. Readers would be impressed with what these young children have learned about verbal expression of their own thought.

The next paper-pencil example is to have students make a *CSI booklet.* One teacher asked students to make CSI booklets to emphasize when to use CSI across the school curriculum. Manning (1984) designated four school uses of CSI. Teachers spend the majority of each day engaging students in academic work. In order to help students of all ages increase their achievement in academics they must *listen* well, *plan* effectively, *work* efficiently, and *check* their work accurately. These four school uses of CSI: listening, planning, working, and checking were identified and discussed in Manning (1984). The booklet is centered around students learning, reinforcing, and extending these four times when CSI is especially required. On the cover of the booklet, the students write WHEN TO USE CSI and draw themselves with a balloon-caption (comic bubble) over their heads saying something helpful to themselves at school (e.g., Do I have all my materials together to start my assignment—a sharpened pencil and paper?). Each of the next four pages of the booklet is devoted (one each) to listening, planning, working, and checking. Each page is labeled with a word, (e.g., LISTENING) to aid students' association with the corresponding self-talk for listening times at school. Depending on students' ages, they draw or cut out pictures of people or they write examples of self-talk for each "time to use CSI." Over each person's head they draw a bubble (like in the comics) and write a task-relevant, helpful self-talk message to self. Some teachers have modified this and used familiar cartoon characters first, then magazine cut-out people, then self-drawings or their own school pictures (movement from an external to an internal focus). The purpose of the booklet is to familiarize students with appropriate school times to remember to use CSI. Some examples from a second-grade class:

Listening	**Planning**
What is she saying?	Do I know what to do?
Do I understand?	What should I do first?
Does this make sense?	I'll do my best on this.
I need to listen carefully.	Let's get going.
Working	**Checking**
I need to slow down.	Does this look good to me?
This looks sloppy. I can do better.	Did I skip anything?
I need to quit staring out the window and get back to this work.	Can I do it a better way?
Looking better.	I'm proud of this work.

Another paper-pencil task is to use *commercial comics* and ask children to rewrite them, based on what the characters are saying to themselves, rather than to each other. This requires monitoring by the teacher and students to make sure they are using private speech and not social speech. This is not an appropriate written activity for K-1 students. This activity may be modified for them as a discussion of the cartoon characters' self-talk, with a follow-up language experience story using self-talk as the focus. In addition, even second- to fourth-grade teachers have reported that their students respond best to this activity if they begin with a comic strip that has only one character per frame. This way it makes more sense that the character might be talking to self, rather than to someone else. However, it is a fun activity for students to write in self-talk when there are two or more characters per frame—it is a challenging and usually a humorous activity. Students enjoy sharing their creations. Teachers begin by saving comic strips. Cut out the strips that appeal to the teacher. Cut out white bubbles to glue over the original captions. Some teachers simply "white-out" the original words and xerox the cartoon for students. Laminate about fifty of these for a classroom set. Try to select ones with one character per frame to be used first and then progress accordingly. Each student receives a strip to use to write the character's self-talk. This activity can be completed in dyads, or small groups. One teacher uses an opaque projector for follow-up discussions of each self-talk cartoon.

A first-grade teacher provides a set of questions at each work station in her classroom. The teacher reports that these questions cause students to reflect on their own school tasks, as they practice metacognitive thinking.

Example 1

TAKING CARE OF MY BUSINESS

Name ____________________

Date ____________________

Good for me! (Students write in something helpful they say to themselves.)

Self-reinforcement ____________________

Work Station: ____________________

LISTENING: Yes or No

_____ Does this make sense to me?

_____ Is there anything missing?

PLANNING AND WORKING:Yes or No

_____ Am I ready to begin?

_____ Do I have all of my supplies?

CHECKING: Yes or No

_____ Did I stay on task?

_____ Is this my best?

_____ Is my work complete?

_____ Is my name on all my papers?

Note: Students respond by writing "yes" or "no" in the blanks and hand in this sheet along with their work pages when their morning work is completed.

Example 2

PRACTICING SELF-TALK:
LISTENING TO TEACHER DIRECTIONS
THIRD GRADE

1. I'm supposed to repeat the teacher directions inside my head.
2. I read the directions along with the teacher.
3. I say each direction over in my head.
4. Does that make sense to me?
5. If it doesn't, raise my hand, and ask for help.

Another paper-pencil task to reinforce CSI is to ask students to make *written posters* for the class. These posters can include anything related to CSI that the teacher and students want to display in the room. One example is to have four groups of students make a helpful poster for each of the four school uses of CSI. Each group is assigned one of the times to use CSI (i.e., listening, planning, working, and checking). They write a draft list of task-relevant, helpful questions and statements-to-self for each of the four areas and propose this list for acceptance. The drafts are evaluated by members of the other three remaining groups to validate the helpfulness of each self-talk entry. If an entry is considered unhelpful or task irrelevant by a majority of students then that entry is deleted. The remaining self-talk entries are written neatly on a poster and displayed as a CSI bulletin board. Four posters, as developed by a fifth-grade class are provided below:

POSTER 1

While Listening:

1. Does this make sense?
2. Am I getting this?
3. I need to ask a question now before I forget.
4. Pay attention.
5. Can I do what he's saying to do?

POSTER 2

While Planning:

1. Do I have everything together?
2. Do I have my friends tuned out for right now?
3. Let me get organized first.
4. What order will I do this?
5. I know this stuff!

POSTER 3

While Working:

1. Am I working fast enough?
2. Stop staring at my girlfriend and get back to work.
3. How much time is left?
4. Do I need to stop and start over?
5. This is hard for me, but I can manage okay.

POSTER 4

While Checking:

1. Did I finish everything?
2. What do I need to recheck?
3. Am I proud of this work?
4. Did I write all the words? Count them.
5. I think I finished. I organized myself. Did I daydream too much?

In a final example, the teacher writes a language experience story (to be used later as a handwriting lesson) illustrating how students are successfully using CSI. The story, using the students' names for characters, focuses on examples of how the students were able to maintain concentration on story-writing in the midst of classroom conversation, etc. Focus on the students' self-talk. On one day "Concentration" may be the theme. Another day "CSI for Listening" may serve as the theme. Other themes may include "CSI for Planning," "CSI for Working," "CSI for Checking," "CSI for Completing Tasks," etc. The students are more motivated to practice handwriting if it is personalized. In the meantime, they are also having their CSI skills positively reinforced.

Art Activities

Please refer to Figure 1 (p. 133) to locate where we are at this time on the CSI model. Art activities are used here to insure that students practice the CSI strategies they have heard and seen modeled for them previously. Art activities and CSI are integrated, because students enjoy expressing themselves through art. They are motivated by the drawing, painting, etc., while CSI is squeezed into the art activity as reinforcement and practice of CSI strategies. Some examples of how classroom teachers, committed to CSI, used art activities are: drawing and painting. Students draw self-portraits with a cartoon bubble over their heads illustrating a CSI statement: "I will remember to wait my turn." Students may also paint their portraits and add a touch of self-talk. Students may be divided into four groups to illustrate on four different murals the four school times to use self-guiding statements (i.e., listening, planning, working, and checking). These murals usually consist of drawings or paintings of students in a school environment with a bubble over each head, with the self-talk written with magic marker. These make beautiful wall displays in the room. One principal was so impressed that she asked to use them in the school foyer for everyone to enjoy and to learn. The last example is to divide a sheet of drawing paper into four sections: "listening," "planning," "working," and "checking." The students are asked to draw themselves for each section and write a CSI statement-to-self or question-to-self.

Rote Rehearsal

The last practicing component is rote rehearsal. Students practice the modeled CSI, following Meichenbaum and Goodman's steps (1971) described previously in chapter 3. For classroom use this means that students practice self-statements aloud, softly, and silently to themselves in order to internalize the process. Meichenbaum and colleagues were successful in improving impulsivity and promoting creativity when subjects were taught helpful, facilitative self-talk. It will not be adequate to stop after teachers or peers have modeled CSI statements. Instead the three steps of student practice in sequence are: (1) practice CSI speaking aloud, (2) whisper CSI statements to themselves, and finally (3) silently rehearse the statements-to-self.

This process may be conducted with the whole class, small groups, or individuals. Meichenbaum used CSI with individuals to reduce impulsivity, therefore working with individual students is not repeated here. A description of using students' rote rehearsal for large group instruction is included. The same classroom process can be used for small groups as well as large groups. The example is "hallway behavior." The class has just returned from lunch and they were excessively noisy, pushing each other, opening doors to other classes, and running over smaller children who were also in the hall. The sixth-grade teacher decides to use a CSI strategy. She's tried everything else. Therefore, she begins by expressing her dissatisfaction with their hallway behavior using I-messages. Next, she describes her expectations clearly: "As you go down the hall tomorrow I'd like you to do five things. They are (1) walk, don't run; (2) remain silent, don't talk; (3) stay together, don't leave the group; (4) stay in a line, don't run into others; (5) keep your hands and feet to yourself, do not touch another. I am going to talk about each one of these separately because they are very important. We must stop disturbing the whole school each time we leave this room. I'll talk to myself as if I were one of you going down the hall. First I'll talk about the need to walk, instead of running. Please listen carefully. Tell yourself to listen to every word I say. If I were you I'd talk to myself like this: 'I walk quietly down the hall. When I run, I endanger my own safety and those I may meet. Sometimes I forget this safety rule. I will remember to walk, not run. I'll monitor my feet by saying, "Walk feet—no running feet allowed. I can do it!"' Now class I'd like you to repeat each one of the statements I just said to myself. I'll write them on the board. We will repeat all the statements aloud together, then I want you to whisper all the statements, and then say all of them silently to yourself. The first one is 'I walk quietly down the hall.' Starting with this one, and reading down the list, repeat aloud together until we finish the last one which is 'I can do it.' Altogether, . . . " The students repeat together using all three forms: overt, faded, and covert self-talk. The same process is repeated for the other four rules for hallway behavior which the teacher described to the students. After each hallway rule is verbalized, following Meichenbaum and Goodman's (1971) steps, the students and teacher return to the hall and practice using CSI statements for hallway behavior.

One reason students do not follow class procedures and rules is because they are not specific, nor have they been explicitly taught by the teacher, modeled by the teacher and perhaps peers, and practiced by the students with accompanying self-guiding speech to self. Readers may be saying, "Too time consuming." It isn't too time consuming if one observes how much time is spent policing, nagging, and pleading with students to behave. In addition to being less time consuming over the long-run, students are learning a means for self-control via explicit, quality exposure to a "self-talk" role model. I believe strongly that if all teachers took the initial time at the beginning of the school year to teach, model self-talk, and instruct practice for all classroom rules and procedures, classroom discipline problems would no longer be the number one or number two problem in our nation, as they have been for the past fifteen years. For a list of rules and procedures that lend themselves well to teacher description, self-talk modeling, and self-talk practice, please refer to Evertson et al. (1988).

For each school function (e.g., lunchroom, hallway, bathroom, water fountain) that requires teacher planning and deliberation about procedures, I believe that teachers must also do something resembling a task analysis for each classroom procedure. The sixth-grade teacher-model for hallway behavior (presented earlier) represented this kind of teacher thought. The behaviors she required in the hall were (1) walking, (2) quiet, (3) staying together, (4) staying in line, and (5) keeping hands and feet to self. Therefore her task analysis of hallway behavior consisted of these five behaviors. If teachers will take the time to (1) analyze other procedures in their classroom, (2) conduct a task analysis to decide what they really mean by appropriate behavior (e.g., in the lunchroom), and (3) clearly articulate these behaviors, (4) model accompanying, facilitative self-talk, (5) insure practice from students in the three forms (aloud, whisper, and silently), (6) role-play the procedures, and then (7) monitor and encourage the use of CSI, a great improvement in classroom management should result. But better still, a means for self-control is fostered.

Cueing

Referring again to Figure 1, the last component of Manning's approach to CSI is cueing. Students have now experienced "teacher and peer modeling" of self-management. They have had first-hand practice of self-management. Now students will need prompts and reminders to insure continued and sustained use of CSI. Prompts can take the form of posted class rules written from a self-management orientation, rather than the traditional other-control orientation, posters, group and individual cue cards, cue audio tapes, and other cueing signals.

The first suggestion is to write classroom rules and procedures in "first person, present tense." For example instead of a rule that reads "Wait your turn" the rule reads "Wait my turn." This facilitates responsibility toward oneself. When second person is used, it is not really a self-reminder; it is a reminder made by someone else. Especially young children, who view the world from an I-orientation, respond much better to rules stated from their own perspective rather than from an external directive. Often when young children read the rule "wait *your* turn" they read it literally to mean that *you* should wait *your* turn but I don't have to. If the rule reads "wait *my* turn," young children realize that that rule includes them as well. In addition, older children also respond more personally to self-directed rules, using "I" and "my" in place of "you" and "your." In addition to first person, rules should be written in present tense: "I raise my hand" or "Raise my hand." Future tense rules, such as "I will raise my hand" foster futuristic thinking and may cause students to postpone adherence to a later date. Many of my creative student teachers have developed outstanding thematic rules that accompany units of study. I wish I could include all of them here. However, one example in particular that I always remember was a first-grade animal unit when the rules were posted on climbing monkeys. One monkey had the rule "I don't monkey around," while another monkey had "I go bananas over finishing all my work" written on their stomachs. The students adored and followed the "monkey rules" stated in a self-directed manner. Nothing can replace the creativity of individual teachers to make CSI really work to foster self-control. Another example of self-directed rules, using pictorial cues to accompany the rules is provided below. These picture rules are very helpful for nonreaders or young learners.

Written Class Rule	**Cue Picture**
I raise my hand.	(Show picture of student with hand raised.)
I listen.	(Show picture of a large ear.)
I wait my turn.	(Show drawing of two students —one waiting for water while the other is drinking water.)
I stay in my seat.	(Show picture of a student sitting quietly, working on a task at desk.)

The teacher-made posters for the four school uses (i.e., listening, planning, working, and checking) are similar to the posters made by students to practice CSI statements-to-self. In this place on the model (see Figure 1) these posters serve a cueing role to remind students to use CSI. Teachers are encouraged to use student-made posters to represent the best self-talk examples for cueing purposes. With younger students (grades K-2) these posters should be introduced one poster at a time and practiced for approximately two weeks to one month before the next poster is introduced. Use teacher judgment as to how fast older students (grades three to twelve) can process the information effectively. One fourth-grade teacher says she puts all four uses on posters—with examples of exemplary CSI—over her chalkboard to guide work habits of students all year.

Her posters contain the following information:

While Listening to Instructions

1. Goal setting: I will listen carefully.
2. Coping statements: I can understand, if I don't daydream.
3. Guiding statements: She is telling us what to do first.
4. Self-questioning: What do I do when I finish?

5. Self-reinforcement: I know what to do now. Good for me!

While Preparing to Work

1. Goal setting: I will get everything organized.
2. Coping statements: I don't have all the crayons I need. What should I do about that?
3. Guiding statements: Put all my materials at my desk.
4. Self-questioning: Am I ready to begin?
5. Self-reinforcement: I have everything ready.

While Working

1. Goal setting: I want this to be my best work/day.
2. Coping statements: This is hard for me, but I'm trying.
3. Guiding statements: Be careful—don't skip a line.
4. Self-questioning: Is this looking right to me?
5. Self-reinforcement: This is really looking super. I'm working hard.

While Checking Finished Work

1. Goal setting: I check over every paper.
2. Coping statements: I'm tired of looking over this. Just two more problems, though.
3. Guiding statements: Yes, that's right.
4. Self-questioning: Where do I put these?
5. Self-reinforcement: I finished all my work and checked over it once. Good for me!

The next discussion will center around cue cards to remind students to use CSI strategies. In the regular classroom, students have behaviors they need to improve. Almost every child has some behavior that needs improvement. Each week, students may decide individually what behavior they wish to address via a cue card reminder. Of course, the regular classroom is not conducive to students talking aloud to themselves all at once. The students are instructed to whisper the self-instructions or to read them to self silently. Examples of cue cards might be, "Stay seated now," "Don't daydream—concentrate," "Try to answer." Cue cards can be individualized to meet the needs of each class member. One teacher uses a clear plastic shoe bag in which she puts categories of behavior reminders on laminated index cards. All are stated from an internal perspective (e.g., Finish all my work). The students are free to get a card when needed and tape it on their desk as a reminder. Occasionally this teacher will choose a cue card for a particular child; however, the emphasis is on child initiative for self-correction. For nonreaders, Palkes et al. (1968) training pictures may be worthy of consideration. In any event, the cue card serves as a stimulus/reminder to mediate behavior.

Cueing may be used in the form of small index cards for individual children, large posters, group cue cards, and other display methods. One teacher uses a large cue card which simply says "I CAN TRY." This card is suspended from the ceiling on poster board. She introduced the card because her first-grade children had begun the unfortunate habit of saying "I can't," even before they heard all of the directions. She reports that the card has been very effective in practically eliminating shouts of self-defeating "I can't! I can't!" She points to the card. Further, she says some of the students point to the card for their peers. The group cue card reminded the children not to defeat themselves before they even attempted tasks. This worked extremely well in changing attitudes about what they were able to accomplish and about the corresponding accomplishments, themselves.

Individual cue cards are used to remind single students. This cueing system is used for three types of classroom reminders. These types are to inhibit inappropriate classroom behaviors, to initiate and to reinforce appropriate behaviors. Depending on grade level and maturity of students, one of these types may be introduced at a time and practiced until students are following their own cues quite easily. However, teachers in third grade and above report that they introduce all three types at once. Some teachers make a set of cue cards for each type and give them to students who exhibit a need for them. Other teachers have asked students to make their own cue cards as needed. These are usually taped on the student's desk and used as a reminder (e.g., raise my hand) until the students and/or teachers believe that they no longer need them. When the appropriate behavior has become automatic the cue card should be removed. Of course, modifications of cue card use are often made by teachers to suit their own particular needs. Modifications of cue cards have included paper bracelets with cueing on the bracelet, group cue cards displayed in the classroom (e.g., I try my best) and cueing folders kept at desks to self-record appropriate behaviors at the sound of a buzzer or timer in the room (e.g., Am I on task? If not, tell myself to focus on my work).

It should be emphasized that in most cases students should work on only one behavior at a time. Therefore, only one cue card should be visible on the desk. A string of cue cards taped to the student's desk is inappropriate and will probably be unhelpful. Teachers and other interested readers may write to me for sample cue cards. I am presently compiling a book of cue cards for publication.

Cue cards may be drawings of animals, stick figures, people, or imaginary characters demonstrating the target behavior the teacher wishes the student to perform (e.g., listening to others). These cue cards are sometimes drawn by teachers or commerical cut-outs may be used. Cards are usually laminated and are the size of a 3 x 5 index card. However, cue pictures may be reduced or enlarged. Pictorial drawings (e.g., a smiling face with one oversized ear to cue "listening") may be used with or without a written prompt (e.g., I listen well) accompanying the picture.

In addition to teacher-made cues, there are some commercial cueing techniques available. The Ralph Bear Training Figures in the Bash and Camp research (1975) are extremely popular with teachers. Teachers like to enlarge these for bulletin boards and other learning displays. They also make excellent individual cue cards singly and collectively. Also Palkes, Stewart, and Kahana (1968) have training pictures that may provide some ideas for classroom cueing of appropriate behaviors.

Long (1984) demonstrates teaching self-control and pro-social behavior by using therapeutic signs and sayings in classrooms for emotionally disturbed children. Some of these are easily adapted or used as they are in regular classrooms. For a complete listing of these, please refer to Long's article. Most of these are stated in the second person (e.g., Listen to Your Controls) and should be changed to first person (e.g., Listen to My Controls). To illustrate how cue cards may be adapted for individual school needs, consider one particular school faculty who were not satisfied with lunchroom behavior. Children were throwing food, screaming, getting under the tables. Therefore, the teachers and/or students made large colorful cue cards, (written in present tense, first person) and posted them in the lunchroom, they prepared centerpieces for the table containing cue cards, they made cue card placemats for the lunch tables, and they prepared reinforcement cards or buttons for children to wear when they demonstrated appropriate lunchroom behavior. They reported a great deal of improvement in their lunchroom atmosphere.

Cueing of CSI may also be conducted using teacher-made audiotapes. Hallahan, Lloyd, and Stoller (1982) have compiled a very helpful manual for teachers on preparing a tape to improve attention of students. The materials needed are a self-monitoring tape and a self-monitoring card. In self-monitoring studies, the Hallahan et al. method was found effective for increasing on-task behavior and academic productivity. Benefits continued even after students stopped using the tape. Tapes with earphones may be used for individual children or tapes may be used with whole classes or small groups experiencing difficulty with attention and concentration. We might call this a "Tape Cueing Activity" for the purpose of encouraging student(s) to attend/concentrate throughout the day and to be aware of their own concentration abilities. The directions for making such a tape are as follows:

1. The teacher prepares a 60-minute tape periodically recording the sound of bell or melodious tone. The ringing of the bell or tone should be recorded at different intervals throughout the 60-minute period. Vary the length of the intervals.
2. The teacher plays the tape throughout the day as needed.

3. When the students hear the bell or tone on the tape, have each student ask him/her self the question, "Was I concentrating or not?"

4. Supply each student with a record sheet. Have each student mark "yes" if he/she was concentrating and "no" if he/she was not concentrating.

5. This procedure may continue until the students' concentration improves (1–2 weeks). It can then be used periodically throughout the year if you so desire.

Please refer to Hallahan for more specific instructions. Also see the self-record sheet provided in chapter 10.

The final discussion about cueing of CSI is the use of color for cueing attention. Zentall and Kruczek (1988) found that color placed on the part of a letter, difficult to form, increased performance for hyperactive, nonattentive students. Color may be used to draw attention to relevant stimuli within tasks. Please note that color used just to make a task more attractive can actually disrupt the performance of many students. However, color may be placed strategically on difficult words in a passage or even near difficult-to-remember objects (e.g., bright yellow dot placed over the light switch to cue children to turn off the lights in their room). A classroom example may be to put a large, bright red, circle over the classroom door to remind young children to wait at the door for further instructions from the teachers before exiting. One teacher used a red dot to cue students, who were hopping up every few minutes, to stay seated for a reasonable period of time. She placed a cue card on the desk with a red dot, picture of person sitting at desk, and the words "Stay seated" on the card. She also placed a large red dot on the floor where the child would turn her foot to get out of her seat. The child was instructed that when she felt the urge to pop out of her seat, she was to touch and read her cue card in a whisper and to look down at the red dot on the floor as she turned in her seat. This child was soon regulating her own "in-seat" behavior and had grown in feelings of self-efficacy.

Cueing is a method used to encourage students to remind themselves to bring their own behavior under their own control. This frees the teacher from excessive policing and allows more time for academic pursuits. The teacher is not continuously reminding students to raise hands to speak, to sit down, to wait their turns, to lower their voices, and so forth. Instead, a system of cueing is implemented whereby students prompt themselves. Cueing is never administered as punishment. Cueing, as with most management strategies, may be abused if used incorrectly by teachers to control students. The aim is just the opposite. It is a means to help children learn to control themselves. Cueing is nonpunitive self-reminders. As students learn to manage their own classroom behaviors, they need reminders. Self-reminder cue cards are nonpunitive tools for the promotion of the self-controlled, self-managed student.

Sample Lesson Plans Using the Manning CSI Model

The first lesson plan is written for kindergarten and is used to encourage "sharing materials."

Teacher: Debbie Bryant
Day 1

Goal: My students improve in sharing materials in the classroom.

Modeling: I begin with adult modeling.

1. Teacher talks aloud and demonstrates sharing behavior at the actual area with materials. An example of self-talk would be "I know Jim needs these crayons to color his picture. We can both use them; I think I will share these with him."
2. Teacher models statements verbally. Have students repeat such statements as "I share my things with others." "I let someone else use my glue." "I remember to share things at school." Students rehearse behavior.
3. Teacher prompts students: "I . . . " to see if children will complete the statements. Students may again practice the sharing behaviors.
4. Teacher whispers prompts; students whisper self-statements. With my kindergarten students, I already have spent time on what it means to whisper.
5. Teacher tells children to say the sharing sentences to themselves; they then display a sharing behavior. Students are in a situation conducive to this idea: art, free play, or working at their tables.

Teacher tells students she learned this from a new friend, the Share Bear. The character is introduced on visual displays in the classroom and is used throughout as an example. The idea is for the children to remember what this character says to himself to help him remember to share with others.

Practicing: Children make and manipulate puppets (stick) of either the Share Bear or their own creations. This gives them an opportunity to practice self-talk as they verbalize what the puppets are saying to themselves. This is done in show form with the teacher suggesting scenarios or simply allowing the children to manipulate freely.

Children are introduced to two new friends, Al and B in a flannelboard story. The teacher creates a story that follows their day at school, including incidents where they do and do not share. When Al and B are using sharing self-talk (like the students practiced to help them remember to share), the students are told to clap their hands.

Children draw or paint pictures of themselves in sharing activities at school or home. Students dictate self-talk dialogue to teacher for writing on the picture.

Cueing: I rewrite classroom rules in "I" form. (I raise my hand to be called on.)

Posters are displayed all around the room, such as at learning centers, free-play area, their individual tables, and the book corner. Posters use the Share Bear character and self-statements to serve as reminders. (I remember to share, I feel great when I share, etc.)

Teacher plays incomplete scenario game with students called "What If." Example: "You are working at the independent table during morning groups. You really need the glue bottle for your work but Mandy has it. Miss Bryant has talked about sharing and waiting for things, but she is busy with the reading group. What do you say to yourself?

Teacher verbally cues students as needed, by giving first word of self-statements. "I . . . "

Day 2

Modeling: This day's modeling involves the use of peers. Teacher calls on a child who is displaying desired behavior related to sharing. Child tells others his/her self-talk used to help him/her remember to share. In addition, the teacher and aide model behavior and verbalize self-talk for real-life situations. Unlike the day before when the adult assumed the role of a child, today the teacher models situations that might occur during the day and how she talks to herself to remember to share.

Practicing: Teacher makes instant photographs of students in sharing scenes to be displayed in classroom. Students tell what self-talk they used in that particular situation. Dialogue is written under the photographs.

I use filmstrips with the stories being read aloud from the teacher's guide. The topics deal with honesty, sharing, fairness, and helping others. These animal characters use self-talk in which they reason and make decisions. This is very appropriate for modeling and practicing speech-to-self, and shows it is acceptable to talk aloud (whisper) to yourself. After viewing, the students discuss the humorous but helpful self-talk the animals used. The filmstrips are easily adapted to use with teacher-created stories. Visual aids would also be helpful using puppet characters, including Timothy Turtle, Sally Skunk, and Roberta Rabbit.

"Selfish Sam" is a game that is played while children are working at centers, art time, or any time when it is necessary to cooperate and share materials. "Selfish Sam" is a little elf hiding in the room watching. He tries to catch boys and girls who are being selfish and not sharing with others. He grows every time he sees selfish behavior. Explain to the children that if Selfish Sam doesn't see any selfishness, he will shrink and finally disappear. A "Selfish Sam" poster is displayed, saying "Don't Let Selfish Sam Catch You!"

Cueing: Again, the teacher uses verbal cues as necessary. Individual cue cards are used in addition to the posters displayed. They are used to inhibit behavior, such as saying "I don't grab." They will encourage initiation of sharing behavior, such as saying "I share with others. I remember to share." These also serve as reinforcers, such as "I am good at sharing. I feel great when I share my things." These also are used with the "Selfish Sam" game. Children are given reward cards for not allowing Selfish Sam to catch them. Examples read "Selfish Sam can't catch me—I share!"

The next lesson plan is for third graders and the goal is to improve self-management of school work habits.

Teacher: Jane Holman
Day 1

Objective: I introduce the concept of self-management by using adult modeling, peer modeling, and a puppet show.

Time: 30 minutes

Materials: School lunch report, Two puppets.
The lesson begins in the morning while I am taking the school lunch report. I pretend to be distracted over and over until I forget what I am doing. I ask the students what would happen if I couldn't stay on task long enough to finish the report. I say, "It is very important for us to learn to stay on task because if we allow ourselves to be distracted, we won't be able to complete anything. I would like you to listen while I talk aloud to myself about this problem. These things that I say to myself help me

stay on task while I am taking the lunch report."

Self-Talk:

Now, what am I supposed to be doing?

Let me see, I need to find out who brought lunches and who is eating school lunches.

I'll ask who brought lunches first and write it down so I won't forget.

It's hard to concentrate with all that noise in the hall. That's okay. I can do it. I'll keep my mind on my work. Ten students brought lunches and no one is absent, so twelve are eating school lunches. I did it! I'm off to a good start today! I ask, "Can you think of a time that you started something and didn't finish because you were distracted by something else?" List examples on the board. Select one example and say "Listen while I talk aloud to myself about this problem. It helps me to say these things to myself and some of these can help you, too."

Self-Talk:

Now, what was I supposed to do?

Let me see, I'm supposed to do this word-search puzzle.

Where do I start? I know what I'll do. I'll do the easy ones first. I can't think while everybody is talking. Just keep my eyes and my mind on my work. Hey, I'm finished. I did a good job.

I ask a student to come up and repeat the self-talk dialogue out loud after me. Then, the entire class will repeat after me out loud. I may choose another example at this point and have one child whisper the self-talk after me. After the class whispers, the individual child performs the statements covertly followed by the class using self-talk covertly.

I close with a puppet show performed by two students selected ahead of time. They act out a skit where one puppet is trying to stay on task and the other is trying to distract him. The first puppet uses self-guiding statements to stay on task until the other gives up and goes away.

I say, "Today we used self-communication to help us stay on task. I'd like each of you to be thinking of some statements of your own that you could use to stay on task. We will be using your statements tomorrow."

Day 2

Objective: The student practices using self-guiding statements. I provide cues as reminders and students make their own cues and a tape.

Time: 45 minutes

Materials: tape, tape recorder, laminated traffic light cue cards, magazines, scissors, glue, index cards, pencils, appropriate and inappropriate statements on cards.

I begin by explaining a guessing game activity. Each student is given a card with an example of a self-talk statement. Students read the statement and identify whether it would help them stay on task. We compare appropriate statements to inappropriate statements.

I explain Dr. Manning's Concentration Thief to demonstrate the concept of concentration. I try to steal their concentration while they repeat to themselves, "I must keep my eyes on my work. I must keep my mind on my work."

Next, I ask each student to write down self-talk statements that they find helpful for on-task behavior. We will make a class tape of the students saying their own appropriate self-dialogue. I say, "If you are working and you find yourself becoming distracted, go to the listening center and listen to the tape. Repeat these statements to yourself to help you stay on task."

In the next activity, students are given materials and instructed to cut out pictures from magazines of people who are working on something. The students write self-talk statements that aid in staying on task using "bubbles" over the head of the magazine cut-outs. These will be displayed on a bulletin board to serve as cues. The students may remove these and use them at their desks when they feel a need for individual reminders.

I introduce Ralph, the bear cue pictures created by Bash and Camp (1975). Each Ralph picture is on a poster demonstrating the four school uses of self-communication. "What am I suppose to do?" reminds students to use self-statements for listening. "What are some plans" serves as a cue for preparing to work. "How is my plan working" encourages self-talk while working. "How did I do?" is a visual reminder to use self-communication while checking work.

To help the students become more aware of how often they engage in off-task behavior, I provide each with a laminated traffic light cue card. At irregular intervals, a tone is emitted that was previously recorded on tape. This is a signal to make a tally mark on the green light for on-task behavior, red light for off-task behavior, and yellow light for each time self-talk is used after marking a red light to get back on task.

The final sample lesson plan is aimed at fifth graders and the purpose is to learn CSI for concentration.

Teacher: Jeane Sammons
Day 1

Objective 1: Students are able to use the five cognitive self-instruction steps (Meichenbaum and Goodman, 1971) to aid in concentration.

Objective 2: Students monitor their concentration throughout the day by marking a "yes" or a "no" on their individual record sheets.

Objective 3: Students use individual cue cards to aid in controlling their concentration.

Procedures:

Objective 1

Materials: chalk, chalkboard, story to read.

1. Teacher asks students what the word *concentrate* means. List answers on board.
2. Tell students that when someone concentrates on something, they "focus their thoughts or give all of their attention to something."
3. Ask students why they believe it is important to learn to "concentrate."
4. Tell students: Sometimes I have a hard time concentrating when I am reading. When I do not concentrate or focus my thoughts on what I am reading, I do not remember what the story is about. When this happens, this is what I say to myself: "It is hard to keep my mind on my work today, but I know I can do it. I will read the story outloud, and then I will be able to understand it. (After paragraph is read out loud) Reading out loud really helped and I understand it now."

   Tell students that "When I talk to myself, it helps me to remember what I am learning."
5. Complete Meichenbaum's five steps.
6. After volunteer is finished, have the entire class practice the scenario like the volunteer student did.

Evaluation: Teacher observes children practicing at their seats.

Objective 2

Materials: pencil, record sheet, tape, tape recorder.

7. Tell students that you have made a tape that

has a "noise" on it. Throughout the day, you will hear the noise and when you do, you ask yourself, "Was I concentrating or not?" If you were concentrating then mark a "yes" on your record sheet. If you were not concentrating then mark a "no" on your record sheet.

8. Give a record sheet to each child and demonstrate the procedure for the children. Tell students that you are not collecting these for a grade, but that you will check them.

9. The students continue this procedure until their concentration considerably improves (1-2 weeks). Then I use it throughout the year at random times.

Evaluation: Teacher checks record sheets each day and also randomly checks a different child each time the "tone" on the recorder beeps and keeps a record.

Objective 3

Materials: cue cards, tape.

10. Tell students that besides the "noise" on the tape recorder, each student has a reminder on the desk to help with concentration. Tell students when I have a hard time concentrating I look at my cue card and I say: "I concentrate on my work and do not play until my work is neatly and correctly done."

11. Tape individual cue cards on student's desks. Students can make their own or use the ones provided by the teacher.

Evaluation: Teacher observation of students' behavior

Materials: "Concentration" matching game.

12. At a learning center, display the matching-card game Concentration for students to play. This gives students a chance to practice focusing their thoughts on one idea.

Closure: Talk about students' record sheets and see how they improved as the day progressed. Was it harder to concentrate some times more than others (i.e., before or after lunch, before recess)? Discuss the Concentration Game. Was it easy or difficult? How did *you* make it easier?

Day 2

Objective 1: Students play the game "The Squirmy Family" to practice their concentration.

Objective 2: Students use the five cognitive self-instructional steps to aid in concentration.

Objective 3: Students use cartoons to practice writing positive self-talk statements.

Objective 1

Materials: chalk, chalk board, Squirmy Family figures.

1. Have students name times or subjects that they have a difficult time concentrating on. Write on board. Discuss and give reasons why.

2. Give Squirmy Family figures to approximately eight students. Read scenario and have the eight students follow along. Participating students are distracted by other students. As a result, many will miss their "part" being announced. Other students can play the game too.

3. After the game, have participating students discuss why it was so difficult to concentrate on their "part." Have observing students tell what they observed as probable causes for the lack of concentration.

Objective 2

Materials: Squirmy Family characters

4. Tell students that you are going to teach them how to ignore noises and people that might be distracting to them and that try to "steal" their concentration.

5. Tell students that sometimes it is difficult to concentrate when there is a lot of confusion or when others are talking or walking around the room. When this happens to me and I am trying to concentrate I say to myself: "I concentrate on my work and get it neatly and correctly done. After my work is done I can play."

6. Use five steps to demonstrate.

7. Play Squirmy Family again with original students and remind them how important it is to concentrate so they won't miss their part. Remind them to talk to themselves when they think they are losing their concentration.

8. Have students discuss how they concentrated on the game. What strategies did they use?

Evaluation: Teacher evaluates students the second time, by observation, to see if their concentration improved.

Objective 3

Materials: cartoons, pencils.
9. Students write their own concentration scenarios from cartoons. Students use self-talk statements to help the character "concentrate."

Evaluation: Teacher evaluates self-talk statements to make sure they are written in the "I" form.

Additional Strategies, Approaches, and Suggestions for CSI Instruction

Meichenbaum's Steps for Aiding Concentration

The object of this activity is to model concentration self-talk statements and then give students the opportunity to practice the statements.
Directions:

1. Conduct a discussion with the students about the difficulties of concentrating sometimes. Ask the students if they ever have trouble concentrating. Then ask the children to list some things they could say to themselves in order to help them pay attention.

2. Using the students' suggested self-talk statements, the teacher models the statements. (Cognitive modeling)

3. The teacher then asks for a student volunteer to role-play, concentrating on an assignment while the teacher verbalizes the self-talk statement. (External guidance)

4. The same volunteer then talks aloud to self while working on an assignment. (Overt self-guidance)

5. The same volunteer then whispers the self-talk statements while working on an assignment. (Faded self-guidance)

6. The volunteer finally thinks the self-talk statements while working on an assignment. (Covert self-guidance)

During academic seatwork, Manning (1990b) documented that students who are designated by their teachers as productive workers talk to themselves differently than nonproductive workers. Examples of these differences are clearly seen by the following information. Of course, one might argue that the productivity caused the more task-relevant self-talk, rather than the self-talk motivating productivity. It's another "chicken-or-egg-first" argument. After reading the following chart, readers or students in classes (especially those who have read all this book sequentially) can argue which it is—self-talk or productive behavior first?

Self-Talk for Academic Seatwork

	FOCUS	FOLLOW-THROUGH	FINISH
	Productive workers (+)	(+)	(+)
Problem definition	What did the teacher say to do first? Where do I start?	How much time do I have to complete spelling? After spelling, I will work on math page.	Make sure I finished all the assignments. Check it off with the board.
	Non-productive workers (-)	(-)	(-)
	I don't know what to do. I can't do any of this anyway.	I finished one. Time for a break. I hate working and working all morning.	Finish. That's a joke. I'm supposed to finish five assignments. Be real.
	(+)	(+)	(+)
Self-starting	Get started on spelling. Better get going.	I need to get back to this spelling right now if I want to finish. Stop staring.	Just one more problem. Look up this word first. Then *I'll* be finished.
	(-)	(-)	(-)
	This is really stupid stuff. I'm not going to waste my time.	I'm not going to continue this silly stuff. Keep working, she says. Who cares about me?	Try to finish. No! No! No! I got more than half. That's good for me. I'm slow.
	(+)	(+)	(+)
Self-guiding	Now put the periods this time. Watch out, this looks tricky.	Now, slow down and read this one more time, carefully. Did I skip a sentence just now?	Count the pages 1-2-3. Name on every paper?

	(-)	(-)	(-)
Self-guiding (Con't)	What is this stuff? Mark has finished five already.	Not another definition! I give up! Where IS number three? Forget it.	Andrea will laugh because I didn't finish. Just stop.
	(+)	(+)	(+)
Self-coping	I'm kind of tired today but I'll get started anyway. These look long and too hard, but I can figure it out.	I may not be getting every one of these right, but I'm trying.	It's hard to get it all done today, but I'll make it. Hang in there—just two more.
	(-)	(-)	(-)
	I'm tired. This is going to be too hard. This is too much work.	I'll miss all these anyway; why work on them? I've had it. I quit.	This is too much work. I won't finish again.
	(+)	(+)	(+)
Self-reinforcement	I get started right away, without wasting my time. I'm a good worker.	I can stick with this stuff. Even the intercom didn't bother me.	Yay, I finished. Looks good.
	(-)	(-)	(-)
	I'm far behind everyone else. I'll make another F.	I'm the slowest one is class. I hate all this school junk.	Stupid, that's me! I can't ever finish.

To help students learn to be more productive and self-directed (especially during independent tasks), strategies within Manning's CSI approach (i.e., modeling, practicing, and cueing) are outlined below. Strategies are given for helping students to focus attention, to follow through with school assignments, and to finish the assignments promptly and accurately.

Manning's CSI Model for Focusing, Following through, and Finishing

	SEATWORK VARIABLES		
	Modeling	Practicing	Cueing
Focusing*	Teacher models by talking aloud as she prepares to begin work (e.g., Do I have all my materials ready?). Teacher uses a prepared checklist to self-check for readiness. Teacher demonstrates use of the check-list. Student observes a videotape of peers talking to themselves as they focus attention (e.g., I need to get started right now).	Student role-plays how she will talk to herself aloud as she begins work. Teacher observes and helps supply appropriate self-statements, if needed. Student continues by whispering and then saying self-directives silently to self. Teacher monitors. In addition, student writes examples of what she will say to herself to prompt her attention. This is done in comic-strip bubble over a self-portrait of the student. The drawing should show her beginning work promptly.	Teacher and student make a set of cue cards to be used one at a time on the desk (e.g., Now it is time to work!). Student uses self-recording each day by marking "Yes" or "No" for focusing attention. The student uses the same checklist the teacher modeled earlier.
Following through*	Teacher models self-talk aloud as she persists at a task (e.g., I'd like to stop now but I can work longer.). Self-coping and self-reinforcement statements are emphasized (e.g., I'll keep working even if every one is not correct. I'm	Teacher plays Concentration Thief with the student. Student practices work persistence even when distractors are tempting her to break concentration. Teacher reinforces her and teaches her to reinforce herself when she is able to	Student wears headphones and listens to a tape that has been previously prepared with intermittent tones. When the tone is heard, the student marks whether she was on or off task. If she is off task she either tells herself

	Modeling	Practicing	Cueing
	doing my best. Good for me.).Peer models (video and audio) are used. A small poster is used as a self checklist if student stops the task (e.g., Am I working too slowly? Why did I stop working? Can I get right back to my task?)	keep working when it would be easy to be distracted (e.g., interruption in the classroom). Student draws herself working amid confusion and writes in her self-talk.	to get to work or reads a cue card (e.g., Let's get going, Jill!). She uses the demonstrated self-checklist as a reminder.
Finishing*	Teacher models talking aloud to complete the assignment (e.g., I've been a good worker today. It is such a good feeling to have everything finished). Peers model self-talk for completion of work (videotape) (e.g., Yay! I finished the whole thing).	Student makes her own audiotape of self-statements which instructs her to complete all her work. She is paired with a younger student experiencing difficulty finishing seatwork. She models for the younger student and uses her audiotape to teach "finishing work" cognitive self-instruction. Student draws herself and writes her own words of self-congratulations for finishing seatwork successfully.	Student uses a strip of colored paper for each week. She punches a hole by each day's seatwork assignment that is successfully completed. She may use self-reinforcement cue cards (e.g., I'm so proud, I finished my seatwork. I reminded myself to finish.). A self-checklist is handed in with the day's work.

*Sample materials are found in chapter 10, "CSI Materials for Teachers."

Most teachers will agree that the goal of classroom management is to produce a self-controlled, self-managed student. They will also agree that it is "easier said than done." One of the reasons for this is that teachers have been exposed to very few tools for promoting self-control. Instead teachers have been given mainly behavior modification techniques that promote control by others. Teachers want to promote self-control. Often they haven't known where to begin to help children help themselves. Instead they were often bombarded with "token economies" and "schedules of reinforcement," which have their place and benefits too. However teachers also deserve some theoretically and research-based, teacher-tried CSI strategies to foster self-management in students.

Where Does CSI Fit into the School Curriculum?

Cognitive self-instruction does not need to be separated from academic subjects at any grade level, if we are talking about promoting memory, comprehension, or problem solving. It is impossible to separate the academic subjects from the cognitive processing areas of memorizing, recalling, comprehending, summarizing, clarifying, predicting, or problem solving. For example, when spelling is taught, the CSI strategy of verbal rehearsal needs to also be taught. The subject matter itself is so interwoven with the cognitive/metacognitive skills that one does not really exist in a school setting without the other. However, metacognitive strategies for learning have often not been taught. It is often assumed that students will just finally discover ways to learn for themselves, and some do and others do not. Many students do not just "pick up" these skills. They flunk out and drop out at alarming and increasing rates. And for those who do learn CSI strategies on their own, how much effort was involved? How much smarter would they be today if they had learned them earlier, or faster, or more accurately? Therefore my first belief is that educators should become knowledgeable about the foundations and classroom applications of CSI to integrate CSI with each subject area.

My second belief has to do with CSI for self-control and self-management of classroom behaviors. The definition of subject matter is important to this discussion. I define teaching self-management for school work habits (e.g., persisting at a task) and social responsibility (e.g., waiting turns) to be "subject matter" for early elementary (K–3) grades. For example, I believe teaching kindergartners metacognitive strategies for sharing is "subject-matter oriented" for this age because social responsibility at school is a vitally important "subject" for kindergartners. I can't help but believe the world might be better if children really learned to wait their turns, share materials, and cooperate because of self-management skills, rather than learning to be socially responsible out of fear of the teacher, or because "an adult told me I had to share!" The time it takes to teach self-management—and it does take time—will, in the long run, provide additional time for academics because the teacher will be less frustrated and will be policing, nagging, and reprimanding self-managed children a great deal less. I also believe if a teacher notes a self-management problem with concentration, staying on task, finishing work, etc., then having the skills to directly teach CSI will be valuable for any and every school subject.

In sum, I have two major beliefs about the place of CSI in the school curriculum. First, it should be incorporated as an integral part of academic instruction for all grades to improve memory, comprehension, and problem solving for subject-matter areas. Second, CSI should be taught as generic lessons in early elementary to directly teach self-guidance of school work habits and social responsibility. In addition generic CSI strategies to promote self-control should be instituted at any grade level when self-management deficits are evident.

Cognitive Analysis: Definition of Terms

*Note that all terms are defined in light of Manning's classroom approach to CSI

Cueing The prompts and reminders to use CSI. Cueing should be written in first person. Cueing reminds CSI for listening, planning, working, and checking work. Cueing can take many forms. Some examples are cards, tapes, and color. Cueing may be intended for large groups, small groups, and individuals to prompt inhibition of inappropriate behavior, initiation and reinforcement of appropriate behaviors. (Third component of Manning's CSI)

Cueing color The use of color to focus one's attention. In academics parts of letters that are hard to form are brightly colored to cue attention to be extra careful. In behavior management, students may be cued with color (red—stop, yellow—slow down, and green—go).

Cueing tapes Hallahan et al. (1982) present an exact, clear description of making an audiotape used to help students self-monitor their own behavior. The teacher makes a 60-minute tape with a tone placed at various intervals (e.g., every 2 minutes, then every 5, back to 2, wait 10 minutes, 3, 5, 2, 1, etc.) At the sound of the tone, students record on a "self-record" sheet whether they were on or off task. If they were off task they tell themselves to get back to work. They may be instructed to read individual cue cards taped to their desks that say "I need to get back to work." If they were on task they may read a reinforcement cue card that says "Good for me, I'm on-task." As the on-task behavior increases, the tone gets farther and farther apart, until it is no longer needed. The audiotape may be used for groups or with earphones for one student.

Finishing behavior To be able to finish promptly (in a reasonable amount of time) with a high degree of accuracy. These "finishing-school-task behaviors" are important for optimal success in a school environment.

Focusing-attention behavior To be able to screen out the distractions of a classroom sufficiently in order to bring one's attention to a focal point. The focal point, in this case, is the classroom assignment at hand. Students who can focus attention start work promptly and know where they are headed (the goal).

Following-through behavior To be able to persist at a task in order to accomplish gains on an assignment. Once attention is focused, the task is started; then the student must maintain this focus sufficiently to continue the work endeavor.

Four school uses of CSI Manning (1984) designated four times at school when CSI is especially needed. Those four school times are while listening, while planning classwork, while working on assigned tasks, and while checking (evaluating) one's own finished work.

Group cue card Prompt cards as reminders to use CSI to inhibit inappropriate behavior, initiate and reinforce appropriate behavior for a large or small group of students. The group has exhibited a common need (e.g., concentration) that requires the teacher to cue this group to use CSI for concentration.

Inhibitory cueing To diminish or cause a behavior to stop as a result of a reminder. Inhibitory classroom behaviors are ones that should cease for the benefit of the classroom functioning (e.g., inhibitory behaviors—shouting out answers, pushing, disturbing others, cursing, etc.).

Individual cue cards Please refer to the definition given for "group cue cards." The definition is exactly the same except the cueing is intended for only one student who has exhibited an individual need that requires the teacher to cue this student to use CSI.

Initiatory cueing To cause a behavior to start as a result of a reminder or prompt. Initiatory classroom behaviors are ones that should begin for the benefit of the classroom functioning (e.g., cooperation, concentration, focusing attention, waiting turns, keeping hands and feet to self, etc.).

Modeling Purposeful and planned overt self-talk for a school work habit or social responsibility, delivered by the teacher or selected productive peers to influence the self-talk of students. The goal of the modeling is to promote self-managed students who are able to focus, follow through, and finish work promptly and accurately and who exhibit cooperative school behaviors. (First component of Mannings' CSI)

Practicing The direct practice of CSI by students for the purpose of reinforcing these skills. Practice fosters maintenance and transfer of CSI. The practice may include games, role-play, paper-pencil tasks, art activities, and rote rehearsal. (Second component of Manning's CSI)

Reinforcement cueing Reminder or prompts used to acknowledge and encourage the continued use of an appropriate classroom behavior. Promotes self-reinforcement, rather than external reinforcement. Students who adhere appropriately to classroom procedures and rules are reinforced with a self-reinforcement card (e.g., "I helped my friend," "I was a good concentrator," etc.). Reinforcement should be specific, honest, and encouraging (e.g., I wrote more words this week).

Role-play self-talk situations When teachers or students talk aloud usually from a prepared script for a specific problem or classroom situation. This problem/situation has been identified as one that needs CSI intervention as a possible means to remedy or solve the problem.

School work habits These are routines students adopt to focus attention, start assignments promptly, persist at a task, finish tasks with promptness and accuracy. Other school work habits relate to students' ability to concentrate, stay on task, study, organize, plan, and strategize efficiently.

Self-directed rules Reminders in the classroom should be spoken and/or written in first person, present tense. In so doing, students are put into the "responsibility-for-self" mode and realize when the rule is read to self that the rule also includes them (e.g., *I* listen to directions).

Self-talk logs or journals A diary-type written account of self-talk utterances that accompany various human situations. The situation is briefly described and what the student said to himself/herself about the situation is written. This self-talk account may be derived from transcribed audiotapes, spoken into tape recorders as the event is happening, or written immediately after the situation has occurred. Random sampling of self-talk over a period of days may also be taken, using the experience sampling methods (Hormuth, 1986).

Self-talk "modeling" categories The self-talk categories are problem defining, attention focusing, self-guiding, self-coping, and self-reinforcement. Examples of each of these are provided in this chapter. It is important that each of the categories be illustrated for students with numerous self-talk examples modeled for each category by adult and peer models.

Social responsibility These are skills related to how well students function socially among their peers. Social responsibility skills include cooperation, waiting turns, sharing materials and time, giving help, receiving help well, patience with others, respect for others, etc. In early grades (K–2) teaching social responsibility is considered a vital part of the curriculum. Using CSI to teach social responsibility is a viable method.

Spontaneous self-talk situations When teachers or students talk aloud to themselves on-the-spot as a situation is occurring. Later the spontaneous self-talk may be referred to, classified into categories, and discussed by student groups.

Cognitive Synthesis: A Summary

Teachers often ask for suggestions to promote self-control. Classroom management suggestions for teachers are often heavy on behavior modification techniques and light on cognitive strategies to facilitate the self-managed student. Self-regulated learning is defined as self-applied techniques for maintaining concentration, simplifying and reducing material to be learned, and internalizing the material for one's own use. Students can become self-regulated learners through the use of metacognitive strategies. These strategies may be referred to as cognitive self-instruction (CSI). CSI was taught to elementary children by Manning using adult and peer modeling, student practice activities, and cueing techniques. These students became more internal in their beliefs about self-responsibility and they exhibited more on-task classroom behaviors. The self-management benefits lasted over three months' time and generalized to another teacher's class (art teacher) and to home behaviors (as rated by their mothers). These CSI strategies, using Manning's approach, are outlined in detail in this chapter with sample lesson plans, and extensions of the Manning approach. CSI is viewed as an incorporated part of academic instruction for all grades requiring metamemory (e.g., science terms), comprehension monitoring (e.g., listening), and mental problem-solving skills (e.g., mathematics word problems). CSI is also viewed as a separate curriculum area for early elementary grades, and when necessary for all grades, to teach metacognitive strategies for school work habits (e.g., focusing attention on a task) and social responsibility (e.g., cooperation with peers).

8

Cognitive Self-Instruction Teaching Strategies

Overview

Metacognitive strategies, techniques, suggestions, and approaches are presented in this chapter. The CSI strategies are grouped in four categories: those to promote memory functions (e.g., recognition, recall), those to promote listening and reading comprehension, those to promote general problem solving, and those to promote self-management of (1) social responsibility at school and (2) school work habits. Academic subject matter such as spelling, mathematics, reading, and handwriting is a part of the discussion for using CSI strategies in classroom processes.

Self-Questions

1. Knowledge. Name one CSI teaching strategy for each of the following areas: (a) memory, (b) comprehension, (c) problem solving, (d) self-control.

2. Comprehension. Explain a viable verbal rehearsal procedure for teaching spelling. Why has it proven to be very effective?

3. Application. Use one of the CSI procedures for problem solving and apply it to a nonschool population. For example, teach doctors to use dyadic instruction to teach medicine to new interns.

4. Analysis. Compare and contrast the elements of reciprocal teaching (Palincsar) with the five steps of cognitive self-instruction as defined by Meichenbaum.

5. Synthesis. Develop three CSI strategies not mentioned in this chapter to facilitate a school task requiring memory, comprehension, problem solving, and self-control. Define the task first, label the components (e.g., problem solving) and then describe the three CSI strategies to promote the accomplishment of this school task.

6. Evaluation. Judge the merits of a CSI program as a future curriculum and/or methods package for school systems.

In this chapter, the four areas of metamemory, comprehension monitoring, dyadic problem solving, and cognitive self-control serve as the framework for discussing various CSI strategies aimed at student improvement in each of the four areas (e.g., metamemory). Academic subjects, as they are germane to one of the areas (e.g., spelling for metamemory, reading for comprehension monitoring) are included. The CSI strategies are not divorced from academic subject matter in the area of metamemory, comprehension monitoring, and dyadic problem solving. However, in the area of cognitive self-control (classroom management) the CSI strategies are presented as isolated (from academics) techniques to foster the self-managed, self-directed, self-regulated student. These self-control CSI strategies indirectly relate to academic successes because achievement in academic areas often improves when the student exhibits more attentive, more on-task classroom behaviors. Nevertheless, the self-control strategies are presented apart from academic instruction.

Metamemory

Verbal Rehearsal for Academic Subjects

The basic idea is that information children repeat aloud and hear back into their own ears is more readily remembered than the same information repeated for them by another. As the sound waves leave the mouth and return back into the ears, the reafferent cycle stimulates the memory capacity. The word is spoken and received. The brain is activated as the word is spoken and heard. The spoken word semantically sets up associations of meanings as the word is stored for retrieval. The repetition of speaking a word aloud to self for the purpose of recall is called "verbal rehearsal." When teachers are working in any content area requiring activation of a student's memory, a helpful learning strategy is to model, practice, and cue verbal rehearsal strategies. Verbal rehearsal is defined as information spoken aloud to self for the purpose of recalling the information from memory. Information that is verbally rehearsed is much more likely to be remembered. Statistics indicate that students remember 20 percent of what they hear from an external source, 70 percent of what they themselves repeat aloud, and 90 percent if they speak aloud to themselves about a task as they are performing the task. When asked the question: What school subjects lend themselves well to verbal rehearsal strategies? teachers' responses have included learning the alphabet, anything that has to be remembered in sequence, dates in social studies, terms in science and social studies, spelling, mathematics facts and precise steps, vocabulary words in reading, definitions in any subject, etc. I am sure there are many more. Whenever a new term is introduced for any academic subject (e.g., *photosynthesis* in science) the term should be spoken aloud by the students who are hearing the word for the first time. Many excellent teachers intuitively ask students to verbally rehearse.

In observations of student teachers, I have been amazed at how many introduce new, difficult terms and never ask the pupils to repeat the new terms aloud. Often pupils will voluntarily say the new word to themselves. I often think when pupils repeat the word just spoken by the student teachers, that this will prompt the student teachers to ask the whole class to repeat the word for themselves. However, often they still do not.

I became very frustrated in one observation where the student teacher was teaching the ending sound of "f" in a reading lesson to a small group. One child was having difficulty hearing the ending sound. The student teacher kept repeating to this child: "What does this word end in? Now listen, 'Lea*f*.'" The student teacher was exaggerating the "f" sound on the end. She continued to repeat the word over and over for the child. I kept hoping she would ask the child to repeat the word for himself. To me, it seemed such an obvious thing to try next. Finally in exasperation she said to the child, "Say leaf." The child said, "Leaf, oh that ends in a 'f' sound." Children are their own best teachers. They need to create their own metacognitive reality. Verbal rehearsal is a simple, straightforward way to teach children how to remember (recognize and recall) information.

A student teacher developed and implemented a CSI format to teach spelling word recall for each week. She claimed that this method was extremely successful and helped even her "slowest children." Her steps were: (1) discussed verbal rehearsal with the fourth-grade students: what it was, when to use it, and how it helped to recall information (e.g., repeat phone numbers aloud to increase the likelihood of remembering them); (2) asked students to trace with their hands the path of a word spoken aloud to self while studying (out of the mouth, back into the ear); (3) referred to the visual (cueing) reminders on the teacher-prepared poster; (4) described each of the six steps on the poster; (5) modeled the steps aloud to herself using one of the student's spelling words as an example; (6) asked for a volunteer to engage in peer modeling of the six steps using a different spelling word; (7) instructed the students to use overt, faded, and silent verbal repetition, included as some of the six steps. Classroom teachers who have used a similar metacognitive process to teach spelling have suggested modifications in the steps. The modified version is presented next.

CSI Steps for Learning Spelling Words

1. Look at the word, sound out the word and each letter, and then repeat the word aloud to myself.

2. Look at the word again, notice the size and shape of the word, whisper the word and each letter, and then whisper the word to myself.

3. Look at the word again, silently say the word and each letter to myself, and then silently say the word to myself.

4. Close my eyes, don't look at the word, sound out each letter, say the word to myself. Check to see if I was right by looking at the word in the book and sounding out the letters. Is that the way I spelled the word?

5. Write the word on my paper from memory, whispering each letter as I write, whispering the word to myself. Check to see if I wrote the word correctly by looking at the word in the book.

6. See the word in my head. Silently spell the letters to myself. Silently say the word to myself. Check my accuracy. Is that the way the word looks? Did I spell it correctly?

CSI Steps for Teaching Spelling

1. Discuss the meaning of verbal rehearsal: what, when, why, and how to use it for remembering spelling words.

2. Trace the path of a spoken word used in verbal rehearsal (out of one's own mouth, back into one's own ear).

3. Write the six steps, "CSI for Learning Spelling Words," on a poster as a visual reminder. Draw pictures of some of the steps if possible.

4. Review the six steps from the poster.

5. Model the "CSI Steps for Learning Spelling Words" for the students.

6. Request a volunteer student to model the six steps, using the poster as a guide.

7. Instruct the students to use aloud, whisper, and silent voices as outlined in the six steps for learning spelling words.

8. Guide and monitor practice in the classroom as students try out the six steps for learning spelling words.

9. Provide corrective and positive feedback as the students practice CSI for spelling.

10. Review the steps each week until they have become automatic for the students.

This procedure may seem rather cumbersome at first. Students who are already good spellers may not want, nor profit from this type of instruction. However, many students never learn any strategies for recall. They fail spelling tests each week not because they are cognitively limited or poorly motivated, but because they lack the strategic knowledge to recall the spelling of words. Teachers in grades two through eight have reported great success using the CSI methods prescribed above. Teachers should not be hesitant to modify these steps based on their own style and student needs. This is just one example. The main idea is to promote verbal rehearsal because, consistently, rehearsers retain more information. In addition, it should be noted that these strategies to recall spelling can easily be used for any subject matter, requiring recall (e.g., studying geography terms and definitions, learning mathematics facts).

In addition to CSI for studying spelling words, research has documented the effectiveness of student-directed cues for remediation of spelling. For example, students circle in red the portion of the word that was misspelled and compare this cued word with the correct spelling of the word. When this is done for practice tests, students using student-directed cues usually score higher on the test.

CSI for Learning Math Facts

1. While looking at the math fact, I say it aloud.
2. While looking at the math fact, I whisper it aloud.

3. While looking at the math fact, I silently say it to myself.

4. Without looking, I say the math fact aloud while I write it.

5. Without looking, I whisper the math fact to myself.

6. Without looking, I say the math fact silently to myself. I check it for accuracy. Was I saying the correct math fact?

7. I visualize the math fact in my mind.

8. I say the math fact silently in my mind. I double check for accuracy. Do I know this math fact now?

Other reported CSI uses for learning academic subjects that require verbal rehearsal are: learning vocabulary words in reading, repeating directions for class work (termed "child checks"), and learning critical information such as dialing 911 for emergencies. CSI steps for learning spelling or learning math facts can easily be applied to learning vocabulary words for any content area and for learning critical information such as 911, or one's telephone number and address.

Teachers often complain that students do not follow directions. The typical comment is that students "just don't listen." Perhaps for some students this is a true statement. However, many children who do not follow teachers' oral directions have mental processing deficits. They may listen and hear every word, however, they may not have mentally screened the directions via the process of rehearsing the directions (either audibly or inaudibly) back to self to check their own understanding. Therefore, after teacher directions are presented to students, the teacher may ask students to softly or silently rehearse the directions in their heads. Ask students to verbally say the directions back to the teacher. Typical questions are: "What did I say to do first? second? third?" "Raise your hand to tell me *all* the directions for this assignment." "What did I say to do when you are finished?" When the students verbally repeat the directions and hear the directions in their own ears, recall is facilitated. If they repeat the directions aloud, softly and silently, then they are much more likely to complete school tasks as assigned and even to remember what to do when they finish the tasks.

Variations of Verbal Rehearsal

A student of mine once said, "It's really weird how my husband, who is majoring in veterinary medicine, studies. He repeats terms and "stuff" he has to remember in a voice other than his own. He makes great grades but I have to leave home when he is studying." We laughed together. Later, I realized that he probably did this in an effort to aid his memory, his recall, and his retrieval of this information (or perhaps to get rid of his wife—who knows?). Anyway, the manner in which information is stored affects the ease or difficulty with which it is retrieved for later use. My student's husband was making the information vivid as he stored it; therefore, he studied in a "different voice." At least, that is my explanation. I am certainly not advocating that we teach students to study in "funny voices"; however, I am asking that we make information that will need to be recalled from memory (e.g., spelling words, math facts, terms, important information, etc.) vivid, deliberate, and emphatically rehearsed to aid recall. Creative teachers have been doing this for hundreds of years.

Variations in Verbal Rehearsal

1. Choral response. Have all the students repeat words, terms, facts, etc., together in unison. Ask students wearing tennis shoes to repeat together. Students whose last names begin with "r" repeat together, etc.

2. Singing. Ask students to sing the information, putting the information to be recalled to the tune of a familiar song (e.g., *Row, row, row your boat*). Divide the class into groups (3 or 4) and ask each group to put the class directions for hall behavior, etc., to the tune of their favorite song. Groups share their creations with each other.

3. High/low. Rehearse the information in a little, squeaky high voice —like a mouse. Then rehearse using the deepest voice possible—like a huge grizzly bear. Repeat vocabulary words the way Papa Bear, Mama Bear, and Baby Bear would probably say them.

4. Loud/soft. Rehearse the information (on the playground) at the top of students' lungs. Whisper the information in the softest, but still audible, voices.

5. Dramatized. Rehearse information in a father voice, mother voice, teacher voice. Rehearse like a washing machine would say the information, or the vacuum cleaner, or a chipmunk, or well-known rock singer, etc.

In addition to variations in verbal rehearsal, Pressley et al. (1985, pp. 115–116) present a number of strategies for remembering:

1. Single item repetition: repeating material over and over, one item at a time.

2. Cumulative rehearsal: repeating material over and over in a cumulative fashion, rehearsing old items along with new ones.

3. Meaningful organization: looking for meaningful, semantic relationships among items.

4. Hierarchical allocation: studying information in order of its importance, with more important information studied first.

5. Differential effort allocations: expending more effort when studying the material that is not yet learned.

6. Imagery elaboration: making up interactive images that include the to-be-learned items.

7. Verbal elaboration: making up a story to include the to-be-remembered items.

8. Keyword method: transforming information items to more familiar ones and then putting them into relational images with other information.

9. SQ3R: surveying what is to be learned, questioning oneself, reading the material, reciting it, reviewing all important information.

Comprehension Monitoring

Listening Comprehension

A self-check poster, or other display, may help students remember to mentally process directions as they are listening. Review the poster before giving directions and display in a prominent place in the classroom. Frequently remind students of their responsibility to monitor their own listening comprehension. A listening comprehension poster may include some of the following self-questions or self-statements.

Listening Questions

1. Do I understand these directions?
2. What am I supposed to do?
3. Is there anything missing?
4. Do I know how to begin?
5. Do I know every step along the way?
6. What did the teacher say to do when I was finished?

Students verbally rehearse the self-questions to remind themselves to use them while listening. Teachers should model the self-questions for listening, encourage role-play practice of them, and continue to cue (via posters using Listening Questions such as the ones suggested) throughout the year or for as long as is necessary.

Palincsar and her colleagues are investigating how nonreaders in first grade learn to summarize, generate questions, clarify, and predict through listening comprehension, as their teachers read third-grade-level text aloud to the students. In this way comprehension monitoring (using listening) can be learned by nonreaders in the same way that readers have learned reading-comprehension strategies, through Palincsar's et al. reciprocal teaching methodology (explained in previous chapters).

Self-questioning to promote awareness of automatic thoughts is important for all grade levels. At this point we do not know what self-questions are best suited for what grade level. A recommendation is for teachers of a grade level to brainstorm sets of self-questions for memory skills, listening and reading comprehension, including content reading, problem solving, school work habits (e.g., finishing work), and social responsibilities (e.g., respect for each other). Teachers should begin with the areas most critical to them. After self-questions are made for their chosen areas, teachers try them to see which questions seem best for their students.

For example, a group of second-grade teachers used these self-questions with their students for problem solving:

Do I listen carefully?	Cue picture
What do I need to know?	Cue picture
What do I know?	Cue picture
What will I do first?	Cue picture
next?	
last?	
Do I work carefully?	Cue picture
Did I find the answer?	Cue picture
Did I say the answer to myself?	Cue picture
Did I write my answer correctly?	Cue picture

Although not tested yet, these questions may be appropriate for many grade levels for problem solving. Another group of fourth- and fifth-grade teachers used this set of self-questions for map skills:

Did I read the name of the map first?

Did I study the map?

Did I look for keywords on the map that I know?

Do I know what the symbols and key mean?

Where is the compass rose?

Reading Comprehension

Improving instruction in reading comprehension is a concern shared by most educators. One of the promising areas of teaching reading comprehension has been comprehension monitoring, or discerning whether what is being read makes sense and, if not, knowing strategies to correct the problem. Good readers monitor comprehension. They identify when they are not understanding and they use CSI strategies to overcome their problems. Some strategies are knowing when to reread, when and how to use context clues, use of a dictionary. These have been referred to as "fix-ups"—knowing how to fix up one's comprehension problems.

Strategies such as SQ3R (Survey/Question/Read/Recite/Review) are aids for readers before and after reading has occurred. CSI strategies for reading monitoring must also occur during reading. Although there is some evidence that reading maturity brings with it the natural ability to monitor one's own comprehension, monitoring can be taught. In this way, many reading problems may be prevented. One very promising strategy is Palincsar et al.'s reciprocal teaching, whereby students use four distinct steps: *summarize*—stop at intervals during reading and explain in a nutshell what has been read; *clarify*—reread portions that are fuzzy, obscure, unclear or discuss them; *question*—develop questions(s) that teachers may ask; *predict*—foretell likely events and happenings in the material. During reciprocal teaching, the teacher and students rotate turns being the teacher. First the teacher models one of the four steps (e.g., clarifies). Then, the teacher and students silently read a portion of text and the teacher applies these four steps. During this time, the teacher continues to model by thinking aloud, pointing out, and explaining what he/she is doing. Next, the students and teacher silently read the following section of the text. The teacher then asks for volunteers to play the teacher and model for peers the same four steps previously demonstrated by the teacher. This pattern continues with the teacher modeling, and then the students modeling the same strategies for their peers. In the beginning, teachers must prompt and perhaps shape students in their modeling. However, as the students develop skill in the four steps less teacher guidance is needed. This is clearly a progression from other- to self-regulation.

Classroom teachers who use basal reader instruction may be interested in the work of Schmitt and Baumann (1986 p. 23–31) in which they clearly describe how to incorporate comprehension monitoring into basal reader instruction. Their methods are based on adaptation of reciprocal teaching, just described above. These authors break down a directed reading activity into prereading activities, guided reading activities, and postreading activities.

Prereading activities. (1) Activate background knowledge: Do this by finding out what the students already know about the topic to be read. Discuss the title and pictures to ascertain what the group already knows and has brought with them to the story. (2) Make predictions about the content: Use the title, pictures, and prior knowledge to hypothesize what might happen in the story. Record the group predictions or allow individual members to record their own predictions. (3) Set purposes for reading: Tell students they should read with a purpose in mind to help their attention and comprehension. Often the students' predictions serve well as the purpose(s) for reading (i.e., find out if the apple really did turn into a mouse). (4) Generate questions: Ask students to develop questions that they want answered as they read. Students tell what questions they want answered. These too can be listed, to be answered later.

Guided reading activities. (1) Summarize at various points: At strategic places in the story, after a main element has occurred, ask the students to stop and review the main points of their reading. (2) Evaluate and make new predictions: As students read and know more facts, they should verify their predictions and make new ones if necessary. (3) Relate new information to prior knowledge: As new facts are presented students should discuss how this new information fits in with or relates to something they already know about. (4) Generate questions: Encourage students to ask themselves questions about the story as they read.

Postreading activities. (1) Summarize total selection: Students review the whole story stressing the main points. Individual students may summarize the story or group summaries may be sought. (2) Evaluate predictions: Go back to predictions made before and during the story to validate predictions, what caused changes in their predictions, how accurate were they, etc. (3) Return to the purpose set for reading: Provide children with self-questions: Did I find out what I needed to know? Did I meet my purpose for reading? (4) Generate questions for the total selection: Teachers and students ask questions about characters, plot, situation, goal, solution, etc. Students ask each other questions, students ask the teacher questions, and the teacher asks the students questions. Throughout the prereading, guided reading, and postreading activities the teacher tells the students the rationale for these processes (e.g., "stopping reading to review main points periodically is a great way to check your own comprehension").

The next section includes two sample lesson plans that illustrate some of the steps mentioned above. These plans were developed by Jackie Carson and taught to her fourth grade students. The teacher, herself, will speak in the "I."

Reading Lesson Plans
Using Comprehension Monitoring

There are two different formats of lesson plans. The plan with "The Ghost in the Orchard" is what I use with the poor readers. They are passive learners who don't use metacognitive techniques and they need to go through the whole process. The second format, "The Boy Who Wouldn't Talk," is used with my above-average readers. They demonstrate better comprehension skills and don't need to go through the process of questioning group members. I have found that if we draw a story out too long, they become bored with the story. The slower group seems to enjoy the questioning techniques.

On the day before reading a selection from the basal text, students look up vocabulary words and place them and their definitions in their personal glossary notebook.

Cues for reading comprehension are posted in the classroom. Each step to encourage self-evaluation is listed and students are reminded to use it for any independent reading such as social studies and health, as well as stories from the basal reader.

<u>Plan No. 1</u>

1. What do I already know about these words and topics?
   (a) Vocabulary words—repeat aloud.
   (b) Look at the pictures and title. What do I already know about ghosts and an orchard? Student responses:
      - A ghost is a thing that floats around.

- A ghost is a spirit.
- Ghosts scare me.
- An orchard is a bunch of trees in a row.
- (What kind of trees?)
- Peach trees or apple trees.

(c) Let's look at the picture on page 183. What do you see?
- I see a barn so I think the story takes place on a farm.
- I see apple trees.
- It's night because I see the moon and stars.
- A boy is looking out a window and he looks like he's looking at something.

2. What do I think will happen in the story based on the title and pictures?
   - I think the boy is home alone because he looks scared. I think he's going to see a ghost in the orchard.

   (All students agreed with this prediction.)

   What is my purpose for reading this story?
   - I want to find out if the boy really saw a ghost.

   Read pages 183–186. Write two or three test questions to ask each other.

3. Stop reading. What are the main points in the story? What new information have I discovered during reading?
   - Where were Freddy's mother and father?
   - What scared Freddy?
   - What did Freddy think he saw that night?
   - What did it look like?

   What are the main points in the story? Freddy is home with his two sisters. His parents are in town at a meeting. Freddy saw something twice before that he thinks is a ghost, and he's looking out the window trying to see if it will appear tonight.

4. Are my predictions correct?
   - Yes, he saw a white thing gliding in the orchard. I think it's the ghost.

   What do I think will happen next?
   I need to make predictions.
   - I think he'll go outside to try to see it better.
   - I don't, I think his parents will come home.

   Read pages 187–191 to find out if my predictions are correct. Write two or three test questions about new information that I have discovered.

   Repeat Step 3

   Stop reading. What new information have I discovered during reading?
   - Who knocked on Freddy's door?
   - How did Freddy know who it was?
   - Why did Freddy ask Big Peter if he believed in ghosts?
   - What do you think will happen between Freddy and the ghost?
   - Why did Freddy think he had caught a ghost?
   - How did he do it?
   - How did he warn his parents about the ghost?
   - How do you think his parents felt when he told them about the ghost?
   - What was the ghost?

5. Evaluate my predictions.
   Are they correct? What information made me change them?
   We were sort of right. There really wasn't a ghost, but it looked like one. We were right about the story happening on a farm at night.

6. Evaluate the main ideas:
   Characters I think Freddy was brave to try to catch a ghost.
   - I don't. I think he was stupid!
   - He should have told his parents when he first saw it.

Problem The problem was whether Freddy saw a ghost or not.

Goal Our goal was to see if Freddy really saw a ghost.

Solution Freddy told his parents about locking the ghost in the garage. His dad took him to the garage and they went in through the workshop. They saw an animal that looked like a pale reindeer. They called the zoo and found it was a fallow deer that had escaped.

Plan No. 2

1. What do I already know about these words and topics?

   (a) Vocabulary words—repeat aloud

   (b) Look at the pictures and title
   Student responses:
   - The name of the story says that a boy won't talk.
   - He's looking out of a window in the first picture and he looks sad.
   - Another picture shows a city street with three boys standing on a sidewalk.
   - Another picture looks like a family having dinner and they're all looking at one boy.

2. What do I think will happen in this story based on the pictures and titles?
   Student responses:
   - I think a boy got mad at his family and wouldn't talk to them.
   - He looks sad. I think his dog died and that's why he won't talk.

   What is my purpose for reading this story?
   - I'm going to read this story to find out why he won't talk.

   Read pages 84–88.

3. Stop reading. What are the main points in

the story? What new information have I discovered during reading?
Carlos stopped talking because he moved to a new country and no one could understand what he said. He was unhappy. He and his brother met a boy on their way home from school. He asked them to walk him home.

4. Are my predictions correct?
No, Carlos didn't get mad at his family and his dog didn't die. I found out why he stopped talking. He was unhappy because he left his home and nobody spoke his language.

   What do I think will happen next?
   I think he will make friends with the new boy.

   Read pages 89–93 (repeat number 3 above).

5. Evaluate my predictions.
Are they correct?
What information made me change them?
Yes, Carlos made friends with the boy, but I found out something new. The boy's name is Ricky and he is blind. Carlos talked to him so he could take him home. Finally, Carlos started talking again.

6. Evaluate the main ideas:
<u>Characters</u> Carlos was afraid to try to speak a new language because he was afraid people would laugh at him. Ricky helped Carlos by spelling words with blocks.

   <u>Problems</u> Carlos wouldn't talk.

   <u>Goal</u> We wanted to find out why Carlos wouldn't talk. We found out the answer.

   <u>Solution</u> Carlos talked to Ricky because he realized that he needed to help him get home. Ricky ended up helping Carlos by teaching him English words.

Students should monitor reading comprehension based on self-questions, stated in first person. It often helps if the self-questions are written, displayed, and/or visually represented to the students. Students can keep their reading comprehension self-questions on a card at their desk, or taped in their reading book. The self-questions, if general enough, may be displayed in the room over a period of time, or displayed only during reading instruction. One set of self-questions is:

What is the main idea?

Who did what? to whom? why?

How do the characters feel? why?

Does this make sense to me?

How does this story end?

As the literature on reading comprehension monitoring is read, a synthesis of it produces some main strategies for promoting greater student responsibility for their own comprehension. The major comprehension strategies that have evolved are (1) strong, rich quality cognitive modeling, using *think aloud* by the teacher and later by students, (2) informed metacognitive strategy training, (3) guided, interactive verbal dialogues during reading instruction, moving from teacher-student to student-student interactions, (4) self-check questions, and (5) visual representations of the metacognitive processes. These five strategies appeared and reappeared in the literature as effective facilitators of reading comprehension, but never altogether. Perhaps if they were all put together in one reading program, a very powerful methodology would be the result. Each of these five will be briefly described in the hope that some brave educator (somewhere) will apply all of them simultaneously.

Adult and peer cognitive modeling using think aloud strategies. Davey (1983) presents a very helpful tool for teachers. She describes the actual think aloud words of teachers used to help students monitor reading comprehension. The exact words are not intended as words that teachers should actually mimic. However, the words, by example, provide a clear picture of cognitive modeling. Davey's steps are: (1) Select a passage to read aloud that contains some difficult words, or contradictions, or incompleteness. The passage should be short with obvious comprehension stumbling blocks. (2) As the teacher reads aloud, the students follow along in the text. (3) As a comprehension problem is met, the teacher stops and thinks aloud to show identification of a problem and metacognitive strategies for "fixing it." (4) The students listen as the teacher thinks aloud for them. (5) After several think aloud, teacher-modeling sessions, the students work in dyads to practice think aloud, taking turns reading orally and stopping along the way to "think aloud," sharing their thoughts.

Examples of Davey's "think aloud models" (1983, p. 45):

1. *Make predictions.* (Show how to develop hypotheses.)

"From the title, I predict that this section will tell how fishermen used to catch whales."
"In this next part, I think we'll find out why the men flew into the hurricane."
"I think this is a description of a computer game."

2. *Describe the picture you're forming in your head from the information.* (Show how to develop images during reading.)

"I have a picture of this scene in my mind. The car is on a dark, probably narrow, road; there are no other cars around."

3. *Share an analogy.* (Show how to link prior knowledge with new information in text.) We call this the "like-a" step.

This is like a time we drove to Boston and had a flat tire. We were worried and we had to walk three miles for help."

4. *Verbalize a confusing point.* (Show how you monitor your ongoing comprehension.)

"This just doesn't make sense."
"This is different from what I had expected."

5. *Demonstrate fix-up strategies.* (Show how you correct your lagging comprehension.)

"I'd better reread."
"Maybe I'll read ahead to see if it gets clearer."
"I'd better change my picture of the story."
"This is a new word to me—I'd better check context to figure it out."

Davey suggests that parents think aloud as they read to their children, and to listen to children think aloud about their own reading. Although Davey's work is used as an example, many others have advocated the use of cognitive modeling to teach students how to monitor their own reading.

Informed metacognitive strategy training. In this procedure, teachers tell students directly *what* the strategies are, *how* they are used, *why* they are helpful, and *when* to apply them. This procedure of clearly and directly teaching students about the strategies is found very consistently in the literature. Sentences such as "Demonstrate not only how to read, but also why and when you would use such strategies" are found repeatedly. Another example is found in Paris and Oka (1986) when they say: "Children were taught what comprehension strategies are, how to use them, when they are applied, and why they are important" (p. 105). Therefore teachers may consider incorporating a clear articulation of what, how, when, and why to use certain metacognitive strategies to monitor one's own reading. On the other hand, it should be noted that Kendall in Wham (1987) cautions about overemphasizing process to the detriment of product. Kendall's caution is often quoted in the literature. Kendall believes that enthusiasm about metacognitive strategies may lead teachers to teach students about metacognitive skill, rather than leading students to use these skills. I think we should consider Kendall's cautions. However, I am also impressed by the strong research evidence that informed training has been effective and beneficial in the promotion of comprehension monitoring skills. Many students have been helped when they were specifically told what, how, why, and when to monitor their own comprehension.

Guided, interactive verbal dialogues with a progression from other to self-regulation. This procedure is the backbone of reciprocal teaching. This method has been referred to often in this text.

Palincsar's Reciprocal Teaching Method
(Palincsar, 1986, p. 119)

1. Each day, before the dialogue, the teacher uses informed strategy training. Review *what* strategies students are learning, *why* they are important, *how* to use them, and *when* to use them (the context in which the strategies are useful).

2. The teacher, using the title of the text brings out background and prior knowledge, students make predictions about what they will learn in the text; students indicate what they are interested in learning.

3. A teacher is appointed for the first section of text.

4. Teacher and students read the section (silently and/or orally).

5. The "teacher" (student or adult) asks a question about the material to which the others respond.

6. This teacher then summarizes the main points and asks for elaborations on the summary from other members of the group.

7. The students and teacher discuss clarifications that came up during the reading of the text.

8. The teacher and students make predictions regarding upcoming text. A new "teacher" is appointed.

Other guidelines are important: the adult teacher is mainly responsible for initiating and sustaining the dialogue during the beginning days of reciprocal teaching instruction. The teacher models and informs the students about the definitions of summarizing, question generating, clarifying, and predicting as they are used in the context of reciprocal teaching. These definitions, according to Palincsar, are provided in the "definition of terms" section at the end of this chapter. As reciprocal teaching instruction continues, the adult teacher transfers more responsibility for sustaining the dialogue to the students. The teacher continues to provide feedback and to coach them through the dialogue.

These verbal dialogues are familiar ways for children to internalize learning. Children learn and develop intellectually through social interaction as a natural, spontaneous occurrence beginning at birth. Therefore, this procedure is a natural one for students. In addition, the dialogues allow teachers an opportunity to evaluate students' levels of understanding. Cooperative learning, a major component of reciprocal teaching, facilitates strategic learning when teachers and students work together on a mutual problem with the same governing objectives. There is a great deal of empirical evidence that favors guided, interactive instruction over such methods as teacher demonstration and traditional skill instruction (Palincsar, 1986).

Self-check questions. Repeatedly, the use of self-questions to promote self-monitoring by students appears in the literature. If teachers will take the general questions they usually pose to students about the students' reading comprehension, a set of self-questions for students is available from the teacher's list of questions. Teachers often ask, "Does everyone understand?" An appropriate wording of that question for students' self-check is "Do I understand?"

Davey (1983) used student checklists of various types. Her purpose for using the checklist was to involve the students and verify that students perceived that they were using monitoring procedures.

Self-Checklist

WHILE I WAS READING HOW DID I DO? (PUT AN X IN THE APPROPRIATE COLUMN.)

	Not very much	A little bit	Much of the time	All of the time
Made predictions				
Formed pictures				
Used "like-a"				
Found problems				
Used fix-ups				

Visual representations of the metacognitive processes. Teachers often use posters, learning center activities, games, etc., that provide a visual representation of metacognitive steps. Visual representation reinforces the use of metacognition, makes an abstract concept much more concrete, and facilitates a multimodality approach (especially needed with an internal-processing skill like metacognition). For example, a bulletin board display entitled "I Am A Reading Detective" may be used to graphically illustrate What?, Why?, How?, and When? to use comprehension monitoring. Many learners need the visual representation to remind and to consolidate these abstract processes.

Dyadic Problem Solving

Metacognitive problem solving is joint, goal-directed verbal collaboration between a novice and a more experienced member in any given educational context. One researcher who fits within this particular definition of metacognitive problem solving is James Wertsch. He calls his work with adult-child dyads "dyadic" instruction. The dyads were formed as a collaborative problem-solving team. Adults serve as the cognitive guide, structuring the learning through their verbalizations, as the child gradually internalizes the adults' verbal guidance. This internalization empowers children to become their own cognitive guide. The better the quality of the dialogue between adult and child, the better the quality of the child's internal cognitive guides. Inter-Intra. Wertsch has not actually proposed his dyadic instruction for regular education classroom processes. However, I have taught his ideas for years as classroom strategies for problem solving. Let's assume a student is having difficulty with mathematics, specifically with long division. The teacher may use "dyadic instruction," via steps developed by Meichenbaum and Goodman (1971).

Dyadic Instruction for Problem Solving

1. The teacher invites the child to listen and watch as he/she thinks aloud (in first person) the steps to solving the long division problem (or any other problem). The teacher talks to self as the problem is computed.

2. The teacher thinks aloud the steps of a similar long division problem while the student writes the numerals in the proper places.

3. The student talks aloud the steps of another, similar long division problem and writes the answer. (The teacher observes and guides if necessary.)

4. The student speaks softly the steps of the same (or another) long

division problem and writes the answer. (The teacher observes and guides if necessary.)

5. The student says the steps silently to self as he/she computes the long division algorithm (same or new problem). (The teacher observes the computation.)

The decision to keep the exact same problem or to switch to a new, similar problem at each of the five steps is left to the discretion of the teacher. Some students respond favorably to new, similar problems at each step, while other students need the repetition of the same problem for each of the five steps. Excellent teachers have been using steps 2 and 3 for many years. However, they do not often systematically go through the sequence in order from step 1 to step 5. This is important as students need all five steps in order to internalize the problem-solving process firmly in their own minds. Usually, after step 3, teachers are satisfied that students know how to do the problem. This is often not true because there has not been adequate repetition to insure mastery. Meichenbaum calls these same steps "cognitive self-instruction: specifically, step 1 is *cognitive modeling;* step 2 is *overt external guidance;* step 3 is *overt self-guidance;* step 4 is *faded, overt self-guidance,* and step 5 is *covert self-instruction.*

Meichenbaum (1984) foresees the focus of education becoming more study-skill process oriented. He believes that children should be given tasks that require cognitive planning. Assignments should include an element that requires students to describe how they plan to perform the assigned task. When the assignment is evaluated and discussed, the evaluation will center on the planning process, not only the product.

The following teaching situations describe how teachers used dyadic instruction to help students problem solve. It should be noted that teachers most often report using dyadic instruction for individual students experiencing difficulty. Nevertheless, the same process can be adapted for a group of students experiencing similar difficulties in a subject matter area: step 1 remains the same with the teacher thinking the steps aloud at the board. In step 2, either a student (peer model) works the problem as the teacher verbally directs, or each student works the problem on a slate board while the teacher verbally directs and monitors the work carefully (guided practice), or both peer modeling and guided practice may be used. In steps 3, 4, and 5 a peer can continue to serve as a model for overt, faded, and covert self-instruction or students in unison can say the steps aloud, softly and silently, or both peer modeling and individual practice may be used. The key to dyadic instruction is the verbal interactive dialogue and the gradual, internalization of information by the students, moving from teacher guidance to student guidance.

Dyadic Instruction Examples

Teacher 1: I used dyadic instruction with one of my math students. He was having a difficult time recognizing and naming the numerals 1 to 5. I made a puzzle-type game using numeral cards that matched a colorful board. I first played the game, talking aloud the directions using Meichenbaum's self-talk categories: *problem definition* (What do I do with this?), *focusing attention* (Find the first puzzle piece with a 1 on it); *self-guiding* (See if it goes here. No, look at the shape again. Try another piece); *self-coping* (This is not a 1, I picked up a 3. That's okay. See how a 1 looks. It's just a straight-looking line. Here it is); *self-reinforcement* (Good, I know the numeral 1. Now I'm ready to start over with the 2). Next the student attempted to match the puzzle piece 2 with the 2 on the board, while I used a similar dialogue to guide his motor act of placing the 2 correctly. The student talked aloud to himself as he matched 3. I guided him with some helpful self-questions and self-statements when he became frustrated or hesitant. The student spoke softly to himself as he matched the 4, and silently to himself as he matched the 5. He was clearly pleased with his accomplishment. No attempt was made to directly teach the categories of self-talk (e.g., self-guiding). As the student learns facilitative problem-solving skills, I may begin to use the self-talk categories as a natural part of the problem-solving vocabulary.

Teacher 2: I used dyadic instruction during writing class when students were revising their compositions. I talked aloud, to revise my own writing as they listened. I used a series of *problem defining* (How do I want this to come across right here?); *attention focusing* (This sentence needs attention); *self-guiding* (I keep losing myself in this sentence—it's way too long); *self-coping* (This is frustrating, I am having to work so hard. But I'll be pleased when my words say what I mean); *self-reinforcing* (Great sentence right here!). The students worked in pairs and talked aloud about their own and each other's composition as the other person listened and evaluated the self-guiding speech (e.g., "You aren't coping, you are frustrating yourself too much!"). My students (seventh graders) learned the self-talk categories at the beginning of the year. It's probably the most valuable thing I ever taught. My students this year are the most responsible, independent workers I have ever had. Knowing cognitive self-instruction has not only improved academics, their self-esteem is outstanding.

Lockhead and Whimbey (1987) detail ways to teach analytical reasoning through think aloud pair problem solving. The dyads are given a problem dilemma. They talk together to (1) identify the problem, (2) plan solutions, (3) follow the plan, (4) review the solution to see how effective it is. The students take turns being the problem solver, thinking aloud, while the other student listens. The students are able to communicate their thought patterns. The self-talk guides the behavior.

Goldman (1982) recommends a problem-solving metacognitive strategy employing simple stories. Goldman calls this strategy "The Goal Story Interview."

Goal Story Interview (Modified)

Step 1 Ask student(s) to tell or write a story about something they want for themselves. Tell *what*. Tell or write accompanying self-talk.

Step 2 Students describe why they want this particular thing (e.g., new dog, better grades, new home, etc). Goldman calls this the "Motive Probe." Tell *why*. Tell or write accompanying self-talk.

Step 3 Students tell or write a "Plan of Action." Describe the steps for obtaining their want (goal). Tell *how* or write accompanying self-talk. Goldman calls this "Means Probe."

Step 4 Students tell or write about wanting this "something" but not being able to obtain it. Goldman calls this the "Obstacle Probe." *Blocked goal.* Tell or write accompanying self-talk.

Step 5 Students tell or write about overcoming the obstacle and still being able to obtain their "want" or "goal" in the end. Tell *how* the obstacles were circumvented. Tell or write accompanying self-talk. Write self-coping and self-reinforcing if goal is unattainable for student at this time.

Lowenthal (1986) describes additional problem-solving strategies but these strategies are not necessarily metacognitive. They do, however, lend themselves well to easy modifications, to add a metacognitive element. For example, problem situations are presented and students are asked to plan strategies to accomplish goals (e.g., If you want a turn on the slide, how do you get one?). This planning does not really necessitate verbal self-regulation or metacognitive skills (i.e., overseeing one's own mental processes). However, social problem-solving dilemmas can foster metacognition with such teacher comments as "Draw a picture of yourself in this situation, and write down what you are saying to yourself in order to get a turn on the slide. How can you verbally cope if you are unable to have a turn? What would you say to yourself?" One teacher in second grade has a "talking place" where she and students in crisis (e.g., fighting on the playground, cheating, stealing) go to discuss the problem. The place is a "bulletin board with four small posters, each a different color, in sequence from one to four, connected by colorful ribbon. The board is entitled "The Talking Chart for Solving Problems."

Poster 1: Talk about what happened. What's the problem?

Poster 2: What did you say to yourself before you hit, cheated, stole? How did you feel?

Poster 3: What was the result of your actions? What happened? How did you feel?

Poster 4: What could you have said to yourself that might have stopped the hitting, cheating, stealing? How would that have changed the result? Draw a picture or write a plan of self-talk that might help you gain control of this situation.

This board helps to make a problem situation more concrete. In this way, young children can more readily understand their own responsibility. The posters are labeled (1) Problem, (2) Self-Talk, (3) Result, and (4) New Plan to Improve. Remember in step 4 to include a new way of talking to themselves as part of the new plan. Cognitive self-instruction involves either (1) overt or covert self-talk or (2) cognitive modeling of self-talk spoken to self or spoken toward others to guide their behavior.

Blandford and Lloyd (1987) used a self-checklist of self-talk to aid the problem of poor handwriting. This checklist is a self-evaluation used to highlight the important aspects of correct handwriting (p. 344).

Self-Evaluation of Handwriting

Questions-to-Self	Circle one	
1. Am I sitting correctly?	Yes	No
2. Is my paper positioned correctly?	Yes	No
3. Am I holding my pencil correctly?	Yes	No
4. Are all my letters sitting on the line?	Yes	No
5. Are all my tall letters touching or nearly touching the top line?	Yes	No
6. Are my short letters filling only 1/2 of the space?	Yes	No
7. Am I leaving enough, but not too much space between words?	Yes	No

These self-questions may be written on the left side of a card with an area on the right side to mark "Yes" or "No" for each question when a handwriting assignment is due. These cards could be duplicated and stapled to handwriting papers. When students use self-evaluative "questions-to-self," improvements in many areas, including handwriting, are experienced.

The final point in the problem-solving section is that teachers need to talk (model) the CSI language until it becomes everyday school and home vocabulary. Do not be reluctant to use terms such as *monitor, self-question, self-cope, self-guide, self-reinforce* in context often during the school day.

Metacognitive Language in the Classroom

Instead of always saying:	Sometimes say:
"Think about your answer."	"Monitor your thinking."
"Tell me what will happen."	"What are you saying to yourself about this? What do you think might happen?"
"Your work is not up to par."	"You need to self-question and evaluate this. Say to yourself 'Is this my best work?'"
"What were you supposed to do here?"	"Oops! Say to yourself: 'What was I supposed to do?'"
"You need to get to work."	"Tell yourself to get to work."
"You'll be okay. Just calm down."	"Use your self-coping; say 'I'll be okay. I can calm myself down.'"
"Look, put all the capitals on this line."	"Use your self-guiding; say 'The capital letters go on this line.'"
"You did a great job on this drawing."	"Reinforce yourself; say 'I worked hard and my drawing shows it!'"
"I'll read the directions one more time."	"Rehearse the directions again. Repeat them softly to yourself."

This chart is not intended to diminish the spontaneity of the teacher. Depending on the students' ages, academic levels, and emotional stability levels, some of these metacognitive comments may not be appropriate. In addition, the metacognitive language is not intended to replace all externally oriented teacher comments (e.g., You need to work harder. Super job on this assignment, etc.). Students, especially young students, still want teacher guidance and encouragement. However, using teacher judgment and knowledge of your students, developing a natural metacognitive language in the classroom will promote more independent problem solvers. As with all teaching/learning strategies, these methods will work better for some students than others. The teachers' professional judgment and discretion should temper all of these suggestions.

Cognitive Self-Control

In chapter 7 the development of the self-managed student using the Manning CSI approach is described. Therefore, this section is a description of additional CSI strategies, techniques, activities, and approaches to foster the self-directed youngster. If this book were written in Japan, this section very likely would be the first, rather than last. To explain, in Japan social development is as valued as academics. From kindergarten through third grade, lessons on self-control and cooperativeness are considered "lessons," not something that is "dealt with" so lessons can occur (academics). All Japanese students are told they can be successful if they persist and work hard. "Japanese students have the highest science and math test scores in the world. More than 90 percent graduate from high school. Illiteracy is virtually nonexistent" (Kantrowitz & Wingert, 1989, p. 54). Taking a lesson about the value of social development from the Japanese may be worthwhile.

In this section on promoting the self-managed student the topics are: (1) CSI to help the hot-tempered or out-of-control student, (2) CSI to promote attention and on-task behavior, (3) CSI to promote social responsibility, (4) CSI to promote school work habits, and (5) CSI reinforcement.

CSI to Help Out-of-Control Students

Temper tantrums, hitting peers, screaming at teachers are not uncommon in our schools today—sadly so. Often teachers react impulsively, angrily, indignantly, using external control. Perhaps their reactions are perfectly justified. But in the meantime, the "out-of-control" student has not learned how to control these angry outbursts. Externally restraining or punishing the student usually meets the teacher's immediate need to stay in control of the classroom; perhaps not wrongfully so. But external control does not teach a student how to exercise self-control and better judgment in the next situation that sets the student off again. There are CSI strategies that can foster student self-control.

Strategy 1 (Turtle Technique: Schneider, 1974). Young students are taught to visualize a turtle, who withdraws into its shell when disturbed by its surroundings. (A visual cue card of a turtle with limbs inside the shell is helpful). The students are taught to imagine they are turtles, pulling arms close to their bodies, putting their heads down, and closing their eyes. They relax muscles (go limp) and find an acceptable way to express themselves. Therefore the three parts of the turtle technique are to (1) imagine and play like a turtle inside its shell, (2) relax inside the shell, and (3) make a good plan. The teacher introduces the "turtle strategy" through a story about a handsome little turtle who gets in trouble at school because he fights (Robin, Schneider, & Dolnick, 1976, p. 450).

> Little Turtle was a handsome young turtle who was very upset about going to school. He always got in trouble at school because he got into fights. Other kids would tease, bump, or hit him; he would get very angry and start big fights. The teacher would have to punish him. Then one day he met the big old tortoise who told him that his shell was the secret answer to all his problems. The tortoise told Little Turtle to withdraw into his shell when he felt angry and rest until he was no longer angry. So he tried it the next day, and it worked. The teacher now smiled at him and he no longer got into big fights.

The teacher proceeds by modeling the turtle response. The students practice and role-play the response when provided with aggressive stimuli in story form (e.g., What if Sally called you an ugly name?). The cue word is "turtle." The teacher and the peers of "out-of-control" students repeat the word *turtle* whenever they see an incipient fight. The teacher reinforces with praise when students successfully "turtle" themselves or cue their friends to "turtle" when angry outbursts look likely. The students and teacher practice "relaxing" inside the shell to defuse negative emotions. They tense and relax muscle groups. Another excellent relaxation strategy is to take a deep breath through the nose and blow it out as slowly as possible through the mouth making a teeny, tiny space between the lips. Others are (1) count backwards from ten to one and (2) repeat the words *calm down* to self. After practicing relaxation, students learn alternative coping strategies, rather than fighting. Discuss ways in a classroom meeting that are acceptable: count backwards, relax, remove self from the situation to cool off, *tell* the aggressor to stop bothering you, tell someone in authority, use I-messages, etc. The emphasis is on choice rather than on impulsive reaction. One of the best ways to reduce impulsivity is to teach a verbal mediator to allow the out-of-control student time to act in a more meaningful manner. Teach students to talk to themselves when confronted or provoked to fighting (e.g., While in the turtle shell say to myself "Stop! I have a choice! I don't have to hit back! Animals fight! People talk. I can do it"). The teacher (after modeling, practicing, and cueing) can reinforce the use of the turtle technique with visual reminders (e.g., posters, bulletin boards) with the words "Turtle, Relax, Talk to Yourself." An example of one of my favorite posters:

Self-Control CSI Poster

Snail Talk

1. Relax
2. Stay calm
3. I have a choice
4. Stop! Don't hit back.
5. Animals fight! People talk!
6. I can do it. I am strong.

Strategy 2. When students are about to explode, remind them that they were able to control their tempers on a previous occasion (e.g., "Remember, yesterday you had reason to hit James but you two talked out your problems. What did you say to yourself to stop yourself from hitting James, as you usually do? Use that same self-talk again").

Strategy 3. Tape a tiny cue word such as "I'm calm" or "I can choose not to fight" inside the collar of a shirt of a very aggressive student. This should be done nonpunitively, with student consent. Instruct such students to look at the word when they feel a temper tantrum coming on. They are to read the word, repeating it softly to themselves three times, when the aggressive stimulus is present. Teachers often prompt the use of the cue word by touching their own collars as a reminder to students that a "potential outburst" is possible.

Strategy 4. Use peer friends who solve "frustrating situations" (e.g., can't find a lost book) in a rational manner, without explosions of anger, to talk to the "out-of-control" student. Peers model the self-talk they have successfully used to guide their calm, rational approach. This should be done when the impulsive student is calm and wants to be helped by a particular peer. This calm self-talk of peer models may be audiotaped or videotaped to be used as a teaching tool for all grade levels. If students are capable, ask them to make a movie (video) of scenes that usually provoke them. Show the self-talk that leads to explosions versus the self-talk that leads to a nonviolent or even calm reaction.

Strategy 5. Use puppet shows, emphasizing the self-control self-talk of the puppets. Present typical classroom situations that normally cause aggressive behavior. Via cognitive self-instruction, the puppets convince themselves to react and behave sanely. After the puppets have verbally calmed themselves down, puppets use self-reinforcing self-talk (e.g, I didn't waste my time going into a rage over that! I came through this without going crazy this time! Good for me).

Strategy 6. Discuss the following rational ideas with students for whom this is age appropriate:

1. Expressing anger is a choice.
2. All people feel anger and want to explode sometimes but they don't.
3. People would be angry all of the time if they corrected everything that needed correcting in the world.
4. People can disagree without being disagreeable.
5. Be sure you have not misunderstood the person who has provoked you. Clarify before verbally confronting. "I think you just said . . . to me. Is that right? Did you mean...?
6. Talk over concerns when both parties are calm.

Strategy 7. Teach aggressive students critical self-questions. Teaching CSI self-questions requires modeling, practicing, and cueing, just as other CSI strategies do (Manning, 1988). Examples of critical self-questions are: (a) How does my body tell me I am about to explode? (b) Is this really worth getting this upset about? For self-question (a) students should list ways they recognize their own "boiling points" (Petti, 1986). Some signs are tight neck, throbbing temples, racing heart, antsy, etc. For self-question (b) students respond to hypothetical situations and whether or not these situations are worth getting upset about. Knaus (1975) suggests that the student who is often provoked by name calling or teasing may want to use these self-questions: (a) Am I the name someone calls me? (b) If a person teases me or calls me a name, does that statement or act change all my other good qualities? (c) Am I unlikeable if one or a few people tease me or call me names? (d) Why am I making this my problem? (e) Do I think the teaser or name caller would continue if I no longer cared or if I handled it differently?

Strategy 8. Use self-reinforcing statements to self. Learning to use self-control, especially when one has a history of tantrums, requires patience from the teacher and the student. There will be regressions. However, teach hot-headed students to reinforce self for any incident wherein they successfully controlled themselves (e.g., "I did it! I came through that situation with my head clear and my body calm. Better for me and better for everyone").

Strategy 9. If possible, audiotape aggressive students in the midst of a tantrum. Ask such students to look into a mirror. When calm has been restored, talk about what they saw in the mirror and play the tape for them. Often "seeing and hearing" is believing. Seeing what a spectacle they are, may have a favorable impact.

Strategy 10. Teach students to release anger and frustrations on a regular interval basis in acceptable ways such as physical activity (e.g., bike riding, jogging, swimming, etc.) or talking regularly to a close friend.

In addition to these strategies Powell (1984) presents other strategies for teaching students basic social interaction skills to promote self-control. There are some helpful teacher aids in this publication (e.g., affective skills in a developmental progression from waiting turns to demonstrating techniques to control behavior).

Powell's teacher evaluation forms to assess self-control are about the students' ability to speak in a controlled manner in various school situations (e.g., during lunch) and general self-control after confrontative events. Interested readers should refer to Powell (1984).

CSI to Promote Attention and On-task Behaviors

The self-instructed strategies to focus attention and to stay on task have components of self-observation, self-monitoring, self-evaluation, self-recording, self-correction, and/or self-reinforcement techniques. These terms were defined in chapter 6 (text and/or definition of terms section). The CSI procedures take the form of teachers sounding a bell, clicker, noise, etc., at random times during the school day. When this signal is presented, students stop and mark on a self-record sheet whether they were on or off task. If they were on task they mark "Yes." Students are taught to use self-reinforcement and return to their assignment. If they were off task they stop, mark "No," and self-correct (e.g., I am not on task. Please work on the assignment, now!).

For readers who are interested in knowing more about CSI to promote attention and on-task behaviors, please refer to the final chapter in this book. A case study is presented whereby an off-task, nonattentive fourth-grade female was successfully redirected through CSI strategies. The steps, materials, interviews, and results are found in the last section of chapter 10. In addition, Hallahan, Lloyd, and Stoller (1982) have prepared a very helpful manual for teachers on "Improving Attention with Self-Monitoring." This manual was intended for learning-disabilities teachers; but as we know, there are many learning disabled students in regular classrooms.

The following materials are taken from Hallahan, Lloyd, and Stoller (1982). The classroom teacher may first want to formally assess attentive behavior of one or two especially nonattentive students.

A Sample Recording Sheet for Assessing Whether Students Are or Are not Attending to Assigned Tasks*

(Timer Intervals are Designed for 6-Minute Average)

Directions: When the timer rings, MARK the appropriate entry by the time interval observed.

Set the Timer for:	Mark +, –, or 0
4 mins.	________
8 mins.	________
2 mins.	________
6 mins.	________
4 mins.	________
6 mins.	________

*From Hallahan et al., 1982, p. 10

The teacher introduces self-monitoring in a way similar to the following description from Hallahan et al. (1982, p. 12):

> Johnny, you know how paying attention to your work has been a problem for you. You've heard teachers tell you, "Pay attention," "Get to work," "What are you supposed to be doing?" and things like that. Well, today we're going to start something that will help you help yourself pay attention better. First we need to make sure that you know what paying attention means. (Teacher models immediate and sustained attention to task.) And this is what I mean by not paying attention. (Teacher models inattentive behaviors such as glancing around and playing with objects) Now you tell me if I am paying attention. (Teacher models attentive and inattentive behaviors and requires the student to categorize them.) Okay, now let me show you what

we're going to do. While you're working, this tape recorder will be turned on. Every once in awhile, you'll hear a little sound like this: (Teacher plays tone on tape). And when you hear that sound quietly ask yourself, "Was I paying attention?" If you answer "yes," put a check in this box. If you answer "no" put a check in this box. Then go right back to work. When you hear the sound again, ask the question, answer it, mark your answers, and go back to work. Now, let me show you how it works. (Teacher models entire procedure.) Now, Johnny, I bet you can do this. Tell me what you're going to do everytime you hear a tone. Let's try it. I'll start the tape and you work on these papers. (Teacher observes student's implementation of the entire procedure, praises its correct use, and gradually withdraws her presence.)

A target student, Edwin needs help learning to monitor his attention to the task at hand. Hallahan et al. (1982, p. 8) offer a possible nonpunitive way to present self-monitoring:

Self-Monitoring of Attention

Scene: A classroom of students engaged in various activities. One teacher is walking about the room, preparing for her next activity. Some students are sitting in a semi-circle facing another teacher and answering questions she poses. Other students are sitting at their desks and writing on papers or workbooks. Edwin is working at his own desk. The teacher picks up some work pages that have green strips of paper attached to their top.

Teacher: (Walking up to Edwin's desk.) Edwin, here are your seatwork pages for today. I'm going to start the tape and I want you to self-record like you have been doing. What are you going to ask yourself when you hear the beep?

Edwin: (Taking papers.) Was I paying attention?

Teacher: Okay, that's it. (Turning away.) Bobby, Jackie, and Anne; it's time for spelling group. (Starts a tape recorder and walks toward front of room where three students are gathering.)

Edwin: (Begins working on his assignments; is continuing to work when a tone comes from the tape recorder. Edwin's lips barely move as he almost inaudibly whispers.) Was I paying attention? Yes. (He marks on the green strip of paper and returns to work. Later, another tone comes from the tape recorder, Edwin whispers.) Was I paying attention? Yes. (He marks on the green strip of paper and returns to work. Later, as the students in one group laugh, Edwin looks up and watches them. While he is looking up, a tone occurs.) Was I paying attention? No. (He marks the strip of paper and begins working again. He continues working, questioning himself when the tone occurs, and recording his answers.)

The last Hallahan et al. example for self-monitoring is a "Was I Paying Attention" checksheet:

Date ________________

WAS I PAYING ATTENTION?

	YES NO		YES NO
1.	____________	21.	____________
2.	____________	22.	____________
3.	____________	23.	____________
4.	____________	24.	____________
5.	____________	25.	____________
6.	____________	26.	____________
7.	____________	27.	____________
8.	____________	28.	____________
9.	____________	29.	____________
10.	____________	30.	____________
11.	____________	31.	____________
12.	____________	32.	____________
13.	____________	33.	____________
14.	____________	34.	____________
15.	____________	35.	____________
16.	____________	36.	____________
17.	____________	37.	____________
18.	____________	38.	____________
19.	____________	39.	____________
20.	____________	40.	____________

CSI to Promote Social Responsibility

Quite a few CSI strategies to foster social responsibility were suggested in the previous chapter especially since Manning's model addresses both social responsibility and school work habits. Please refer to chapter 7, in addition to this discussion. Social responsibility, in the context of this book, relates to school behaviors such as cooperation, waiting turns, respect for adults and peers, etc. The techniques presented previously, such as self-monitoring, self-recording, and self-cueing may be used to promote social responsibility at school.

Strategy 1. A self-evaluation strategy which combines self-monitoring and self-recording is a bulletin board display with a library card pocket for each student. The students decorate the pockets to add color and put their names on the pocket. Each month, beginning with the first month of school, a different social responsibility is highlighted.

I am responsible for:	
September	Getting to know others
October	Sharing my materials
November	Cooperating in the group
December	Waiting turns
January	Respecting my teacher
February	Respecting my friends
March	Listening to others
April	Being patient
May	Saying good-bye

Each month's theme is put in large letters across the board with the decorated library pockets underneath. Popsicle sticks with cues for inhibiting inappropriate social behavior, and initiating and reinforcing appropriate social behaviors are kept in three different boxes (i.e., (1) initiating, (2) inhibiting, and (3) reinforcing). As the students interact, popsicle sticks are given to the students as needed. The cues relate to the month's social responsibility theme. For example in September "I am responsible for getting to know others" is shown on the board with a decorated pocket for each student. The pockets will hold the popsicle sticks. Students might earn a stick from the inappropriate box if they wouldn't sit by a particular student (e.g., I'm getting to know everyone, not just a few people). Students might earn one from the appropriate box if they introduced themselves to a new student (e.g., I made a new friend) and the reinforcing box if the "getting to know" behavior is predominant, noticed by others or the teachers (e.g., I am a good friend to everyone in my group). The teacher can easily jot down a related cue sentence (in first person) to be read by students. Students may wish to develop their own "cue," depending on their ages and/or maturity levels. At the end of the week, a time is set aside to ask students to evaluate their social behavior for that week by sorting out the popsicle sticks. In some cases, the teacher may wish to conference with individual students. The bulletin board display serves as a concrete way to teach social responsibility. This method serves as a means for teaching self-evaluation of social responsibility. In addition the strategy is flexible enough to be very teacher-controlled or very student-controlled (e.g., teacher gives out cues, writes cues, talks about progress or needed improvement; or students may give cue sticks to self or peers as self-assessed, write own related cues, and self-evaluate progress at the end of each week.) Of course, combinations of teacher and student responsibilities may occur at the discretion of the teacher.

Strategy 2. Teachers may use paper-pencil assignments for various social responsibility scenarios presented to the students: "Tilly, Arlene, and Mike have been a threesome at school for several years. They like their desks to be next to each other. They share their secrets. They often study together. A new student, Sebastian wants to be included in this group. Tilly, Arlene, and Mike aren't sure." The scenario is discussed in small groups. Next, each student is requested to write in responses for four self-questions posed by a favorite character, such as Garfield. They are requested to write responses and any accompanying self-talk. A sample worksheet with the four self-questions is provided on p. 215. This worksheet may also be cut into halves to be used in conjunction with sending a student to time-out, isolation, or opportunity rooms. The isolated child works on the first two questions of the worksheet: What is my problem? and What is my plan? In this way, the student reacts to why he/she was sent to time out and what they plan to do to work out the problem. When these two parts are filled out to the teacher's satisfaction, the student may rejoin the group. The second two questions: Am I following my plan? and Am I proud of myself? can be used as follow-up self-evaluation for this same student.

Strategy 3. The Bash and Camp (1975) training figures may be used to promote waiting turns, cooperation, etc. These figures are also found in Meichenbaum (1977). Similar cue cards, developed by the classroom teacher that are more closely related to a specific classroom context may be used. Using these cue cards, students write original stories about what is

Gaining Control/Solving My Problems

Name ______________________ Date ______________________

Cue picture here ______________________

What is my problem? ______________________
Describe or draw a picture of ______________________
the problem.
____

Cue picture here *My plan is* ______________________

How can I do it? ______________________
Describe or draw a picture of ______________________
the plan.
____

Cue picture here ______________________

Am I following my plan? ______________________
Describe or draw a picture of ______________________
my steps.
____

Cue picture here ______________________

Am I proud of myself? ______________________
How did I do?
Describe or draw a picture of ______________________
my success. ______________________

---

happening, what the characters are saying to themselves, etc. After the assignment, students discuss the self-talk as it relates to social responsibility at school. Cue cards like these might be made by the classroom teacher for each of the nine themes mentioned in Strategy 1, this section.

Strategy 4. One kindergarten teacher has incorporated self-guiding speech into her behavior-management system:

1. Each child has his/her name on a paper arrow.

2. Each child begins the day with his name arrow on the green light.

3. If a child must be reminded more than twice to get him/herself "in control" and to remember the rules, then he/she must move his/her arrow from the green light to the yellow light.

4. If a child must be reminded again after his/her name arrow is on the yellow light, then he/she must put his/her arrow on the red light and go to the time-out chair for five minutes.

5. At the end of each week the teacher sends home a sheet noting a child's behavior for each day during that week.

6. At the beginning of the year when the teacher introduces the behavior-management system, she also teaches appropriate self-talk for each light through role-play.

7. If the situation calls for a self-talk sentence not included in those sentences already learned by the class, then the teacher will help the child practice it.

8. *Green Light.* When students see their name arrow on green light. They tell themselves positive statements they have rehearsed.

Prerehearsed statements for Green Light

I am in control of myself.

I respect others' space.

I can control my voice.

I know how to use class materials.

9. *Yellow Light.* When students must put their name arrow on yellow light, they say to self prerehearsed yellow-light sentences or another sentence that may be more appropriate for a particular situation. These statements focus on the students' controlling of a particular misbehavior and avoiding placement on red light and in time out.

Prerehearsed statements for Yellow Light

I need to slow down.

I need to work quietly in my area.

I need to be respectful of others.

I am going to ignore things that distract me.

10. *Red Light.* When students must put their name arrow on red light, they must go to the time-out chair and must say to self prerehearsed red-light sentences or another sentence that may be more appropriate for a particular situation. These statements focus on increasing the students' positive feelings about themselves and on encouraging themselves to regroup and return to the group with a fresh resolve to behave in a controlled manner.

Prerehearsed statements for Red Light

I promise to control myself.

I start over again with a fresh start.

I plan to have a good rest of the day.

CSI to Promote School Work Habits

For additional information, please refer to chapter 7, this text. School work habits involve routine, everyday school tasks such as focusing attention, staying on task, listening to directions, organizing materials, persisting at a task, and finishing work promptly and accurately. The proficiency of such tasks results in a self-directed, self-managed learner. Most educators would agree that the promotion and development of independent, self-starting, self-regulated learners are primary goals of education. The following CSI strategies are described as possible means to facilitate these goals.

Strategy 1: Classroom Game. Who or what am I? Characters such as Connie the Concentrator are drawn or written on an index card. Students draw one of the characters. They must describe the character and the other class members must guess what school work habit is being described. For example, Connie the Concentrator—"I try not to look up if I hear another student talking while I am doing my work. Who am I?" Other characters may be Lanier the Listener; Opie the On-tasker; Owen the Organizer; Daisy the Dallier; Denise the Direction Follower; Frank the Finisher; and Paul the Piddler.

Strategy 2: Classroom Game. What Is Wrong with this Picture? Use a feltboard with velcro attached to cut-out classroom characters (e.g., teacher, students, aide, etc.) Depict classroom scenes where students are bothering friends who are trying to work, interrupting others, etc. The teacher asks: "What is wrong with the picture I see of this classroom? How can we fix it?" The teacher emphasizes CSI as part of the plan to deal with distractions.

Strategy 3: Classroom Game. What Time Is It? When the teacher says "Stop, what time is it?" the students must reply with "It is time for me to tell myself ____________________." Students fill in the blank with proposed self-talk.

Strategy 4: Fun Activities. Jig-Saw Puzzles. Homemade puzzles with theme characters illustrating appropriate self-talk, such as "I am concentrating," "Where do I start?," and "If I work hard I can get it right," are provided.

Pack the Suitcase. To practice having ready pencils, crayons, paper, etc., make suitcases (from snack-cake boxes, candy boxes, etc.) each for a different class (e.g., mathematics, spelling, reading). On top of the lid write "Do I have everything I need for (class)? Inside the lid repeat the same question and provide answers in the form of a checklist already checked off: __✓__ pencil, etc. Have a group of cards with pictures of possible items needed for these classes. Students can practice thinking through what they normally need for each class and putting the right cards in a suitcase. Then they check the cards against the checklist in the suitcase.

Strategy 5: Cards. Concentration. Make two decks of the same cue cards, using pictures and words to promote appropriate school work habits (e.g., stay on task, picture of child studying). Students use the two decks to play Concentration, whereby they turn both decks of cards face down. A player begins by turning over any two cards, looking for matching pairs. The idea is to remember where certain cards are and to try to get the most pairs. May be played singly, in dyads, or in small groups.

Scooby Do and Scooby Don't Matching Cards. Opposite school work habits (e.g., on task and off task; following directions and not following directions) are illustrated on two decks of cards. Students are given the "don't" cards and they must match them with the "do" cards; or Concentration, as described in strategy 5 may be played. Teachers will probably think of many more ways to use these cards.

Strategy 6: Self Checklists. (See p. 219 for an example.) Students make their own checklists for materials at school and materials to carry home (homework).

CSI Reinforcement

Teachers provide external reinforcement for compliance when students perform as directed or asked. Students need just as much or more positive and

Self-Management Checklists
"I am responsible for school materials"

	School Materials Do I have?	Homework Materials Do I have?
Monday	______	______
	______	______
	______	______
	______	______
Tuesday	______	______
	______	______
	______	______
	______	______
Wednesday	______	______
	______	______
	______	______
	______	______
Thursday	______	______
	______	______
	______	______
	______	______
Friday	______	______
	______	______
	______	______
	______	______

corrective feedback for learning to be responsible for themselves. Teachers need to keep recalling the true definition of helping: helping others to help themselves. Good parents and good teachers work themselves right out of the job of being parents and teachers in the sense that they teach children to become independent, in less need of the parent or teacher. Of course, dependency needs must be well met before independence can flourish. Good parenting and good teaching foster independence, a "responsible-for-self" human being. Often this philosophy is difficult to adhere to (e.g., when the last child is leaving home, when the students no longer need the teacher). However, when the child who is leaving home and the student who is moving to the next grade progress forward with independence and a sense of responsibility for self, then the parenting and teaching have been successful, by one measure at least.

Because independence is recognized as an important goal, teachers (and parents) need to praise and encourage responsibility toward self and toward others. When students direct and guide their own learning and behavior, acknowledge this (verbally, in writing, nonverbally, by giving self-reinforcement cue cards, sending notes home to parents, etc.). Positive feedback should be specific, genuine, and mostly private:

> I noticed you checked to make sure you organized all your materials before class.
>
> You never even looked up from your work when the bell rang. You must have really been concentrating.
>
> Great attention to the story. You kept your eyes on the pages and even your posture said you were into your work.

One classroom club that seems to be on the right track is the ICMM club (Bradley, 1984) developed by a classroom teacher. ICMM stands for I Can Manage Myself. Since I read about this club, I have passed the idea on to many classroom teachers who have used ICMM with great success. This is the kind of reinforcement self-managed students need, especially when they are first learning the skills of self-management and self-control.

Cognitive Analysis: Definition of Terms

Afferent The part of the "spoken word/reafference cycle" when the spoken information enters the ear.

Clarifying (Palincsar, 1986) Discerning when there has been a breakdown in comprehension and taking the necessary action to restore meaning (e.g., reading ahead, rereading, asking for assistance [p. 119]).

Efferent The part of the "spoken word/reafference cycle" when the spoken information leaves the mouth.

Goal story interview (modified) Students tell or write what, why, and how they plan to obtain a goal. They tell or write how they plan to cope if they are unsuccessful at reaching their goal. Students write their self-talk as they discuss their goal-directedness.

Guided reading activities The CSI activities that occur during the reading of a story in a basal reader during a directed reading activity.

Mental processing deficits Difficulties in one's own metacognitive monitoring and overseeing of mental functioning during the reception or expression of information.

Predicting (Palincsar, 1986) Hypothesizing what the structure and content of the text suggest will be presented next (p. 119).

Prereading activities The CSI activities that occur before students read a story in a basal reader during a directed reading activity.

Postreading activities The CSI activities that occur after the reading of a story in a basal reader during a directed reading activity.

Question generating (Palincsar, 1986) Self-questioning about the type of information that is generally tapped on tests of comprehension and recall (p. 119).

Reafferent cycle The cycle of sound waves and semantical context of words, as this verbal information travels from self or others into the speaker's or listener's ear. As the information is received there is general activation of the brain, which in turn causes a more vivid storage of this information. The meaning of the information when received in the ear provokes past associations and also affects storage.

Reciprocal teaching The four components are to summarize, to clarify, to generate questions, and to predict during verbal interaction between and among teacher and student(s). The role of the teacher is sometimes played by the classroom teacher and sometimes played by students who rotate turns being the teacher.

Self-checklist A series of questions stated in the first person, used to stimulate self-monitoring and self-evaluation. Self-checklists are usually written and students mark "Yes" or "No" as a way of proofing or evaluating their planning, or ongoing, or finished performance.

Self-correct To become aware of one's own inappropriate behavior and to remedy that situation by stopping or changing to an appropriate behavior.

Self-monitor To keep a watchful eye on one's own thinking as the processes of memory, comprehension, problem solving, and self-control are occurring.

Self-record To keep a written account of one's own incidences of a specific target behavior (e.g., number of times on task when a timer is heard randomly throughout the day).

Self-reinforce To praise or encourage one's own efforts and abilities through verbal messages provided to self (e.g., "I stayed calm").

Summarizing (Palincsar, 1986) Identifying and paraphrasing the main idea in the text (p. 119).

Turtle technique When confronted with aggressive stimuli, students are taught to imagine and play like a turtle inside its shell, to relax inside the shell while making a nonaggressive plan of action (e.g., obtain a third person to be a mediator). This technique aids impulsive, physically aggressive students for whom the strategy is age appropriate.

Verbal rehearsal Information spoken aloud to self for the purpose of aiding recall of the information from memory.

Cognitive Synthesis: A Summary

CSI strategies that are feasible in the classroom to promote memory, comprehension, problem solving, and self-control are outlined in this chapter. In general, verbal rehearsal, organization, study allocation, elaboration, keyword, and SQ3R are the main thrusts when considering the development of CSI strategies to enhance memory abilities. In the area of comprehension, self-questioning, informed training, and reciprocal teaching seem to be the main lines upon which other strategies are developed, extended, and modified. Problem solving (when limited to problem solving with an element of metacognition, and not general problem solving) is characterized primarily by dyadic instruction, moving from other- to self-regulation. CSI self-control strategies include elements of cognitive modeling, rote practice, indirect practice and cueing techniques.

Specific strategies are detailed as suggestions only. Teachers are urged to develop CSI strategies for their own students, based on the teachers' professional assessments of student strengths and needs.

9

Cognitive Self-Instruction by Grade-Level Divisions

Overview

In this chapter, the reader will find a series of lesson plans geared toward CSI programs and strategies by grade-level division. The grade-level classifications are preschool, early elementary, middle school, secondary/college, and adults. For each classification there are general teaching suggestions and specific sample lesson plans written by inservice teachers, representative of the grade-level focus.

Self-Questions

1. Knowledge. Name one CSI strategy for each of the five grade-level classifications in this chapter (i.e., preschool, early elementary, middle school, secondary/college, and adults).

2. Comprehension. Explain why younger children need more cueing of CSI strategies than do older students.

3. Application. Take one of the lesson plans for early elementary stu-

dents and modify it for a younger or older classification of students (i.e, either preschoolers or middle schoolers).

4. Analysis. Consider the components of modeling, practicing, and cueing CSI strategies, and tell how a selected lesson plan in this chapter addresses each of these three components.

5. Synthesis. Write a lesson plan for a middle school student who is reading at a first grade level and is socially very immature for his/her age. Give a rationale to explain why the CSI strategies I develop are appropriate for this child. Include the components of modeling, practicing, and cueing.

6. Evaluation. Select any of the sample lesson plans and critique the plan based on feasibility, importance, and creativity.

In this chapter, CSI ideas are presented by grade-level divisions (i.e., preschool, early elementary, middle school, secondary/college, and adults). Teaching suggestions, sample lesson plans, modeling techniques, guided and independent practice of CSI strategies, and CSI cueing ideas are outlined for each grade-level classification. As is true of all the CSI strategies in Part Three, each suggested strategy is based on theoretical and research considerations.

Preschool

Children in the preschool setting have the ability to learn to use self-verbalizations to foster learning; however, the average learners do not spontaneously produce verbal self-guidance for themselves. Therefore, teachers need to supply the verbal self-guidance initially. However, if teachers approach the guiding of children this age from a Vygotskian perspective (other- to self-regulation), they can facilitate verbal self-regulation. For example, instead of always giving external commands (e.g., You need to sit over here) teachers can foster the development of responsibility through such comments as the following: "Alice remind yourself to sit over here. Say to yourself: 'My seat is next to the window and I need to sit in it during story time.' Alice, tell me what you will say to remind yourself to find your seat? Can you repeat what I said? Let's play Copy Cat. Please repeat after me: 'My seat is next to the window' (child repeats aloud, whispers, and silently). 'I need to sit in it during story time.' (child repeats aloud, whispers, and silently)." Teaching the precursors of verbal self-guidance is beneficial and possible. However, this kind of teaching is time consuming and requires a lot of patience. In the greater scheme of things, however, the preschool teachers who care enough to teach the "vocabulary of self-control" spend much less time externally directing children later in the school year.

The emphasis during this preschool age is on the combination of internal with external control. The external problem solving agent (the teacher) as a cognitive model is crucial, especially at this time. The adult verbally structures the learning. The greater the quality of this learning "scaffold" the greater the quality of the child's subsequent self-guiding problem-solving abilities. In addition to serving as a rich cognitive/verbal model, teachers of preschoolers must also provide the vocabulary of self-control in a very direct manner. In short, teachers of preschoolers must model self-guiding self-talk, provide verbal mediators for the students, and oversee and reinforce overt, faded, and covert practice of verbal self-guidance. In addition, preschool teachers must serve as one of the members of a collaborative problem-solving unit, with the preschooler(s) as the other member(s). The instruction should be pitched in advance of the students' development because students are able to problem solve on a higher plane during collaborative, dyadic instruction.

Teacher: Chris Ogilvie
Day 1

Goal: To teach CSI skills to preschoolers to promote waiting for assistance from the teacher when appropriate to do so.

Objectives:

Students observe teacher modeling of how she uses CSI skills to help her "wait."

Students observe and participate in repeating the teacher's self-talk example of staying in seat while waiting.

Procedures: Teacher introduces the lesson by asking if anyone has ever had to wait for something and how they felt during the wait. After taking several responses, teacher says, "I have to wait sometimes too, and it's not easy! Let me tell you some things I say to myself when I need to wait for something." Teacher will then model several scenarios and demonstrate the self-talk used during the wait.

1. Standing in line at the water fountain: "I don't like standing here. Maybe I can cut in

line to get my drink. No, I need to *STOP* and *WAIT.* It'll be my turn soon. I'm glad I can wait my turn.

2. In large group: "My teacher asked a question. I want to yell out my answer so I can be first. No, I'll *STOP* and *WAIT.* Miss Ogilvie will like it if I raise my hand. I'm glad I can wait!
3. Going to play: "I can't wait to play but I'm stuck at the back of the line. If I cut in line, I'll get outside sooner! No, I'd better *STOP* and *WAIT.* Miss Ogilvie will be proud of me if I wait in line. I am proud too!"
4. Waiting to use the glue: "I need that glue right now, but Bryan has it. I can grab it out of his hand but I need to *STOP* and *WAIT.* Miss Ogilvie likes us to share and wait our turn. Hey, I'm waiting and it's almost my turn! I can wait!"
5. Sharing work: "I can't wait to show Miss Ogilvie my good work! She looks busy but I can interrupt her. Oops, I need to *STOP* and *WAIT.* She can see it later and will be extra proud that I did not interrupt.
6. In need of help: "I don't know what to do on this paper. I'll get up and go find my teacher. No, Miss Ogilvie said to *STOP* and *WAIT.* I will raise my hand and she will come help me. Hey, here she comes! I waited!"

Teacher stops here and asks the children if they heard what was said when she talked to herself about waiting. Teacher then picks a child as a peer model to try talking to self as the teacher did. Teacher sets up the scenario where the child needs help and explains that he is going to talk to himself as he pretends to do a "hard" math paper. Children attempt to model the same self-talk used, as teacher sits with them and has them repeat what she said about waiting. Teacher repeats this same scenario using different children to peer model as the rest of the class is taught how to use self-talk to "stay in my seat and wait."

After the modeling exercises, teacher leads a short wrap-up session on the importance of waiting and staying in my seat. Teacher also reviews what should be said when we talk to ourselves about waiting.

Expectations: I enthusiastically introduce my children to the cognitive-monitoring process of self-talk. By modeling negative and positive thoughts, they will better identify with me and realize that if teachers can talk to themselves, they can too. In these examples, they can understand what is being said in my self-talk and that it directly relates to what they should be saying to themselves.

I evaluate during the peer-modeling step and am able to see if they are grasping the concept. This is easy to detect by how much prompting I do after several children have modeled. I explain that we will be working on this some more and that they can "practice" (model) throughout the day with a partner if they'd like to continue "talking to themselves." I observe and evaluate during these times as well.

Day 2

Objectives: Students practice saying self-talk statements out loud as they repeat what teacher says.

Students practice whispering self-talk statements concerning staying in their seats and waiting for help.

Students observe teacher modeling and peer modeling as they learn how to use cues to remind them of the target behavior.

Procedures: Teacher begins lesson by asking if anyone remembers what was learned in the previous lesson. This leads us into a discussion on self-talk and the modeling (or pretending) that was done. For a quick review, we use one or two peers to model the scenario from Day 1.

The teacher then explains that we need to "practice" what we say to ourselves so we can remember better. She then leads by having the children repeat after her as she states the self-talk concerning waiting at their seats. (Example: "I need to *STOP* and *WAIT*." Children repeat, "I can wait." Children repeat, etc.)

The next step involves the children whispering the examples of self-talk. Since many young children do not understand the concept of whispering, it is necessary that the teacher model and the children repeat. A peer also models whispering the statement. Games are played where the children whisper to a partner and try not to let the teacher hear them. After some examples have been demonstrated, we end the practicing step and move on to cueing.

Teacher asks children what they should do if they forget what to say when they are trying to wait. She receives answers and then models what she would say if she forgot what to do. (Example: "I want to go over to my teacher and ask for help, but Miss Ogilvie told me to say something and do something, I can't remember!" At this time, teacher brings out large cue card of a girl holding a STOP sign. "I know. I'll look at that poster that says STOP. I remember now, I'm supposed to *STOP* and *WAIT*. I did it. I remembered what Miss Ogilvie said to do!") At this time, teacher discusss the cue-sign and where it is placed in the room.

Peers then model what they need to do if they forget, as teacher prompts them to look at the cue sign. Teacher also prompts self-statements when necessary, to make sure that students all recall what they say to themselves.

Teacher asks what she could do if she can't see the big cue sign. After taking suggestions, she holds up small, individual cue cards to place on the desks. She models and explains that "these can be put by my seat to remind me to *STOP* and wait in my seat." Teacher instructs children to color neatly and make the cue cards look like themselves. She passes out cues and reviews while children are coloring. Teacher also tells children that she is looking for people who are staying in their seats and waiting as well as people using self-talk to *STOP* and *WAIT*.

Another teacher taught CSI strategies to foster responsibility for school work:

Teacher: Bonnie Crowe Andersen
Day 1

Goals: From these lessons on CSI, I expect students to accomplish two goals. First of all, I expect them to stop feeling so helpless when faced with school work which may be difficult or not fun for them. Second, I expect the students to feel more confident while working, by talking to themselves, and saying they can do the work and do it well (to the best of their ability).

I know at times preschoolers are faced with work that is developmentally inappropriate. In situations when the students really can not complete a task, I help them make a cue card that says "I am trying." This way, the students do not feel totally helpless and feel better about themselves.

My overall goal for using cognitive self-instruction in the kindergarten class is to help the students realize they are worthwhile people, to build their self-esteem and self-image.

Objective: Students observe the modeling of appropriate self-talk. Then they practice CSI for typical school day occurrences.

Materials: "I can" (made previous day), math paper, writing paper, pencil, lace-up shoes, story written on chalkboard or chart paper, puzzle.

"I can" is made by covering a tin can with construction paper (e.g., small orange juice cans). The colorfully decorated cans prompt children to say "I can" instead of "I can't." Children and/or teachers reinforce the use of the verbal message "I can" by dropping buttons, dried beans, etc., into the "I can" cans.

Purpose and Introduction: Today we are going to start learning a way to help you do better work and feel better about your work and yourself.

Procedures: Teacher leads discussion, asking students to relate situations in which they feel helpless and may have said, "I can't do this." Allow time for sharing experiences. Teacher relates experiences, also (e.g., learning to drive, school projects, cooking, reading a long book, etc.). Teacher models several situations in which she uses self-talk to tell herself she can complete a task. Students watch. Example situations are as follows:

1. Completing math paper: "Miss Crowe gave me this paper and she told me how to do it. Let's see, I need to color the things on top yellow and the ones on the bottom red. This is easy! I can do this."
2. Putting puzzle together: "First I need to find the corner pieces. I can do that. Now I need the outside pieces. I can do that, too. I'll put the outside pieces together first, then work on the inside. I can put this puzzle together. Miss Crowe told me I could and I can."
3. During P.E.: "Coach said for me to bounce this ball ten times without stopping. It's going to be hard to do, but I can if I try."
4. Tying shoes: "Cross the laces. I can do that. Now make a loop and go around it with the other lace and pull through. I can do that, too! There, I tied my shoe."
5. During Music: "I'm supposed to beat this drum in time to the music. I can do it. 1-2-3-4. That's right. I *can* do it."
6. During Art: "Draw a circle. Hmm. I need to go around like this. I can make a circle. It's easy."

7. In line for lunch: "Oh, no! We're having soup for lunch. I'll have to walk slowly or I'll spill soup all over me. I can walk slowly. I know how. There, I made it."
8. Sitting on floor for story: "I sure am tired. I'd really like to lie down. No, Miss Crowe won't like that. I can sit still for a few more minutes. I can listen a while longer."
9. Copying story from board: "This is not my favorite thing to do, but I can do this, then Miss Crowe said I would color a picture. I like to color."

Teacher models #9 above using "I can" can as cue. Explain that the can is there to help remind me what to say to myself.

Choose a student to model self-talk in situation #9. Use "I can." Prompt students as needed. Make sure student says "I."

Closure: Teacher asks how using self-talk can help solve problems. Ask students if they ever talk to themselves and ask them to share what they said to themselves. Ask if their self-talk helped them in that situation. Ask students if they think the self-talk modeled would help solve the problem or not.

Evaluation: Teacher observation of students while she and peers are modeling. Teacher assessment of answers given during closure. Do the students have any idea what is going on?

Later in the day the students will have an opportunity to make their own "I can" for use in tomorrow's lesson.

Day 2

Goal: Students use appropriate self-talk to eliminate feelings of helplessness and replace these feelings with confidence.

Objective: Students practice appropriate self-talk and practice using "I can" as a cue.

Materials: "I cans," paper, pencil.

Purpose and Introduction: Yesterday I showed you how to talk to yourself to solve problems. Today you are going to practice talking to yourself to help *you* solve problems. I will also show you how to use your "I can."

Procedure: Review situation #9 from previous lesson. Have a peer model again, using own "I can." Teacher says each statement and students repeat aloud. Do this several times and make sure all students are participating.

Teacher says each statement and students whisper. Repeat several times and make sure all students are participating.

Teacher says each statement and students say them silently. Remember to allow time for students to say each statement in their heads. Repeat several times.

Teacher asks how the students will remember to say "I can" to themselves. Introduce cue. Repeat activities listed above using cues. Again, go through each step several times to insure students are participating and understanding what they are doing. Stop and question students throughout, "What are you saying to yourself?," "What is this can for?,"etc.

Closure: Ask if anyone can say what they have learned. Tell students they can not only use the "I can" when they are writing, but other times as well. Get students to say what these other times might be. Have students write a different story and use their "I can."

Evaluation: Teacher assessment of practicing. Did the students participate in practicing? Did they use "I can" while writing a story? Did they talk to themselves at all?

Next is a teacher's account of how she plans to use CSI to help a kindergarten boy who is not thoughtful about his and others' belongings.

The classroom teacher describes the problem and how she plans to teach self-management skills to improve responsibility for personal belongings at school:

Problem: Some preschoolers have a limited concept of personal belongings—those of themselves and those of others.

Case in point: Jason is an average five-year-old child who is away from home in the school-type setting for the first time. He has one sister who is thirteen years his senior. Jason has a very easy-going personality and mixes and interacts well with the other children. Jason has, however, one very annoying and typical problem. He has little respect for others' belongings and will not take responsibility for his own belongings. There are several times during the school day when Jason interrupts the class and the teacher with his problem. The most disturbing to others is when the class is engaged in the morning work time. The class works in three small groups which are (1) teacher centered, (2) aide centered, and (3) student centered. During this time of day Jason's problem really comes into focus. Every child has his own "box" which contains crayons, scissors, pencils, and other belongings, as well as an individual cubby in which to put their papers and workbooks, etc. Jason pays attention to the directions and seems to know what is expected of him. The problem comes when he begins to implement his task. Jason will open and use any box within his reach. If he needs a red crayon and Matt's happens to be in sight then its Matt's crayon he will use. If next he needs a blue one he might put Matt's back into Jenny's box and pick up Jenny's crayon,and so it goes until all belongings are mixed up and other children are very indignant. This is very upsetting to the other children and also to the classroom atmosphere.

Another problem occurs when it is time to leave school for the day. Jason will leave his papers, letters to parents, coat, etc., if not prompted by the teacher to check his cubby and take home his belongings.

Procedure for altering Jason's behavior: In order to help Jason change his behavior there are several CSI strategies employed by the teacher. First of all, the children are given a brief talk on the respect of others' belongings. The teacher identifies objects which she considers her personal belongings such as her scissors, her markers, desk, pocketbook, etc. It is stressed that these things are not to be used by anyone other than the teacher except with permission. Next the teacher points out the students' personal belongings. The teacher then refers to her things as "my desk," "my scissors," etc. She is therefore becoming a model for Jason to imitate.

Next, I give the children a situation involving the use of others' belongings and allow the students to role-play the situation and discuss why we don't use others' things, and the consequences of using others' things, (example, broken and lost crayons, etc.) All of these strategies are a general overview for the entire class. The teacher has a private talk with Jason about his new role in changing his behavior. Jason is presented with a card which contains a picture and the words *Jason's Things*. This card is given to Jason to be kept at his seat and referred to during the day. Jason is encouraged to think about the message of the card, "Jason's Things," and to remember to use his own things when completing his work tasks. The teacher also has a copy of the card and holds hers up to remind Jason to use his things during the day. In order to help Jason to remember his correct behavior he is taught the same dialogue that the teacher uses when doing her tasks,: "I use my scissors to cut out this picture" or "I put my pencil or book back up since I am finished," etc. These same techniques are used at the end of the day to help Jason learn responsibility for taking his things home. The teacher shows her card, and says "I take my

```
things home." Jason also holds up his card and
repeats "I take my things home."

After several days of this prompting and dialogue by
the teacher, Jason became more prideful and respon-
sible for his own belongings and those of his peers.
```

After implementing and evaluating this plan for Jason, the teacher reported a great deal of improvement in Jason's responsibility for his and his peers' belongings.

Other classroom suggestions for using CSI with preschoolers are found in the following teacher comments:

> *Teacher A*: When students have problems understanding mathematics (i.e., counting), I ask them to count out loud so that they might be able to work out the solution by hearing themselves talk about it. I found that having these young children repeat things out loud really reinforced their learning.
>
> *Teacher B*: I prepared and provided each of my six kindergarten students with 5 x 8 cue cards which they used as self-reminders during teacher-directed lessons only. Since these children's reading abilities are limited, I designed these cards with pictures on them. On each card, I drew pictures of an ear, a closed mouth, and an extended upward hand. I told my students that the card was to remind them to tell themselves to listen carefully, to keep their mouths closed when someone else was speaking, and to raise their hand when they wanted a turn to answer a question.
>
> Before I used cognitive self-instruction with my students I found that I was having some trouble managing their behavior during formal instruction. During "center time" and other more child-centered activities, these cue cards are not necessary. However, during teacher-centered or teacher-led activities these cue cards were the answer to my problems. The students were able to control their own behavior without a great deal of interruption and distraction.
>
> *Teacher C*: I finally experienced the difference between cognitive modeling of an assigned task and giving directions for an assigned task. Teachers of preschoolers (and all ages, for that matter) should use cognitive modeling instead of giving directions. When I think out loud about a task, while children listen, I have found that they are much more attentive. They like to hear me think aloud. Teachers just have to shed those inhibitions and get in there and be a good "thinking" role

model for children. The best way to do this is to think aloud. A second advantage is that I often realize obstacles that the students may confront as I model aloud how to do an assignment. A third advantage is that I am providing vocabulary—"language for thinking." I'll never give directions again to young children. I'll "think aloud my plan for doing the assignment" for them, instead.

Early Elementary

Students at this grade level are capable of learning CSI strategies to improve academics, socialization skills, and school work habits.

The first two lesson plans are excerpted from a teacher whose goal was to use CSI as a means for learning and recall of multiplication facts, especially the facts giving her students problems (e.g., 7 x 8 = 56).

Teacher: Mary Anne Smith
Day 1

Objective: The students are able to talk to themselves during a variety of activities as the teacher models; intended to improve memorization of multiplication facts.

ACTIVITY I:

During this activity the teacher introduces and models talking to herself. The teacher writes this statement on the board while demonstrating self-talk: "We are going to learn our multiplication facts."

Dialogue: Teacher: "I need to put this statement on the board." While writing the statement on the board, the teacher says "Let's see, how does this look? Are my letters straight? Yes. Is my handwriting big enough? I don't know. Let me step back here and look. Yes, I believe that is big enough. Let's see, did I make any mistakes when I wrote this? 'We are going to learn our multiplication facts.' Yes, I forgot to put the period there. I can't believe I forgot that period. Let me put it at the end of the sentence. Now class, did you notice anything in particular that I did as I wrote on the board?"

Student: "Yes, Mrs. Smith, you were talking to yourself the whole time that you were writing."

Teacher: "You're right, I did just talk to myself, and what was I talking about?"

Student: "You were talking to yourself about that sentence you just put up on the board."

Teacher: "Yes, that's right. Talking to myself helped me to get that sentence up correctly. Do any of you ever talk to yourself?"

Student: "I talked to myself when I got up this morning."

Teacher: "Great! And what did you say to yourself?"

Student: "I told myself I wanted to go back to bed but I had to get going or I'd miss school."

Teacher: "Good, it's helpful to talk to yourself. I am always talking to myself about something. I'll bet you all do, too." Let's play a quick game. Get out your pencil and paper. Now, for the next five minutes, I want you to write down the words that you are saying in your mind; ready, let's write."

Teacher and students write for approximately five minutes. After the time is up, the teacher and the students share what they wrote on their papers.

ACTIVITY II

Materials: (1) student snapshot, (2) markers, (3) colored construction paper, (4) white balloons cut from drawing paper, (5) glue

Procedure: Teacher passes out materials and says, "What do you suppose that you are saying to yourself right now in this picture? Think about it a minute and then write what you think you're saying to your-self on the white bubble I've given you. I'll tell you what I'm saying, 'Boy, my desk could really stand to be cleaned up, it's a mess!' When you have written what you were saying, glue the picture and the bubble to the construction paper." When the students finish, they pin their pictures and captions on the bulletin board with the caption, "What did I say?"

ACTIVITY III

Materials: (1) poster-sized pictures of people, (2) large bubbles from white paper, (3) magic markers

Procedure: Teacher says, "What could these people be saying to themselves? I'll bet this man is saying, 'What am I doing at the circus?'" Teacher asks for a volunteer to come up and write what he thinks a person is saying, and then attach it to the picture. Each child that wants to will get a chance to write the self-talk.

Day 2

Objective: Students practice steps two through five of Meichenbaum's CSI while applying these steps to multiplication facts through practicing, cueing, and verbal rehearsal.

Before these two days' activities, the teacher has assessed the students on the multiplication facts. The teacher will have a listing of what each child needs to work on. The multiplication facts that many children exhibit problems with are the facts that we actually work on in class; that is, when we go through the CSI steps.

ACTIVITY I

Procedure: Students repeat after the teacher: "I can talk to myself. It's OK to talk to myself. Talking to myself can help me to remember hard multiplication facts." The students whisper these words, and then the students and teacher say these words to themselves.

ACTIVITY II

Materials: (1) chalkboard, (2) chalk

Procedure: CSI

1. Teacher says "9 x 7 = 63" and writes the problem on the board. Students observe.
2. Teacher says, "Students, write this problem. Now, listen to me while I say, '9 x 7 = 63.'"
3. Teacher says, "Now class, watch while John comes to the board, writes the problem and says the problem out loud." John writes the problem on the board and says, "9 x 7 = 63."
4. Teacher says, "Now class, watch while Joan comes to the board, writes the problem, and says the problem in a whisper." Joan writes the problem on the board and whispers, "9 x 7 = 63."
5. Teacher says, "Now class, watch while I write the problem on the board and you and I say '9 x 7 = 63' in our heads."
6. The teacher and class repeat this procedure with several of the identified difficult multiplication facts.

ACTIVITY III—ART

Materials: (1) colored markers, (2) white drawing paper

Procedure: Each child writes a troublesome multiplication fact on the drawing paper. Teacher says, "Students, I want you to write a multiplication fact that gives you trouble. If you have trouble remembering, I can help you write one. When you have written it, copy it in bubble letters like this." Teacher then writes a multiplication fact on the board in bubble letters. "When you've done this, color or decorate the math fact that you bubbled, sort of like I'm doing on my paper. If you like, write the fact in other different ways and decorate. See, isn't this fun? When you have finished, we'll put these on the wall to help you remember these troublesome facts."

ACTIVITY IV—VERBAL REHEARSAL

Materials: (1) blackboard, (2) pencils and paper

Procedure: "We write each multiplication fact, one

at a time, until we have written the entire table. I write one fact at a time on the board. You write the same fact on your paper. I say the fact and point to it, then you say the fact and point to it. For instance, I write 7 x 8 = 56 on the board, you write it on your paper, then I point to 7 x 8 = 56 and say it, and then you point to 7 x 8 = 56 and say it. Today we follow this procedure for every fact in the seven table."

Cues:

1. Each "multiplication table" is written on a poster with a familiar cartoon figure. The cartoon figure, Porky Pig says, "I-I-I-know my 4's. I-I-I can even say them to myself."
2. The caption over all the artwork in activity 3 reads, "HEY—THIS IS EASY FOR ME!!!!"
3. The identified problems for each child are written on stickers and placed on the child's desk.
4. A mobile extends from the ceiling. It consists of a head with math facts written on the forehead, the caption reads, "I listen to myself during math!"

Please note that these plans are to teach a process for memorization of multiplication facts. These plans do not take the place of mathematics lessons for "understanding" mathematical concepts. During those lessons, students will need to manipulate materials and go beyond the verbal rehearsal of the facts. Verbal rehearsal is to aid retention of the math facts themselves.

A teacher interested in CSI to promote self-control and self-management skills used the following lesson plans:

> During the first week of school, I follow plans for day one and day two. Before I introduce the self-instructions, I administer the Nowicki–Strickland Locus of Control Scale. Then I administer it again after one month and after three months. The results help me to determine whether or not I have been successful in teaching the students to use their self-talk in order to become more internally controlled. After completing the lesson plans for day one, I proceed to day two and to each classroom rule as soon as approximately 85–90 percent of the students are able to perform the task automatically without the use of cueing.

If 85–90 percent of the students are not able to perform the task automatically, I reteach self-instruction for each classroom rule as needed. I also work with students individually or in small groups if they are having problems after I reteach.

One example of a remediation activity is to work with students individually to help the students make positive self-statements and to record these statements. I ask the students to listen to these statements at least two times each day.

Other classroom rules to be taught by self-instruction are:

1. Respect property of others.
2. Walk inside.
3. Keep my feet, hands, objects, and unkind words to myself.
4. Follow directions.
5. Wait my turn.
6. Stay on task.
7. Share my classroom materials.
8. Clean my work space.
9. Listen to my teachers and my classmates.

In addition, students are observed in an effort to determine which ones will benefit from using positive self-statements to overcome shyness, to increase self-motivation, to build self-esteem, etc. CSI is a valuable tool for use in these areas.

Teacher: Gretchen Campbell
Day 1

Goal: Students use self-instruction to help them follow the classroom rules.

Objectives:

1. Given adult modeling, the students demonstrate self-instruction overtly, faded, and covertly for the classroom rule: Stay in my seat.
2. Given classroom scenarios, each student pro-

duces at least one appropriate self-statement to inhibit getting out of their seat, to initiate staying in their seat, and to reinforce themselves for staying in their seat.

3. Given the game "Betcha Can't Stay in Your Seat," students role-play by using self-statements to help them stay in their seats. (Cue cards are used as a reminder.)

<u>Introduction</u>: "Today, boys and girls I want to teach you some ways to talk to yourself so that you can follow our classroom rule that says 'Stay in my seat.' Have you ever talked out loud to yourself? Have you heard people talk out loud to themselves? (Allow time for student responses.) That is very interesting because I talk out loud to myself a lot. I talk out loud to myself when I am cooking, and this helps me to remember if I have forgotten to add something. I also talk to myself when I am driving my car. I talk out loud to myself many times every day."

"Remember, I told you that I go to school at night. Sometimes I have a hard time remembering to stay in my seat when I am in my class. I want you to listen as I talk to myself about staying in my seat."

<u>Procedure</u>: Adult models staying in my seat. "I want you to make believe that I am at my school and Ms. Loggins (classroom aide) is the teacher. While the teacher is writing on the board, I want to get out of my seat and walk around in the room. It is hard to stay in my seat, but I can do it if I try. Now I talk to myself about staying in my seat. 'Stop. I *can* stay in my seat. (Teacher models staying in seat.) Good for me; I am staying in my seat.'

"Now I want you to talk to yourself about staying in your seat. We will play a game called 'Copy Cat.' I will say something and also perform an action. Look at me. Listen, then say and do exactly what I say and do. 'Stop.' (Students repeat.) 'I can stay in my seat.' (Students repeat.) 'Good for me, I am staying in my seat.' (Students repeat and stay in their seats.)

"Now let's play Copy Cat and whisper instead of talking out loud." Teacher models and whispers "Stop" (students repeat by whispering) "I *can* stay in my seat." (Students whisper.) "Great for me, I am staying in my seat." (Students whisper and remain in their seats.)

"Now I want you to talk to yourself by 'thinking'. You say the things that we have been saying to ourselves about staying in our seats. Remember to say these things to yourself, inside your head. You are not talking out loud now." Teacher models covertly by sitting in seat (points to head as though thinking). Students demonstrate covert self-talk. (Kindergarten students may not be able to do this step. May need to stop during the fading step. Teacher can ask, "What did you say to yourself when you were 'thinking' about staying in your seat?")

Teacher chooses a student to role-play staying in my seat while teacher models by verbalizing out loud the self-talk to match the student's action.

Student will role-play staying in seat and will talk aloud to self.

<u>Scenario</u>: "The teacher is having reading groups, and you want to get out of your seat. What would you say to yourself to keep from getting out of your seat?" (Call on students for response.) "What would you say to yourself to help you remember that you can stay in your seat?" (Call on students for response.) "What would you say to yourself after you stay in your seat?" (Call on students for reinforcing statements.) *If this is done with the entire class, teacher may need to use more scenarios. For example, the teacher is talking with a visitor, and you want to get out of your seat, etc.

Adult explains the rules of the game "Betcha Can't Stay in Your Seat." (Developed by teacher.) Adult tries to get students to stand up when a song also directs them to "stand up." Students use cue cards to remind them to stay in their seats. If student stands up, he/she is out of the game until end of song. Winners are those who stay in their seats until end of song.

Closure: Adult reviews inhibitory, initiatory, and reinforcing self-talk by discussing with students.

Reinforcement:

1. Make individual or classroom charts with students' names listed. During a period of time when students are supposed to stay in their seats, set the timer at different intervals. When it goes off, check to see if students are in their seats and place a star or smiley face by their name if they are in their seats. (Could also set the timer and observe students or have students keep the record for themselves to see if students stay in their seats for the entire time interval.)
2. Students work in small groups to create murals that show them in a situation where they need to stay in their seats. Teacher observes and questions students as they work.
3. Students make booklets by drawing pictures of themselves in different situations where they need to stay in their seats. Students dictate sentences about their picture and teacher writes sentences.
4. Display a red sign as a reminder for students to indicate that it is time for everyone to stay in their seats. Display a green sign during activities in which students are allowed to get out of their seats.

Evaluation:

(Objective 1) Teacher observation/assessment of student's ability to demonstrate self-instruction overtly, faded, and covertly.

(Objective 2) Teacher assessment of each student's ability to produce at least one appropriate self-statement to inhibit getting out of seat, to initiate, and to reinforce staying in seat.

(Objective 3) Teacher observation and questioning to evaluate how well students are able to use self-instruction and cue cards to help them stay in their seats.

Day 2

Objectives:

1. Given adult modeling, the students demonstrate self-instruction overtly, faded, and covertly for the classroom rule: Raise my hand.
2. Given paper, pencil, and crayons, students are able to draw themselves in a situation where they need to raise their hand.
3. Students produce at least one appropriate self-statement to inhibit talking without raising their hand, to initiate raising their hand, and to reinforce themselves for raising their hand.
4. Given the game "I Spy," students role-play by using self-statements and cue cards to help them remember to raise their hand before speaking.

Introduction and Purpose: "Today, boys and girls I want you to tell me what you have learned to do that helps you stay in your seat." (Students respond: lead them to discuss self-talk.) "Today I want to teach you some ways to talk to yourself so that you can follow another classroom rule: Raise my hand to speak." (Raising hand is used during discussion or questioning whenever it would be inappropriate for students to call out the answer or for all students to talk at the same time.)

Procedure: "Sometimes I want to shout out answers instead of raising my hand. It is hard to raise my hand, but I can do it if I try. When I am at night school, I talk to myself about raising my hand. Listen as I talk to myself about raising my hand. 'Stop. I can raise my hand.' (Adult raises hand.) 'Good for me, I raised my hand. Great!'

"Now, I want you to talk to yourself about raising your hand. We will play Copy Cat again. Remember to listen to what I say, then you say exactly what I do. 'Stop!' (Students repeat.) 'I can raise my hand.' (Students repeat and raise their hands.) 'Good for me, I raised my hand. Great!' (Students repeat.)

"Now, let's play Copy Cat and you whisper exactly what I whisper. (Adult models and whispers.) 'Stop.' (Students repeat.) 'I can raise my hand.' (Students repeat and raise their hands.) 'Good for me, I raised my hand. Great!' (Students repeat.)

"Now, I want you to say the things that we have been saying about raising my hand. Remember to think these things, do not say them aloud." Teacher models covertly by sitting and pointing to head as though thinking. Then teacher raises her hand. (Students demonstrate and raise their hands.) Kindergarten students may not be able to do this step.

Teacher chooses a student to role-play raising my hand. Teacher models and verbalizes out loud the self-talk to match the student's actions. Student will role-play raising my hand and will talk aloud to self.

"Pretend or make believe that you are at school. The teacher is doing calendar time and you know the answer; you want to answer the teacher's questions. You start talking to yourself about raising your hand. Draw a picture which shows you that you remember to talk to yourself." (Teacher and aide walk around and question students about their self-talk.)

Teacher explains the rules of the game "I Spy." (Teacher will choose objects in the room and say excitedly, "I spy something . . . red, yellow, etc.) Who can tell me what it is?" (Teacher will try to get the students to tell the answer without raising their hands.) Winners are those who raise their hands before answering.

Closure: Teacher reviews inhibiting, initiating, and reinforcing self-talk by discussing with students.

Evaluation:

(Objective 1) Teacher observation/assessment of students' ability to demonstrate self-instruction overtly, faded, and covertly.

(Objective 2 and 3) Teacher assessment of each student's ability to produce at least one appropriate self-statement to inhibit talking/answering without raising hand, to initiate and reinforce raising hand to speak.

(Objective 4) Teacher observation and assessment to evaluate how well students are able to use self-instruction and cue cards to help them raise their hands to speak/answer questions.

Reinforcement:

1. Students make booklets by drawing pictures of themselves in situations where they need to raise their hands.
2. Students work together in small groups to make murals by drawing pictures of themselves as they raise their hands. Students tell about their pictures or dictate sentences.
3. Explain the I Can Manage Myself Club (ICMM). Make little cards and print ICMM on the cards. Print a message such as I Can Manage Myself: I raised my hand today. (Kindergarten students need to be reinforced externally on a daily basis. Could use the ICMM cards daily for whatever rule was being taught.)
4. Students cut out cartoon characters or pictures from magazines, glue them on construction paper, and draw bubbles. Teacher writes statement in the bubble. Students dictate

self-statement to teacher. This activity could be used for any of the classroom rules.

The goal of the next two sample lesson plans was to improve students' school work habits (i.e., planning and organizing for the school day and listening and paying attention during class).

Teacher: Ginger Jackson Leftwich
Day 1

Objective: Students practice using cognitive self-instruction to assist them in planning and preparing for the day.

Materials: "Am I prepared?" poster cue card, "Ralph the Bear" poster cue cards on wall, overhead projector, children's supplies.

Time: approximately 30 minutes

Procedure:

1. When the students enter the room ask them to be seated, but not to get ready for class yet. While the children are waiting, the teacher models adult self-instruction by talking to herself while preparing for class.
2. After Opening Exercises are dispensed with, the lesson begins. "This morning we're going to talk about how we get ready for class every day. Did anyone notice what I was doing while I was getting ready today? Yes, I was talking to myself. Sometimes I do this aloud and sometimes I do it inside my head. Either way it helps me plan what I need to do."
3. The teacher points out "Ralph the Bear" posters. "My friend, Ralph, talks to himself, too. He uses these four questions to help him in lots of situations." Discuss these cue cards and Ralph's use of the four questions.
4. "Now I'm going to pretend I'm a student and I'll show you how I use Ralph's questions to

help me." Teacher models behavior and uses overt self-instruction. "What am I supposed to do? I need to get all my things ready for class. What are some plans? I'll need my pencils and paper at my desk. I'll keep my homework at my desk, too. How is my plan working? This is okay, but I want to sharpen my pencils and put my bookbag away. I'll do that now. How did I do? I'm all ready for school. I did a good job."

5. The teacher selects a student to act out the process of getting ready while the teacher says the verbalization.
6. Redirect the students' attention to the "Ralph" posters. The students all repeat the questions together.
7. The teacher chooses several students to model self-instruction by getting themselves ready for class and using self-talk to work through the process. The other students observe and listen to their comments. Afterward allow these children to repeat some of their statements that answered Ralph's questions. List these on the overhead projector.
8. The teacher asks the entire class to look at Ralph's posters again. This time they whisper the statements aloud.
9. The teacher selects half of the remaining students to get ready while whispering to themselves. She reminds them to use Ralph's questions and add their own answers. Add comments to the list on the overhead.
10. Repeat the process of whispered self-instruction with the rest of the class.
11. Repeat Ralph's final question, "How did I do?" and have the students compliment their work.
12. The teacher displays the "Am I prepared?" cue poster. She explains that it will be in the front of the room in the mornings to remind everyone to prepare for class. Ralph's questions remain on the wall.

Evaluation: The teacher evaluates by observing the students' participation in the activities. She also observes to see if they maintain the self-instruction on subsequent mornings.

Notes: This lesson is designed for use near the beginning of the year. However, prior to its use the students will need their supplies, and they will need to have some trust in the teacher in order to accept the idea.

Furthermore, the teacher needs to follow up and reinforce the lesson on subsequent mornings. The "Am I Prepared?" cue poster will only be displayed in the mornings. Finally, when morning preparation has become a routine task the children will discontinue whispering, the cue will no longer be needed, and follow-up lessons may be discontinued. Then cognitive self-instruction may be applied to a new area. Individuals who experience difficulty may need individual cues.

Day 2

Objective: Students practice using cognitive self-instruction to aid in listening and paying attention in class.

Materials: "I listen" cue mobile, posted classroom rules including "I listen and pay attention," overhead projector, crayons, small cards, Bobby Bear paper.

Time: approximately 45 minutes

Procedure:

1. Define "listening" and "paying attention" through the following discussion. The teacher points to the class rules and probes, "We have rules that say 'I listen and pay attention'. What is listening? What part of your body do you use when you're listening? Do we use anything besides our ears? What is 'pay-

ing attention'?" The teacher accepts and guides children's answers to establish that "We use our brain and other parts of our bodies to help us pay attention."

2. The teacher models an example and a nonexample. "OK, who would like to tell me something that happened to you? You can decide if I'm listening." The teacher models nonexample by not listening, looking at floor, wiggling, etc. "Do you think I was listening? How do you tell?" The teacher asks the child to repeat his story. This time she looks at the child, nods, shows interest, etc. Afterward she responds to the child's story and thanks him for helping. The class may discuss how we can tell if someone is listening.
3. The class proceeds to identify times when it is difficult to listen and pay attention. The teacher makes a list of students' suggestions on the overhead. These ideas will be used for scenarios throughout the lesson.
4. One answer will certainly be, "It's hard to listen when someone is talking to me, while the teacher is talking." The teacher models listening and talking to herself to help her pay attention. "What am I supposed to do? I need to listen to the teacher, so I'll understand this language lesson. I wish my friend would stop talking. I'll just ignore him. I'll keep looking at the teacher. I can talk to myself about what she's saying. Do I understand it? A telling sentence ends with a period. Yes. Good for me—I am listening."
5. The teacher models the verbalization for a child who is demonstrating the act of listening. Other children act as distractors, while the rest of the class observes.
6. The entire class becomes actively involved at this point. The teacher states the examples of self-talk and then students repeat them aloud. This familiarizes the children

with types of appropriate self-statements.

7. Before proceeding, another scenario is selected from the children's suggestions. (listening when I'm tired, listening when I have a stomach ache, etc.) One child is chosen to role-play the situation using overt self-instruction and showing the appropriate behavior.
8. "Now we're going to play a game. We're going to see if you can listen—even when others are trying to distract you." Distribute bear paper and crayons. Ask children who have already modeled to serve as distractors. You may also play lively music in the background as a distraction. Explain to the students, "I am going to tell you how to color this paper, but I'll only say each direction one time. While I'm talking, your friends will try to distract you. If you can talk to yourself in a whisper voice it will help you listen and pay attention to the directions. If you don't let your friends distract you, you win." Halfway through the directions, the teacher stops. She reminds the children it is a game and their papers don't have to be perfect. She suggests talking silently to themselves to see if they can still beat the distractors.

<u>Directions for coloring Bobby Bear</u>:

1. Bobby Bear has big blue eyes. They're just as pretty when he cries.
2. He has pink inside each ear. (His aunt always rubs them and says, "Oh you little dear!").
3. Trace Bobby's mouth and make it bright red. This is where he always gets fed.
4. Bobby Bear has a little black nose. Where the honey is, it always knows.
5. Bobby has a little brown button on his belly. Behind it, is where he keeps his jelly.
6. Draw Bobby a little t-shirt. On this he may get a little dirt.

7. Color his shirt nice and blue. His dad just bought it and it's brand new.
8. On his feet Bobby wears tennis shows that are bright green. He leaves footprints everywhere he's been.
9. Bobby Bear is wearing orange shorts. He puts these on whenever he play sports.
10. Up in the sky is a big yellow sun. Whenever the sun is shining Bobby Bear likes to run and have fun!

When the children finish with Bobby Bear, discuss the game. Was it fun? Was it difficult to listen and pay attention? List their self-talk statements on the overhead projector. Go through the directions again and let students check to see how many they got right. Emphasize positive reinforcement and that every correct mark means "I was listening." Exhibit the cue mobile. Explain that this will remind everyone to listen and pay attention when they look at it. Explain that they can make their own "cue cards" to help them with listening. The cards may have words or pictures or statements that remind them to pay attention. While the children make cards, the teacher circulates, assists students, and praises their efforts.

Evaluation: In order to evaluate children's understanding of the process of self-instruction consider their participation in the activities. Did they contribute comments? Did they demonstrate self-instruction (overt, faded, covert)? Did they make an appropriate cue card?

Notes: Do not evaluate by grading the Bobby Bear activity because failure may indicate an inability to follow or a misunderstanding of the directions, rather than lack of understanding of self-instruction.This is an initial activity for training children to use cognitive self-instruction to aid in listening. It is certainly not the only lesson taught. I know that more practice is necessary to incorporate the process into the child's way of monitoring concentration.

Other teacher comments about CSI strategies to promote excellent school work habits:

> *Teacher A*: I begin my math lessons by asking students to think before they speak. They are to ask themselves two questions, "Have I thought through my answer?" and "Did I raise my hand?" To help them remember I show a picture of a forgetful elephant with the cue question. This sparks their interest.In general they remembered to raise their hands and give good, thoughtful answers. Prior to CSI cueing, I had a problem with students raising their hands when they really did not have an answer ready.
>
> *Teacher B*: I used a cognitive self-instructional strategy with Felicia, a student in a small reading group. In previous lessons, this student had problems staying in her seat and on task (no major disruptions, just little annoyances). I designed a colorful, octagonal-shaped STOP sign, with a stem to hold it by. I laminated it. Prior to the lesson, I told her that I was going to try to help her stay in her seat during group time. I asked her to look at the sign and remember to stop and think before she got out of her seat. We read the word STOP together, and she agreed to try to remember. Felicia really enjoyed having something special and different from the other children. She was very consistent in remembering to look at the sign and soon made a game out of it. When she forgot and started to hop out of her chair, she would look at her sign and say "STOP" very deliberately, then sit back down on her own. It helped her remember the rules and take responsibility for her actions.

The final classroom teacher entry comes from a teacher who wanted to use CSI ideas to improve the self-concept of her early elementary students.

Teacher: Susan Marshall

Goal: To institute a CSI program to improve the self-concept of early elementary students.

My objectives for the students are: (1) they believe they each are special, (2) they realize that what they say to themselves affects the way they are, (3) they understand that although others have an effect on them, they can control what they believe. Inner speech is beneficial at school, at home, and in social situations. The class is exposed to all three types of situations.

The beginning instruction is modeling—first by an adult, followed by a peer volunteer. After an introduction, explain that what we think about ourselves makes us what we are. I show them what I mean by an example of how I used to talk to myself and believe what other people said about me.

Teacher modeling: "I made bad grades on my math tests. When I told my mother, she said 'It's OK, you're just not a math person. I didn't do well in math either.' I thought to myself, 'I can't do well in math because I am not a math person. It runs in the family.' Now I say to myself, 'I know I need to check my paper. Everyone makes careless mistakes. I can make an A in math if I try. I am a smart person.' Now I am successful in math. I did make an A."

Following this illustration is a peer example of how he/she talked to him/herself in a negative and positive way, and how this changed behavior. With the peer actor's permission, I tape his example of positive talk for a learning center. Other activities for the center include:

- a garbage bag for old self-talk
- a group poem for the bulletin board following the pattern "I used to think ________, but now I know ________."
- write a success story about yourself 5 years from now to be aired on the classroom news.

Small groups get together and share "the nicest thing ever . . . (1) they did for somebody else, (2) somebody did for them, and (3) they did for themselves. These examples can be from home, school, or with friends. Each group shares one example with the class.

A game for practicing positive self-talk to improve self-concept is "Confidence Thief." The children imagine the face of someone who has put them down in the past and say, "No matter what you say or do to me, I'm still a worthwhile person." When they get used to saying this, I interject common negative labels after which they say the aforementioned sentence with conviction (i.e., You forgot your lunch again? That's typical). Children respond with "No matter what you say or do to me, I'm still a worthwhile person."

Another method of practicing is a discussion on how to finish an incomplete scenario (i.e., what do you say to yourself when (1) you drop your tray in the lunch room and everyone applauds, (2) you are the last person picked on a team in P.E., (3) you forget your homework and are donned "class spacecase"?). These situations are sure to test one's self-confidence.

To remind them of their incredible self-worth, the students write a paragraph on their "assets." This goes into their positive folder to be read whenever they need a boost.

To share our achievements with others, we divide into small groups and exchange stories of recent successes.

Students may need to be cued often (different times for different people). For this reason, we keep our positive notebooks in our desks at all times. At the beginning of the year everyone writes something they think is special or nice about each person in that person's notebook. Older children could later change these to "I" statements. The "My Assets" paragraph and any recent success stories also go in the positive book. Any time a student's self-confidence begins to fall, he/she can take out the positive folder and read praises.

A cue for self-esteem, which requires overt self-talk is the "Magic Box." The magic box contains important people in the world (a mirror). When a child looks into the box, he/she says, "I am an important person in the world."

A constant reminder of self-worth is the "IALAC" (I am lovable and capable) sign students pin to their shirts. Each time they let themselves believe a negative statement about themselves, they must rip off part of their sign. The object is to complete the day with the whole sign.

The result of this teaching is an awareness of feelings, attitudes, and beliefs they previously didn't realize. Our class becomes "closer" as a result of the students increased respect for themselves and each other. The high self-esteem in my classroom also aids in the learning of subject matter. The children are more willing to take chances—and if they fail, are able to rebound faster.

Other teacher comments about the use of CSI for early elementary include:

> *Teacher A*: I have a child in my class who is constantly asking questions. He asks questions just to get my attention; he already knows the answer when I probe. He and I discussed how many questions seemed reasonable for the morning and then again for after lunch. Together, we decided five questions for each half of the school day. I gave him a strip of paper with the numerals *1, 2, 3, 4, 5* across it. When he decides to use one of his five questions he crosses out a numeral, beginning with the *5*. In this way, he keeps up with how many more questions he is allowed for that time period. This has really worked well. I am getting so much more work done now and so is the student.

Middle School

The CSI strategies presented in the previous section (i.e., early elementary) may be adapted for use with some older students. The average middle school student is very capable of learning CSI strategies to aid memory, comprehension, problem solving, and self-control. Indeed, most of the research on reciprocal teaching to promote reading comprehension monitoring had junior high students as subjects.

<u>Predicted outcomes of the CSI program</u>

1. Implementation of self-communication in each academic area. Students become more indepen-

dent learners as a result of using self-talk in the classroom. There are fewer problems with listening and understanding directions, questions that have already been answered being asked again, and more academic success for *all* students.

2. Implementation of self-communication to change habits. After our initial presentation of self-talk and use of self-talk, students use it to change habits that are a problem to them. This is done on an individual basis. Much of the language of self-talk transfers from the initial encounter. In this phase, students learn to use self-statements that are written and tape talk to make these behavioral changes. As an ultimate goal, students become more stable adults because they make this a lifelong method of monitoring themselves.

   Students do not receive a formal evaluation of this project. They receive teacher feedback on a regular basis, probably once a week after the first month of implementation. Students also write an assessment of how, or if, the program is helping them and in what ways. The teacher holds individual conferences to talk about these assessments. This is especially important to do at the onset of the program. Students keep their assessments so that they can see the progression of their self-talk program.

Goal: Children gain an understanding of using self-communication to monitor work habits and assignments.

Unit Objectives:

1. The student identifies uses of self-talk and labels examples of self-talk as positive (helpful) or negative (not helpful).
2. The student writes self-talk of comic strip characters and explains the positive or negative effects of the self-talk.

3. The student role-plays positive uses of self-talk from teacher-given scenes.
4. The student writes daily self-talk in his or her diary.
5. The student designs and makes a mural entitled, "What Are You Saying to Yourself?"
6. In small groups, the student makes a list of sample self-talk in the four school-use areas.
7. The student uses group cue cards to monitor a mathematics assignment.
8. The student uses self-talk to monitor a day's worth of assignments in each academic area.

Teacher: Fran Abercrombie
Day 1

Objective: The student identifies uses of self-talk and labels them as positive (helpful) or negative (not helpful).

Materials: 3 x 5 index cards, pencils, chalkboard, chalk, self-talk handout

Procedure: The teacher says "Good morning boys and girls. I have something really exciting for you to learn. It takes us a while and it may seem kind of strange or unusual but, it is a strategy that helps you with your school work, as well as carries over and helps you at home and anywhere you go. Hopefully, it is something that will help you for the rest of your life. Remember to keep your minds open at all times and don't give up on me until you've heard all about this wonderful strategy."

Get the supply clerk to pass out the index cards. "Now boys and girls, I want you to think of times that you have talked to yourselves. Yes, I mean it. Think of times when you said things inside yourself so that no one could hear you, or times that you said things to yourself outloud. Everyone does it, so don't think that you're weird. Alright, now listen to this scene and tell me something that you might say to yourself. Talking to yourself is different than thinking. Remember I want to know what you would say to yourself, not what you would think.

"The class is coming in from P.E. You are a little upset because you fell and skinned your knee at P.E. playing baseball. Some of the kids laughed at you. Now you've almost made it back to the classroom and you fall up the steps to the classroom and hurt your knee again. What do you say to yourself?"

The teacher listens to and discusses students' oral responses to make sure that they understand the difference between talking to yourself and thinking.

"Now, let's listen to another scene, but this time I want you to write what you would say to yourself on the notecard that you have on your desk.

"You talked your mom into letting you wear your new pair of pants to school today. You promised that you would not get them dirty or let anything happen to them. During recess you got really involved in a soccer game and accidentally fell in a puddle. Your new pants are soaked with mud. What do you say to yourself?"

After students' responses are written, they share their responses and some of them are listed on the chalkboard. The teacher also shares a response. Responses are discussed as to whether the response is a helpful one to solve the problem or not helpful in solving the problem.

"Sometimes we say things to ourselves that help us to handle the situation that we are in but most times we say things that are very negative and are not helpful at all in handling the situation we are in.

"Take for instance if I am trying to work this math problem, 142 + 986 =______. What are some things I can say to help me and what are some things that I can say that won't help at all? Listen and see if you can figure them out."

Sample dialogue would include: "You know you're not good in math." "Why did Miss Abercrombie pick me to do this problem, I can't do this." "Now, let's see. I must start adding in my one's column, 2 + 6 = 8. Good." "This is too hard." "I hope I get this problem right because if I don't I will be embarrassed."

The class then discusses the dialogue and cites helpful and unhelpful examples of self-talk.

The teacher then uses Meichenbaum's Five-Step Instructional Model with another math problem using only helpful self-talk. Students discuss the difference between this problem and the other problem. Students are given a sheet that has sample self-talk and labels the self-talk as helpful or unhelpful (see Self-Talk I below).

This sheet is discussed in terms of why each statement is labeled as either helpful or unhelpful and what kind of effect each statement has on the person who says it. We also turn each unhelpful statement into a helpful one.

Self-Talk I:

"I'm just no good at Science. It's much too hard for me to understand."

"Let's see. I know I can do this; I'll just take my time and figure it out."

"Boy, I did great on that Spelling test. I only missed one word."

"I hate being here today. I wish that I was still at home in the bed."

"What were we supposed to do next? I'm so stupid. I can't remember anything."

"Next I need to finish my Social Studies questions and I'll be almost finished with all my seatwork."

A second middle school teacher wanted to teach his eighth graders the language of metacognition, as he called it. His lesson plans are presented below:

Teacher: Ronnie Head

Goals: Students become "aware" of the concept of metacognition. Students understand the various uses and importance of metacognition in the students' and the teacher's world. Students understand the power of helpful and unhelpful self-talk in their personal lives.

Objectives:

1. The student is able to identify the definition, types, and uses of metacognition.
2. The student is able to identify what is meant by locus of control, and the words *internal* and *external* in regard to locus of control, also the type of student who functions best (internal or external).
3. The student is able to demonstrate—overtly, faded, and covertly—for at least one target classroom behavior.
4. The student is able to identify an appropriate classroom behavior for each inappropriate classroom behavior listed and discussed.
5. The student is able to produce at least one appropriate self-statement to inhibit inappropriate target behaviors, one appropriate self-statement to initiate appropriate behavior and one appropriate self-statement to reinforce appropriate behavior.
6. The student is able to produce appropriate statements listed in Objective 5 on cue cards.
7. The student is able to explain the theory of verbal self-regulation.
8. The student is able to give examples of the result of helpful and unhelpful self-talk either from their own experiences or someone else's.
9. The student completes a personal improvement project by changing their unhelpful self-talk (see Helmstetter, 1987).

Day 1

Introduction: Metacognition is a concept describing how students can "check on or spy on" their own thinking.

1. Meta means "being aware of."
2. Cognitive means "to think or ponder."
3. An example of a metacognitive experience would be if you found yourself reading a book and you begin to notice you are not understanding what you read.
4. Another example of metacognitive experience would be . . . (I would allow the students to come up with another example on their own after listening to and/or participating in a classroom discussion.)

Procedure: Students and teachers engage in a discussion about the use of metacognition to become aware of and control one's own thinking. When we "think about our own thinking" during instruction, we can help ourselves to understand, or to know when we are not understanding something.

In small groups the students develop at least five school examples when they realized for themselves that they were not understanding something. What class (academic subject) was it? What did students say to themselves? What did students do to help themselves understand (e.g., reread, etc.)?

Use these examples to teach additional CSI strategies (verbal rehearsal, dyadic instruction, reciprocal teaching, and Manning's CSI approach for self-management).

Note: This teacher did not detail how objectives 2-9 were to be accomplished.

The final teacher example for middle schoolers is a CSI project to help students improve their self-concepts and change locus of control to a more internal perspective (i.e., accepting more responsibility for one's own successes and failures). The following is a teacher's first hand account of that CSI program:

Teacher: Christine Fuentes

My objectives for this project are mainly affective. I want my students to first become aware of what they "think" about themselves and who they believe is responsible for their behavior (themselves).

Second, I want to help my students to begin thinking about what is special about themselves and initiate helpful self-talk about behaviors they want to change.

Last, I want my students to practice helpful self-talk for solving school-related problems and to reinforce their own helpful self-talk.

Though this class includes many different types of students, I want to concentrate my efforts on those students who have had few academic successes because of lower mental capacities and who have poor self-concepts. I believe all students benefit from this project but by concentrating on this specific group of students I can build some success into their lives. Our current educational reforms are emphasizing all the "wrong" ideas about education as far as these children are concerned. I hope that by improving their self-concepts and giving them greater control over their own learning they will be better able to survive in a system that usually means failure.

According to Meichenbaum (1977), Hanel in 1974 changed the attribution style of fourth graders who had marked fear of failure and poor academic records through self-instruction. He was able to teach the students to talk to themselves differently, to problem solve and to change their motivational style and academic performance. My project accomplishes some of these same goals by emphasizing self-talk for a positive self-concept and for changing behaviors. A progressive outline for five sessions follow. Two sessions which include modeling are in full detail.

<u>Session One</u>: The purpose is to create an environment of self- and other-acceptance in the classroom. This will be done the first week of school.

Activities:

1. Circle Game Everyone sits in a circle including the teacher. Each person introduces the person before her and then herself. When introducing, she names the person and what that person can do well (i.e., My name is Christine. I play softball well. [Next] My name is Joan. I can write neatly. This is Christine, she plays softball well. [Next] This is Christine . . . This is Joan . . . My name is David and I am good at Math.) The game is done in an atmosphere of acceptance. If someone doesn't remember who she is introducing, that person gently reminds her. (Cumulative rehearsal metamemory strategy)

2. Silhouette of Self A silhouette of each student is made. The student then fills the silhouette with pictures, words, statements about self. These can be positive or negative. The focus is on learning about self and acceptance of self.

Session Two: The purpose of the session is to help the student focus on being unique and special.

Activities:

1. Teacher administers the Nowicki Strickland Locus of Control Scale (1973) instrument.
2. Teacher models why she feels special today. I give the students five statements of what I say to myself that helps me feel good.

I say these statements to the middle school students:

I am unique from the top of my head to the bottom of my toes.

I may sometimes sound like others and look like others, but I am not them. I am me!

I like how I feel. I like how I look. I like how I do things.

I can do anything I believe I can do! I can work hard and do great things. I can be the best me there is.

I smile a lot. I am happy and everyone knows it!

After modeling these statements and discussing times that I need to say them aloud (when people are mad at me, when I make mistakes, or when I am sad), I ask some students to discuss what they say to themselves to help them feel good and do good work.

As a class, we work on getting peer self-statements recorded on the board that we feel are positive and helpful.

I in turn have a peer put these statements on a tape to be put in the listening center for students to listen to and talk aloud along with. Because of Vygotsky's belief that internalization of verbal commands is critical to voluntary control of behavior, I encourage students to not only listen and talk with the tape, but to say these statements to themselves while they are working (softly and silently).

We use Meichenbaum's five steps for behavior control during this session and in subsequent sessions as needed (such as revising the tape or working on an individual problem).

<u>Session Three</u>: The purpose of this session is to have the students identify one positive behavior to initiate.

<u>Activities</u>:

1. Students use their journals to write about one thing (school related) that they were unable to do last year that they want to be able to do this year. The teacher helps students to identify a goal that is realistic and easily attainable.
2. The teacher introduces the Ralph Bear posters as a plan for reaching the goal. The teacher explains a goal she is working on and models as she works through each step:

   (a) What is my problem? "I want to be able to finish all my work and not worry about it." (goal-setting)

(b) What are some plans? "I can make a schedule—decide what has to be done and what can wait. I can organize my work." (guiding)

(c) How is my plan working? "This is not so easy, but I'm getting better. I am not worrying so much." (coping)

(d) How did I do? "I finished everything I had to do. That feels great." (reinforcing)

3. We discuss this in a group. Teacher asks if students have some examples to share. We role-play several examples.
4. Students are given a sheet with four sections so they can write their own self-talk statements. Teacher circulates to help students generate positive and helpful self-talk.
5. When finished with dialogue, students are encouraged to share aloud with small groups their self-talk or to practice alone if they prefer.
6. As a reminder, students are given blank cue cards. On these they write, "I can . . . "on one side and on the other draw a picture of themselves accomplishing their goal. I believe, as Helmstetter said of Level IV self-talk, if we depict ourselves with the new behavior long enough, then we believe it sooner or later.

<u>Session Four</u>: The purpose of this session is to reinforce the changes students are seeing in themselves.

<u>Activities</u>:

1. As students begin accomplishing goals and starting on others, they make "I cans" which they decorate on their own and fill with things they can do.
2. Students also make a collage of themselves which shows all their new changes and positive things about themselves.

<u>Session Five</u>: The purpose of this session is to focus on the "new me."

Activities:

1. Students will design a commercial for themselves. The commercials will advertise why it is great to be "me."
2. Teacher will administer the locus of control instrument again to the students.

From this point on through the next couple of months, the students learn to use the cognitive self-instruction strategies for other learning activities. The teacher introduces the four school uses of cognitive self-instruction and shows how Ralph fits in and can help us. Each section has peer-generated statements which are modeled, practiced, and cued. Lastly, the students work on projects that can be shared with other students to help them. They devise comic strips and cue cards that show positive, self-regulating self-talk.

After the completion of these phases, the teacher again administers a locus of control scale to be compared to the pretest and the one-month instrument. I have seen a gradual trend towards more internal control in my students over the three-month period. Moving towards internal control in my students has the same effects as on adults in that my students become more confident, develop greater self-esteem, have lower anxiety levels and believe that they have control over the events in their lives.

These changes are much easier for some students than for others. Students who have already experienced success in school and have positive self-concepts find it easier to take the leap of faith to believe in this process and try it. Students who are starting without these successes and who are on the bottom of the self-concept scale can be motivated to try this process, however. They can begin to feel good about who they are and these feelings are manifested in increased self-control of behavior and increased academic motivation in the classroom.

I am very excited about the research and literature presented on cognitive self-instruction. I have long believed that the best gift we can give our students is the belief that they alone are responsible for who they are and what they do with their lives. Cognitive self-instruction gives students a plan and a process for accomplishing this, instead of just hearing a teacher "preach" it. Cognitive self-instruction is a means that can easily fit into an elementary school teacher's busy schedule and not interfere with the "product" we "must" teach. I believe that if our students learn a reliable process for learning early in life that it will carry them through all of the events of their lives. I think that in the face of QBE and other present educational reforms, which focus on the "product" regardless of the individual, that if, as teachers we do not concentrate on a process for learning we will be hurting the students we want to help most with our reforms. What's most exciting though, is: if teachers believe in CSI for their own lives, then they can't help but teach it to their students.

A middle school teacher used cognitive self-questioning during a language experience lesson and during a math lesson. She made the following comments:

Teacher A: During my language experience lesson I found that when the children were giving the group sentences, they would all speak at once. So, during my next language experience lesson I used the CSI cue cards. I wrote the cue on a piece of paper and told them to ask themselves before speaking, "Is another person speaking?" I also told them the purpose for it: that everyone in a previous group had all given the sentences at one time and no one could hear. They responded well! I also used this during my math lesson when I was questioning.

Also during my language experience, we were working on using descriptive words in the ghost story we were writing. I showed them another cue card that said, "Before giving a word, stop, ask yourself: is the word a descriptive word?" Students improved by giving me descriptive words, instead of nouns, etc.

Cognitive self-instruction worked really well for me. I believe that it helps children to think and monitor themselves and their work. I used the following cue cards:

Before Speaking

STOP

Ask Myself:

Is another person speaking?

Before giving a word for the story

STOP

Ask Myself:

Is the word a descriptive word?

Secondary/College

Adolescents and young adults often do not know important CSI strategies to aid their own learning. The college students I teach often do not know helpful ways to study. They are unfamiliar with verbal rehearsal techniques, collaborative problem solving, and such. They too, profit from modeling and practicing CSI techniques. However, they do not tend to need cueing as much as elementary and some middle school age students. The general trend (for the average learner) is that with age, the need for cueing of CSI diminishes. Typically, high school students and college students are able to apply CSI strategies they learn about, without having to see/hear the strategies modeled or having to practice them to a great extent. It should be noted however, that although not always essential, modeling and practicing CSI can be very facilitating, even for older learners. One very bright college student said to me: "The best professor I ever had thought out loud to us about the content we were learning. He asked himself questions and then answered them. He allowed us to experience his thought processes. Most professors are not able to do that. I learned so much more because he was brave enough to share his 'think aloud' with a class full of college students."

Nielsen (1984) has a helpful, short publication entitled "Teaching Adolescents the Skills of Self-Management." She says that often teachers are skeptical about promoting independence in youth. The teachers feel threatened by responsible, assertive youth who know how to manage their own lives and learning. Often the compliant, submissive youth is reinforced. Nielsen provides strategies for thinking/self-management skills: (1) teach adolescents to set their own realistic, attainable goals, (2) students need to set goals slightly beyond their present level of performance, (3) if needed, students develop behavior self-checklists to help guide their plans of action, (4) students set self-reinforcement schedules and penalties for their self-management plan, (5) students write self-messages as cues to reach goals (e.g., "Open me to graduate" on a textbook), (6) students learn to write positive self-talk messages to replace negative self-talk.

Some self-talk suggestions for adolescents to use when studying:

"Not studying cannot possibly improve my grade."

"I do better on tests that I study for."

"I spend time every day going over the information."

"I do not let distractions disturb me while I am studying."

"I do well on the test."

"I remember most answers to the questions."

"I recall this information if I spend time studying it aloud over and over."

"I verbalize questions aloud that I do not understand."

"I have the ability to get these questions correct if I will put forth extra effort."

"I can do it!"

"I do not expect myself to be perfect."

"I just do the best that I can."

"I am relaxed while studying."

"I am relaxed while taking the test."

Practice Sheet for Changing Negative Self-Talk

1. Describe the situation:

____

____

____

____

____

2. Describe the negative self-talk you usually say to yourself about this situation.

____

____

____

____

____

3. Write a counter message (positive, helpful) for each of the negative self-statements written above:

____

____

____

____

____

____

Adults

Adults who are deficient in metacognitive processes may be taught CSI strategies in the same manner that high school and college students are taught. Adults need to know, for example, that verbal rehearsal aids retention, self-questioning aids comprehension, verbal collaboration with a more experienced peer aids problem solving, and helpful self-talk facilitates self-control. In addition adults may be interested in a program by Tice (1980) entitled "New Age Thinking: For Achieving Your Potential." This program is very adult oriented and contains twenty-four videotapes. One of the videotape programs has to do with the "self-talk cycle." This particular program focuses on becoming acutely aware of the harmful effects of negative self-talk, how to change it to positive self-talk, and how to talk to self responsibly, choosing intentionally the facilitative self-talk which leads to success, not failure.

Cognitive Analysis: Definition of Terms

Cognitive modeling of oral directions Mentally planning how to respond on an assigned task. These mental (cognitive) deliberations are performed (in first person) by speaking the plans aloud while students, who must complete the task, listen to the cognitive model.

Collaborative, dyadic instruction When an experienced member of a two-person unit verbally structures, guides, and reinforces learning and/or problem solving for a less experienced member. The collaboration initially begins with external regulation with the intent of progressing to verbal self-regulation.

Giving oral directions Externally directing the step-by-step procedure for completing an assigned task. Directions are stated in second person and often are simply read to the students with no further explanation or comment.

Language of metacognition Using the vocabulary and terms related to metacognition on a daily basis until they become automatic and natural for students to use and understand. Metacognitive terms should be defined and then used often (e.g., self-monitor, self-coping, self-reinforcement, mentally check, verbal self-guidance, etc.).

Vocabulary of self-control Words and terms that denote internal perspectives and control. Speaking to students as if they are the ones responsible for their classroom behavior (e.g., Tell yourself: Wait my turn).

Cognitive Synthesis: A Summary

Five age divisions (i.e., preschool, early elementary, middle school, secondary/college, and adults) are designated for purposes of providing sample lesson plans to teach CSI strategies. These sample lesson plans were written originally for a specific group of students; therefore modifications, deletions, and extensions are expected before they are applied to another group of students. It should be noted that some lesson plans for a certain age group classification may also be appropriate for other age groups as well. These lesson plan examples are offered to present the flavor of teaching CSI strategies and to stimulate teachers to develop their own CSI lesson plans.

10

Starting and Maintaining a Cognitive Self-Instruction Program

Overview

The content of this chapter is aimed at answering the following question: "How do I set up a CSI program in my own classroom?" The following steps are suggested and explained.

- Step 1 Provide introductory CSI strategies
- Step 2 Provide a self-communication classroom environment
- Step 3 Take action to diminish or eliminate negative, task irrelevant self-communication
- Step 4 Incorporate CSI philosophy and perspectives into academic subject matter instruction
- Step 5 Implement CSI as a classroom management option to promote social responsibility and productive school work habits
- Step 6 Transfer CSI use for academics, social responsibility, and school work habits from the school to the home.

Suggestions are also given to teach students how to (1) prepare for studying, (2) organize study sessions, (3) study, and (4) evaluate the preparation, organization, and implementation of study sessions.

A case study of an off-task, nonattentive fourth grade girl is outlined. This student was engaged in a year-long application of CSI to teach her cognitive self-management skills. This CSI program was very successful in helping this particular student become a productive, happy, self-confident student. CSI materials (including response sheets for collecting on-task behaviors, student and parent interviews, display and instructional materials) are presented as stimuli for teachers as they develop their own CSI programs.

Self-Questions

1. Knowledge. List the six steps recommended by Manning for CSI implementation in a school setting.

2. Comprehension. Choose three of the six steps and explain what is involved (e.g., activities) in the implementation of each.

3. Application. Describe ways to prepare a group of students for independent study sessions to be conducted outside of the school context (e.g., how to collect materials, organize, study, and evaluate their readings) for tests and other school assignments.

4. Analysis. Diagram in a matrix (with focusing attention, following through, and finishing work [down the side] and modeling, practicing and cueing CSI [across the top]) CSI activities for each cell. For example, what CSI activities will be planned for modeling to aid focusing attention behavior?

5. Synthesis. Develop an argument for using CSI as a classroom management option. Present this argument to someone who is sold on traditional behavior modification.

6. Evaluation. Judge the advantages and disadvantages of requiring that CSI be instituted in all schools in a certain school system.

The questions related to CSI that I am asked most frequently are "How do I get CSI strategies started in my classroom?" and "Where do I begin?" In this chapter, some suggestions are provided for implementing a CSI type program in classrooms.

Since CSI may be used to improve memory, comprehension, problem solving, and self-control, teachers must decide if they want to focus on one, several, or all of these simultaneously. I recommend using some generic introductory activities first, followed by the incorporation of CSI into the educational fabric of academic subject matter (e.g., verbal rehearsal when teaching spelling, reciprocal teaching for reading comprehension, and dyadic instruction for problem solving). In addition, from the beginning of the year, I would implement CSI as a classroom management system to foster student self-control and responsibility. Each of these specific lines of endeavor are discussed in previous chapters and are not repeated again; however, a suggested chronological order of events is the focus for this chapter.

To introduce CSI to any age group the following generic strategies are recommended. As with all the CSI strategies mentioned in this book, modification may be needed for specific groups of learners.

Step 1: Provide Introductory CSI Strategies

Strategy 1. Ask children if they ever talk to themselves. When do they talk to themselves? List on the board or a poster examples of what they say to themselves.

Strategy 2. Share with children examples of adult self-communication. For example: "I tell myself to slow down and read carefully when the material is difficult for me to understand. I ask myself, Does this make sense to me?" Adults may tape their self-communication to share with children. Use a variety of situations. Self-communicate when:

1. Following a difficult recipe
2. Traveling an unfamiliar route
3. Balancing a checkbook
4. Reading a tedious assignment
5. Typing a long letter
6. Completing a laborious task
7. Finding a lost object
8. Looking up a dictionary word, phone number, etc.
9. Building a model
10. Programming on the computer

Strategy 3. Audiotape examples of children using self-communication while performing a school task. You might ask children to speak to themselves aloud as they solve a math problem. Play the tape and point out how the self-communication helped solve the problem. Students who use self-guiding speech to stay on task and/or to stay in their seats may be asked to talk aloud, in order to model for others. Play the tape for your group, pointing out how the self-guiding speech aided children in performing the target behaviors.

Strategy 4. Talk to the children about the four school uses of self-communication and give suggestions orally and/or on posters to remind them when to utilize self-communication. Examples are taken from actual third grade self-communication posters.

Four School Uses of Self-Communication

While listening to directions:

Do I have all the information I need?
Do I understand?
I don't get this.
This will be easy (hard) for me.

While planning work:

If I don't daydream, I'll be able to do this.
If I really work hard, I can do this.
If I quit staring at my girlfriend, I can finish on time.
This is going to be fun to do.

While working:

I'm working hard at this.
I'm not doing so well on this.
Slow down!
I need to ask a question about this.
I need to quit staring out the window and get back to work if I'm going to finish.

While checking work:

Does this look right to me?
I need to do this one over.
I'm getting this.
Can I do it a better way?

Teachers may want to give several suggestions for each use and then encourage students to contribute their own. A poster for each of the four uses, displayed around the room, has been reported by teachers to be helpful reminders to students.

Strategy 5. Introduce games and activities with incomplete information. Remind children to ask themselves the following questions when listening to directions: Does this make sense? Is anything missing? What's missing? Interject the incomplete directions with complete directions to insure that children can discriminate between the two sets of directions. Markman (1977) provided directions for a card game and a magic trick with missing directions which were crucial to enacting the game and trick. For complete information, please refer to Markman's work. Briefly, she gave the following incomplete directions (provided below) for the game. Then she asked the students if they could play. By doing this she could tell which students were able to monitor their own listening comprehension.

Card Game (Markman, 1977, p. 989):

We each put our cards in a pile. We turn over the top card in our pile. We look at cards to see who has the special card. Then we turn over the next card in our pile to see who has the special card this time. In the end the person with the most cards wins the game.

Strategy 6. Children draw pictures of themselves as they communicate with themselves at school. Sheets of drawing paper, divided into four sections are given to children. They are asked to draw themselves at school while listening, while planning work, while working, and while checking work. Children may be told to use cartoon-like bubbles over their heads to write in what they are saying to self. After the drawings are complete, the sections are cut apart, and a mural for each of the four areas (listening, planning, working, and checking), are displayed in the classroom. With younger children (K–2) it may be more appropriate to deal with one of the four areas in isolation. A first grade teacher who has found this strategy helpful introduces self-communication for listening first, and works in this area for approximately one month before she proceeds through planning, working, and checking in that order.

Strategy 7. Save cartoon-strips. The dialogue between characters is blanked out by gluing white paper shapes over the bubbles. These may be laminated for repeated use. Children write in what the characters may be saying to themselves. After the cartoons are completed, children may categorize their responses into one the four areas: listening, planning, working, or checking. In some cases, there may be overlap and this needs to be explained to the children. For example, while listening, children may use "What's missing?" and while checking they may also use "What's missing?" In fact this particular question may be appropriate for all four areas. The context of the cartoon usually provides the meaning necessary for children to tell you if their character is talking to themselves while listening, planning, working, and/or checking.

Strategy 8. Have one student speak aloud to him/herself as directions are given for making a peanut butter and jelly sandwich. Audiotape the self-communication. Play it back for the class, stopping the recorder at intervals to discuss whether the self-communication is self-questioning, self-reinforcement, or goal-setting (Flavell, 1976). An "other" category may be needed for self-communication for dialogue that does not seem to fit appropriately into any of these three.

Examples taken from actual dialogue:

What do I do next? (self-questioning)
I'm hungry. (other)
That worked okay. (self-reinforcement)
Is this the right one? (self-questioning)
I need to finish this. (goal setting)

Younger students (K–2) may have difficulty using classification systems. It will depend on the intellectual level of your children. Even some older children may have difficulty with this assignment. As the teacher, you will be in a better position than I, to determine the appropriateness of this strategy for your children.

Strategy 9. Have students keep a log of what they say to themselves during one school day or portion of the day. The teacher must remind and provide time for this activity. A learning center on self-communication has worked effectively for some teachers. Give a cognitive task at the center, teach children to turn on the tape recorder and record themselves as they talk through the task. Transcribe the statements and questions-to-self on a log sheet. Classify, if appropriate for four school uses and/or self-questioning, self-reinforcement, goal setting, self-guiding, or self-coping.

Strategy 10. Periodically encourage rote-practice of self-communication when performing a school task, such as a typical spelling lesson. Students are shown posters of suggested self-communication. Before starting the lesson, review the four posters (Strategy 4) for listening, planning, working, and checking. After students have listened to directions, stop, ask students if they remembered to use self-communication. Remind them again to look at the posters and use the statements and questions as they prepare to work, while working, and while checking. When students hand in their spelling, ask them to tell you an example of self-communication they used when checking over their work. Many students finish work and do not spend any time proofing what they have done. Self-communication habits must be encouraged and deliberately addressed by the classroom teacher if students are to become proficient at regulating their own behavior.

Strategy 11. Students complete Self-Communication booklets. These may include compiling drawings, cartoons, logs, examples of questions and statements typically used for listening, planning, working, and checking work. Very young children relate well to including pictures of animals, favorite characters, and magazine people talking to themselves. For children who cannot write, adults may transcribe the self-communication for them.

Strategy 12. Students who display inappropriate classroom behaviors such as talking-out, getting out of seat too often, etc., can use self-communication to aid in bringing their behaviors under control. Ask impulsive students to tell you what they might say to self when they are inclined to speak out or jump up. If they can think of nothing or will tell you nothing, suggest a statement, such as "Not now!" "Stay in my seat!" Write these words on an index card and tape it to the student's desk. If you believe this will embarrass students put a red dot on the card, give the card to students to keep, and place a matching red dot on their desk top. An extra benefit, probably the most important one, is that students are held responsible, and when their self-communication succeeds in bringing behavior into an appropriate classroom range, the students feel they have done it ALONE! The students use their own speech-to-self to help themselves. The teacher does not make the students stay in their seats. The students use their own speech-to-self to regulate classroom behavior. A sense of self-accomplishment is often the result.

Step 2: Provide A Self-Communication Classroom Environment

Having taught for seven years, I realize the concern about the noise level in classrooms if thirty students talk aloud to themselves. Depending on the age level of students, and the difficulty level of tasks, all the students will not need to talk aloud. Teach students to whisper if they need to talk aloud through a problem. If a particular student is having difficulty with a problem, provide a self-communication corner or section of the room. Make it attractive and comfortable; perhaps a large chair, couch or bathtub with pillows. Allow students to go there to talk through a problem to themselves. They can return to their seats when the problem has been solved. Let the students see teachers using the "self-communication corner" at times. Teachers should model for students how to talk aloud through very difficult problems. Students who have been told to be quiet since entering school may be reluctant to talk aloud. It is also socially unacceptable to be heard talking aloud to one's self. In the right environment with a determined teacher, these factors can be overcome.

Step 3: Take Action to Diminish or Eliminate Negative, Task Irrelevant Self-Communication

Research evidence supports that productive workers use more positive/task relevant self-talk; while nonproductive workers use more negative/task irrelevant self-talk. Therefore the following recommendations are suggested:

1. The negative self-talk more than likely originated from students' prior social interactions. Before students label themselves "stupid," some other person suggests that particular label to them. Therefore, teachers need to monitor what they say to students. What we as teachers say to them about themselves today, they will internalize and repeat to themselves, about themselves, tomorrow.

2. Insure successful experiences for every student in order to provide positive verbal interaction between teacher and student. Tell students their strengths. This external verbalization becomes internal verbalization later.

3. Interrupt students' negative self-talk. Tell them it is unacceptable to talk to themselves in that manner. Help students substitute a neutral, task relevant self-statement and then a positive, task relevant self-statement. Teachers do not allow one student to call another student a disparaging name; however, we often overlook disparaging self-reference. Such self-statements are perhaps causing equal or more negative results than are the names called by someone else. Let students know that the teacher will not tolerate negative labels applied to others or to themselves.

4. Teacher models neutral/positive task relevant self-talk while performing tasks such as writing on the board (e.g., "All the work is on the board. I did not leave out anything, did I? Let me check once more."). Tell the students that you are guiding your actions by mentally planning/talking to yourself about the tasks.

5. Audiotape and/or videotape peers who have demonstrated neutral/positive, task relevant self-talk during independent school tasks. Use this tape at a center on "School Work Habits" as an appropriate model.

6. Role-play appropriate neutral/positive task relevant self-task after the teacher presents typical classroom scenarios (e.g., "You have thirty more minutes to finish your seatwork and you feel panicked because you don't think you can finish. What would be helpful things to say to yourself at a time like this?").

7. Have students, experiencing poor self-management say orally or write helpful self-talk for themselves to use when focusing, following through, and/or finishing their independent tasks. Drawings of self-portraits with appropriate self-talk may also be completed by students.

8. Have these students self-record for themselves their on/off task behaviors and also their corresponding self-talk. Use a timer or a tape with earphones with intermittent tones recorded. At the sound of the tone, students stop, write down what they were saying to themselves and whether they were on or off task. If they were "on," they proceed by saying, "Good for me!." If they were "off," they say, "I need to move on now."

9. Use self-directed rules (e.g., Focus my attention promptly) instead of externally oriented rules (Focus your attention promptly). The students read the self-directed rules, find them more personal and aimed directly at themselves. Use "I" and "my," instead of "you" and "your." When very young elementary students (K–2) hear/read externally spoken/written rules they often assume that they are meant for everyone except them (e.g., "Finish all *your* work" not "I should finish all *my* work").

10. Cue students to remind them to use neutral/positive task relevant self-talk via cue cards (Camp, Blom, Hebert, & Doorninck, 1977; Palkes, Stewart, & Kahana, 1968).

Teachers willing to invest time to eliminate negative, task irrelevant self-talk and provide neutral/positive task relevant self-talk in its place, may be helping more than they realize. Not only should the student improve engaged academic time, with by-products of higher achievement and self-esteem (Berliner, 1987); but even more importantly the student may break out of a negative pattern of self-talk with its by-products of panic, stress, and depression (Ellis & Harper, 1975). In short, the teacher may have encouraged a lifelong habit of positive self-talk which can improve the quality of life (Butler, 1981; Helmstetter, 1986).

Step 4: Incorporate CSI Philosophy and Perspectives into Academic Subject Matter Instruction

The rate at which CSI is incorporated into subject matter teaching is left to the discretion and good judgment of teachers. However some assimiliation of CSI into subject matter will occur naturally, especially if teachers are knowledgeable about CSI theory, research, and application. Some examples are:

Spelling: teach/use verbal rehearsal techniques

Mathematics: teach/use verbal rehearsal techniques and dyadic instruction

Reading: teach/use reciprocal teaching techniques

Language Arts: teach/use verbal rehearsal for vocabulary; teach self-questioning techniques

Social Studies & Science: teach/use collaborative problem solving in cooperative learning groups; teach verbal rehearsal, elaboration, keyword, etc., for terms, dates, etc.

Handwriting: teach self-questioning for self-evaluation

Step 5: Implement CSI as a Classroom Management Option to Promote Social Responsibility and Productive School Work Habits

Reread chapter 7 because the entire chapter deals with Step 5. Two additional classroom examples are provided below that illustrate the use of CSI: modeling, practicing, and cueing (Manning, chapter 7, this text). The first example is a kindergarten teacher's CSI plan to foster social responsibility in her classroom:

I have been a kindergarten teacher for four years and feel strongly about the effectiveness of CSI. Although the self-management skills for school work habits are not covered extensively until elementary grades, I do feel that teaching young children self-guidance is a very beneficial experience for them, as well as for me.

My introduction to self-communication includes starting with the questions, "Have you ever talked to yourself?" "When?" We talk about their experiences and then I tell them the importance of self-communication: For young children to have a better understanding of CSI we role-play different situations in which they employ self-talk.

I incorporate CSI with the rules in my classroom which are:

1. Use quiet voices
2. Follow directions

3. Play cooperatively
4. Keep hands, feet, and objects to myself
5. Use materials for their purpose

Then I integrate my rules with the five self-talk categories of CSI (i.e, problem defining, attention focusing, self-guiding, self-coping, and self-reinforcing). A child, for example, is about to take a toy from another child which breaks rule #3, above.

This child is verbally guided through the following process. Initially the teacher verbalizes these statements aloud as child plays Copy Cat and repeats each statement aloud, softly, and silently.

Problem defining: "I want to play with the toy. Should I take it from him?"
Attention Focusing: "I can take the toy, but is that following the rules?"
Self-guiding: "Just wait to play with the toy later."
Self-coping: "This is hard to do, but I know I must share."
Self-reinforcing: "I'm glad I didn't take the toy. I feel good about that."

This is time consuming; however children ultimately internalize a self-management system that causes them to grow in responsibility for themselves and others. It is much easier for me to say, "Leave that toy alone." But then the child has learned nothing about problem solving. Of course, sometimes I do say, "Leave that toy alone!" I use CSI as a tool in my classroom, not as something I am forced to do in each situation. I use the following ideas to teach self-talk to my kindergartners.

<u>Ideas for Teaching Self-Talk</u>

<u>Modeling</u>

1. Real Life Adult (Teacher) Modeling
2. Teacher Role-Play
3. Peer Modeling
4. Peer Role-Play

Practicing:

1. Games
   (a) Concentration Thief The teacher tries to distract the students from their academic work. The students need to say: "Don't look away," "Do my work," or "Keep my mind on my work."
   (b) Scenarios Read incomplete scenarios and have students finish them.

2. Art Activities
   Example: Drawing pictures to go with the heading "On My Own."
   Teacher writes down children's dictation of their self-talk to go with their pictures.

3. Cueing
   1. (Use I statements)
   2. Group posters
   3. Individual cue cards

4. Cueing examples (For kindergarten, cue cards and posters should be visual drawings or pictures along with words or no words.)

   Boy 1: He hates to make mistakes. Cue card: "I did my best!" "It's okay to make mistakes."
   Boy 2: He talks so much that he doesn't finish his work. Cue card: "I can finish my work!" "Stop—don't talk—WORK!"
   Boy 3: He rushes through his work. Cue card: "I did my best work."
   Girl 1: She doesn't like to share toys. Cue card: "I need to let other children play with this toy." "I shared and I feel good."

The second example is an eight-day intensive CSI program (Manning, 1988) for fostering exemplary school work habits (e.g., task persistence, task completion, etc.).

Day 1
Teacher models self-instruction to inhibit inappropriate classroom behaviors: five target inhibitory.

Students practice this self-instruction overtly, faded, and covertly through role-play. Example: "I do not shout out answers."

Day 2
Teacher models self-instruction to initiate appropriate classroom behavior: five target initiatory. Students practice self-instruction overtly, faded, and covertly through role-play. Example: "Raise my hand."

Day 3
Videotaped peers model self-instruction for inhibiting inappropriate behaviors: five target inhibitory. Students practice self-instruction overtly, faded, and covertly.

Day 4
Videotaped peers model self-instruction for initiating appropriate behaviors: five target initiatory. Students practice self-instruction overtly, faded, and covertly.

Day 5
Teacher presents typical classroom scenario and models cognitively staying on task. Students develop self-instructional statements and questions and role play staying on task: overt, faded, and covert for ten target behaviors. Use cue cards to practice self-instruction for the game Concentration Thief. Videotaped peers model self-instruction.

Day 6
Teacher reviews ten target behaviors on a poster, written in a self-directed manner, (e.g., Raise my hand, I concentrate). Students copy behaviors on cue cards. They also draw a picture of themselves, including self-instruction written inside a comic strip bubble over their heads and a reminder to themselves.

Day 7
Students work on an assignment. They practice using the cue cards (Day 6) during class scenarios described by the teacher. Each of the ten target behaviors are included. Students view videotaped peers using self-instruction for each target behavior. Students prac-

tice reading cue cards to self faded and covertly. Teacher models self-instruction for (a) listening to the teacher, (b) preparing to work, (c) while working, and (d) while checking over work.

Day 8
Students work on an assignment. They are reminded to engage in self-talk to stay on task. The teacher takes students singly outside the room to verify that, without prompting, each can produce an appropriate overt verbal self-instruction, similar to the ones that were introduced during Days 1–7.

To foster concentration specifically, Dagley (1988) offers CSI steps that have proved beneficial:

Goal: Students pay full attention to a task without becoming distracted in order to accurately and efficiently complete their work.

Ways to Begin:

1. Ask children the meaning of the word "concentrate."
2. To concentrate means to focus one's thoughts or give full attention to something.
3. Ask children to demonstrate how a person looks when he/she is concentrating.
4. Ask children to explain some things that they might think about inside their heads when trying to concentrate.
5. Ask children to give examples of distractions that may keep them from concentrating.
6. Tell children some things you say to yourself to help you concentrate.
7. Ask children to brainstrom several self-talk statements that would help them concentrate.
8. Have children construct their own cue card with their individualized self-talk statements.
9. Practice using the cue card to prompt concentration during an assigned task.
10. Provide corrective and positive feedback for self-management of one's own concentration.

Step 6: Transfer CSI Use for Academics, Social Responsibility, and School Work Habits from the School to the Home

As students gain skill in using CSI for self-direction at school, model, practice, and cue CSI for home. One of the most logical places to begin is "how to study." Students go into a variety of home environments from school. Therefore, the home use of CSI must be general enough to apply to a wide range of heterogeneity. For example, exercise caution when role-playing home scenarios because the stereotypic notions of families (e.g., a mom, a dad, 2 children, and a dog) are unrealistic in our society today (e.g., by 1990, 60 percent of all school age children will live in single parent homes). The transfer of CSI skills must focus on self-direction of study habits at home. Possible topics for home studying are as follows: using CSI to organize and prepare for studying; using CSI while studying, using CSI to evaluate one's own studying. Before students have assignments due and tests to respond to, teachers may need to think aloud and provide other classroom activities to promote good study habits away from school.

1. Preparation and Collection of Important, Related Study Materials

   (a) Teachers think aloud as students listen and take notes (if students are old enough). Always speak in first person in "think aloud." "I have a test in history tomorrow. What do I need to take home? Let's see, I'll need my history book. Got it, check. My notebook, got it. Check. etc."

   (b) Teachers present students with a self-checklist for study preparation. The checklist may be turned in at the end of each week for assessment and sent home for parents' signature. This way the students' self-guidance is evaluated, redirected if necessary, and/or positively reinforced.

   (c) Students practice self-talk aloud, whisper, silently in the classroom.

   (d) Make cue cards if needed.

2. Organization of Study Session

   (a) Teachers role-play how to organize for studying at home, using think aloud.
   Find a good place to study: "I need my own space to study."
   If the study place isn't quiet, model self-talk for coping with distraction: "This test is very important, I'll just pretend my room is empty of all noise."

Self-check as study materials are gathered: "Do I have everything I need?"

(b) Give students a list of self-check questions.

(c) Students practice self-talk aloud, whisper, silently in the classroom.

(d) Use self-checklist as a cue, if needed.

3. Studying the Information

(a)Teacher continues to model aloud:
"First decide how well I must know this information. Will I need to recognize it, recall it, explain it, extend it?
After thinking to myself the question above, I use verbal rehearsal to repeat what I must know: spelling words, terms, main points, etc.
Elaborate on the main ideas.
Outline the chapter for main points.
Underline or circle in red, the main points in my notes, etc."

(b)Students take turns role-playing how they study information by describing their steps first and then thinking aloud what they say to themselves while studying.

(c)After several student volunteers role-play CSI while studying, the students make a poster for the room which provides "Tips for Studying/Thinking Aloud."

4. Evaluation of the Preparation, Organization, and Implemention of the Study Session

(a)Teachers model self-evaluation questions:
Do I feel prepared?
Did I go over all the words at least three times?
Did I highlight the main points?
Did I outline the dense parts?
Did I spend enough time putting this information into my head?
Did I check myself to see if I was understanding? recalling?
Am I ready?
What else do I need to do?

(b)Students use overt, faded, and covert practice of the self-evaluation questions.

Case Study: Using CSI for Attention Problems

The next section of this chapter describes an experience of a regular classroom teacher (fourth grade) who was "going crazy" trying to help a student who was off task and who did not do any written class work on most days. This teacher, Ms. A. began a CSI program and was very successful in helping her student become productive and self-directed. Portions of this case study appeared first in Manning (1990a):

Jill was nine years and three months in September when the case study began. She is a white female. Both her parents work outside the home. She has one younger brother, age five. She is considered low SES by the school, based on the free/reduced lunch program, of which she eats free lunch. Jill is a fourth-grade student in a class with twenty-three other students, taught in a mobile unit of large K–5 elementary school in the southeastern United States. Her teacher, Ms. A., is a black female in her late twenties with five years teaching experience. Jill has an intelligence quotient of 122 and has attended the same elementary school since kindergarten.

Prior to applying CSI strategies, each of Jill's former teachers (K–3), the school principal, Jill's mother and Jill were interviewed individually. The following perspectives were gathered: *former teachers* unanimously agreed that she was an eager cooperative child when her learning was being directed and controlled by the teacher. In other words she could "do the work" if the teacher stayed with her continuously. The fact that she performed well when prodded but did not continue such work independently, caused teacher frustration. The kindergarten teacher said she realized very early that Jill could not/would not work independently. Two of the teachers termed her "lazy," "unmotivated."

The *school principal* knew Jill very well in spite of the large enrollment (i.e., 871) at this elementary school. Over the years, Jill had been sent often to this female principal for neglecting school work. The principal was hopeful that Jill could improve. She expressed concern for what would happen to her in future years if she continued her present school work habits.

During the interview Jill's *mother* was emotional. Her voice quivered and she told about the numerous ways she had tried to help Jill. On the other hand, she mentioned her lack of time to become involved with her children due to her long work hours and fatigue. The mother urged us to help her daughter quickly because for four years she had heard the same report: Jill is capable but does not perform independently.

The initial interview with *Jill* revealed an energetic, perceptive child. She said "What are we going to try now to get me to do my work? My teachers have tried everything." She was fully cognizant of her school problems. Her interests were reading, horses, and daydreaming. Her favorite part of the school day was riding the bus. She was not socially isolated but sometimes preferred to be alone. Her score on the Nowicki–Strickland Locus of Control (Nowicki & Strickland, 1973) was twenty-eight indicating a higher than average externality score before the CSI program. On-task ratings, collected and averaged for ten consecutive school days, during thirty minutes of independent seatwork time was 15 percent It was hypothesized that a CSI program would improve Jill's autonomous work habits, specifically to focus, follow through, and finish independent seatwork tasks, without teacher prompting.

Criterion Variables during Independent Practice

Focus attention. This was defined as the subject's ability to begin work promptly without a teacher directive aimed specifically at her (e.g., "Jill, get started on your work"). Corno (1987) defines a classroom self-starter as one who "seems to know what to do and who does it almost without being asked" (p. 249). Jill's baseline focusing attention behavior (collected from 8:00 to 11:00 a.m. for three weeks every other day) was as follows: (1) For six of the eight days she did not get beyond her name and heading of the paper, even though the classroom teacher directed her to get started, approximately every thirty minutes. (2) On the other two days she wrote three sentences and five sentences, with the teacher urging about every nineteen minutes. (3) Instead of beginning the assigned tasks, Jill stared blankly out the window, seemed to move in slow motion, played with her clothing and spiral on her notebook, arranged and rearranged materials on her desk, doodled with her pencil in the margin, and put her head down on her desk. She did not disrupt others. (4) When the teacher asked her to begin her work she most often ignored the teacher. Occasionally, she would shift in her desk and simulate "focusing attention" behavior; however, as soon as the teacher looked away she assumed her original nonfocusing behaviors.

Follow through. Due to the sequential nature of the criterion variables each was a prerequisite to the next (e.g., Jill had to acquire focusing attention skills before she could follow through on tasks). Follow through is defined here as maintaining concentration sufficiently to persist at an independent school task, without teacher prompting. In addition, at least 50 percent of the entire assignment must be completed successfully as assigned by the teacher. Prior to CSI, Jill was not able to meet this criterion.

Finish independent work. The final criterion variable was that Jill be able to finish her independent seatwork most of the time (4 out of 5 days) with 85–100 percent accuracy.

Cognitive Self-Instruction (CSI)

For each of the three criterion variables (i.e., focusing, following through, finishing) Manning's model of CSI (Manning, 1988) was applied. This instruction is presented in chapter 7.

There were across-the-board positive effects of the CSI program for this particular student, lacking in self-management skills. Jill's scores on the Nowicki–Strickland Locus of Control Scale and a Behavior Rating Scale reflect in a quantitative sense the improvement Jill made. The positive repetitive pattern of improvement across time and context provides a multiple convergence of the facilitative effect CSI produced for one particular nonconcentrative student.

In a more qualitative vein, the interviews provided a similar scenario. Jill's teacher felt that Jill had broken out of her self-defeating pattern of poor self-management skills. She believed the reason this CSI program had been successful in promoting Jill's focusing, following through and finishing seatwork habits was because Jill became cognitively aware and responsible for her work. As indicated by Jill's locus of control score before the CSI was applied, she was quite external. In short Jill did not believe that she was in control of her successes and failures at school. When she failed to produce classwork, she did not see it as her own responsibility. Jill's preinstructional interview supported this viewpoint. When asked who was responsible for seeing that she did her school work, Jill responded that her teacher was. At postinstructional interview Jill responded that she, herself was responsible. After CSI instruction, Jill's locus of control score was more internal and remained more internal across time. In an earlier experimental study with fifty-five elementary children, Manning (1988) obtained similar locus of control results from the application of a CSI intervention.

Although Jill's mother rated her higher on a behavior rating scale after the CSI instruction, her post interview revealed that she did not think Jill was more responsible at home. Possible explanations might be that the CSI training was very specific to independent seatwork of focusing, following through, and finishing work and did not relate sufficiently to home behaviors. During CSI instruction with Jill, home behaviors were not trained. Likewise, Kendall and Braswell (1982), using a cognitive behavioral strategy obtained generalizations to the classroom but not to the home.

The CSI materials used by Ms. A, to help Jill are:

Focusing:

FOCUSING ATTENTION/MODELING

Sample Teacher Model "Now I'm on my own. No one is here to make me get started. I get started on my own. I can do that. Let's go. I have my pencil, paper. I listened to the directions and asked questions if I did not understand. Let me review what I need to do. First, I look up five spelling words and write a story using the words. The assignments are written right in the corner of the board if I forget. I'll put the heading, date, and my name on this paper first. Now, check the five words I wish to look up and get started. This will be fun. I'm going to write a neat story—one about my weekend fun. Watch out, I'm starting to daydream. Look up the words and then I can think about my story for a minute."

FOCUSING ATTENTION/PRACTICING

Sample Self-Portrait
with Self-Talk

Jill uses a school picture of herself with a bubble over her head. She writes a self-talk message (e.g., "I start right away!").

FOCUSING ATTENTION/CUEING

Sample Cue Card

Drawing of a frog. The words on the card say: I'm Hopping to Get Started on my WORK!

Sample Self-Record

1. Did I start right away?	Yes	No
2. Did I have all my materials ready?	Yes	No
3. Did I head my paper correctly?	Yes	No
4. Did I put my name on my paper?	Yes	No
5. Did I do the first one as soon as possible?	Yes	No
6. Did I start without the teacher reminding me?	Yes	No

Following Through:

FOLLOWING THROUGH/MODELING

Sample Teacher Model. "I'm getting tired of this, but I am making progress. Just take one at a time and do the best I can. There, that looks correct. I'm getting through this stuff and I'm learning some things. See I can keep working, even when there is some noise. It is fun to see if I can keep on track, even when the intercom interrupts me. The intercom does not care about my work, but I do. I am being careful but I am working quickly, too. This part is boring but everything can't be exciting. Just keep working. I'm going to see if I can make this my best work. I can do that!"

FOLLOWING THROUGH/PRACTICING

Concentration Thief. Directions for this game can be found in chapter 7 of this text.

Sample Self-Portrait Amid Distractors. Jill draws herself with her nose in a big book. The drawing shows the intercom blasting, a visitor knocking at the door. Jill writes on the drawing: "I keep my mind and my eyes on my work."

FOLLOWING THROUGH/CUEING

Sample Self-Record Rating

ON/OFF TASK SELF-RECORD

Directions: When I hear the tone I mark the right box. Circle the "on" or the "off." If I mark "off," I tell myself to get back to work. If I mark "on" I say to myself "Good for me" and I continue working.

♪♪	1	2	3	4	5	6	7	8	9	10
	On	On	On	On	On	On	On	On	On	On
	Off	Off	Off	Off	Off	Off	Off	Off	Off	Off

Sample Self Checklist

1. Am I working fast enough?	Yes	No
2. Am I working too fast?	Yes	No
3. Did I skip anything?	Yes	No
4. Did I work without delays?	Yes	No
5. Did I daydream?	Yes	No
6. Did I get right back to work if I stopped?	Yes	No
7. Am I pleased with the way I am sticking with this?	Yes	No
8. Am I doing the best I can?	Yes	No

Finishing:

FINISHING/MODELING

Sample Teacher Model. "Wow, I'm almost finished. Good for me. Look, just two more sentences. I have really made a lot of progress. I am a good worker. I concentrate by keeping my mind and my eyes on my work. I am not easily distracted because I want to finish. It is such a good feeling to have all my assignments finished. I have completed excellent work. I am very pleased with it."

FINISHING/PRACTICING

Self-Reinforcement. Jill uses another school picture of herself with the bubble drawn above her head. In the bubble she has written, "I am doing my very best work."

FINISHING/CUEING

Sample Assignment Sheet for Completion of Seatwork

Assignment/Completion*

Monday

Spelling	•
Reading	
Mathematics	•
Language Arts	•
Social Studies	•
Science	
Other ________________	

(Repeat for Tuesday through Friday)

---

*Dots indicate hole punch for successfully completed work.

Sample Self-Reinforcement Cue Card

Jill draws herself with a huge smile. The words in the bubble say "I did my best! And I also finished! Good for me!"

Sample Self-Checklist for Finished Work

1. Did I do all the assignments?	Yes	No
2. Did I do my best?	Yes	No
3. I was in control of finishing my work.	Yes	No
4. I reminded myself to finish.	Yes	No
5. I like the way my work looks.	Yes	No

Structured Interviews

PREINSTRUCTIONAL

Former Teachers

1. Do you remember Jill ________________?
2. What do you remember?
3. What were her most serious weaknesses at school?

4. What was Jill's attitude toward her learning problems?
5. What was your attitude toward Jill's problems?
6. What did you do to help Jill?
7. Did anything help? If so, what?
8. Are you surprised she is still having problems?
9. What would you recommend for Jill now that she is older?
10. What do you expect will happen to Jill?

School Principal

1. Do you know Jill ________________?
2. What do you know about her?
3. How old was she when she was first sent to your office for not doing her work?
4. What are other reasons she is sent to you?
5. Are you surprised that she has continued her pattern of poor self-management skills?
6. What might help Jill?
7. What was Jill's attitude when she was sent to the office?
8. What do you expect will happen to Jill?

Current Teacher

1. Why did you call me about Jill?
2. What is her main problem?
3. What have you tried?
4. Has anything helped? If so, what?
5. Why did you think CSI would be helpful for Jill?
6. What do you want her to improve?
7. In what ways can I be the most help?
8. Who will be responsible for the CSI intervention? Let's talk about our roles.

Art Teacher

1. Do you know Jill ________________?
2. What do you know about her?
3. Is she what you would call a self-starter? good worker? independent worker? Why? Why not?

4. How have you worked with Jill?
5. Does Jill begin promptly and finish her art activities?

Mother

1. What have teachers told you about Jill's school work habits?
2. What does Jill say about their comments?
3. What do you think is the main problem?
4. What have you said to Jill about her school work habits?
5. How does Jill work independently at home?

Jill

1. What do you like best about school?
2. What do you like least about school?
3. Who is responsible for seeing that you do your school assignments?
4. Tell me about the mornings at school when you are left to work on your assignments, while the teacher has reading/math groups? What do you usually say to yourself?
5. Why do you suppose your teachers are often telling you to get busy or to get back to your work?
6. Why don't you work well by yourself on your school assignments?
7. What have teachers, the principal, and others done to help you be a "better worker"?
8. Did these things work? Why? or Why not?
9. Do you want to improve in your school work habits?
10. How important is it to you?

POSTINSTRUCTIONAL AND MAINTENANCE INTERVIEWS

Current Teacher

1. Describe Jill's independent seatwork habits now.
   (a) Focusing attention
   (b) Following through
   (c) Finishing assignments

2. Do you feel less or more involved with over-seeing her attention to and concentration on her seatwork?
3. What has been your attitude toward the CSI strategies? Were they too time consuming? hard to teach? etc.?
4. Do you believe that her improvement will be long lasting or short lived? Explain.
5. How does Jill feel about herself? How do you feel about Jill?

Jill

1. Describe the way you do your independent seatwork now. What do you say to yourself?
   (a) Focusing attention
   (b) Following through
   (c) Finishing assignments
2. Do you feel more in charge/control of what you do during seatwork time?
3. Tell me how you would teach CSI to one of your friends if he/she were having trouble focusing, following through, and/or finishing his/her seatwork.
4. How do you feel about yourself?
5. Do you think you can keep these improvements working for you? How long?
6. Who is responsible for seeing that you do your school assignments?

TRANSFER INTERVIEWS

Art Teacher/Near Transfer

1. Tell me about Jill's abilities to focus, follow through, and finish her independent art projects?
2. Do you find yourself reminding her to "get busy" as often, less often, more often than before?
3. Have you noticed any other differences in Jill's work during art class? If so, what?
4. Do you ever hear/see her talking to herself during her independent work? If so, how often?

5. Has she talked to you about how she has taken more responsibility for her work?

<u>Mother/Far Transfer</u>

1. Have you noticed any changes in Jill's home behaviors recently? If so, describe the changes?
2. Have you noticed Jill talking to herself more often?
3. Does she seem (more/less/about the same) responsible for home related tasks (e.g., making her bed)?
4. Does she spontaneously do more things (e.g., brush her teeth, put away clothing), without a reminder from you or her dad?
5. What does she say about her school work, especially her independent seatwork?

The final section of this chapter includes a variety of CSI materials and helpful suggestions that readers may find extremely useful as stimuli when developing their own CSI strategies for their own particular classrooms.

CSI Materials and Helpful Aids

Reminders for Self-Communication Instruction:

1. When using self-instructional procedures, it is important to insure that the child does not say the self-statements in a mechanical, rote, or automatic fashion. He/she should use inflection and meaning.

2. The rate at which you proceed with the self-communication training procedures can be individually tailored to meet the needs of the child.

3. How much information do you provide in self-statements?

(a.) Initially, the teacher should model and have students rehearse simple self-statements, such as "Stop! Think before I answer!"

(b.) Gradually, the teacher models (and students rehearse) more complex sets of self-statements.

(c.) Sometimes students become embarrassed maintaining the overt speech in the self-instructional training. May need to proceed rather quickly to whispering and covert speech. Teacher can then query students as to what they are telling themselves.

(d.) Try saying "think out loud" instead of "talk out loud to yourself" if children appear confused about what you are asking them to do (from Meichenbaum 1977).

Procedures for Self-Communication Training (Meichenbaum and Goodman, 1971):

1. An adult model performs a task while talking to self aloud (cognitive modeling).

2. The child performs the same task under the direction of the model's instructions (overt, external guidance).

3. The child performs the task while instructing self aloud (overt, self-guidance).

4. The child whispers the instructions to self as he/she goes through the task (faded, overt self-guidance).

5. The child performs the task while guiding performance via private speech (covert, self-instruction).

The next collection of materials is helpful for assessing on-task behaviors and conducting student and parent interviews about self-talk and self-management.

Target Classroom Behaviors

STOP (RED LIGHT) (INHIBITORY)	*GO* (GREEN LIGHT) (INITIATORY)
SHOUTING-OUT	RAISE HAND
JUMPING-UP/OUT OF SEAT	STAY SEATED
DAYDREAMING/STARING	KEEP QUIET/LISTEN
PLAYING AROUND THE ROOM OR DESK	KEEP WORKING/CONCENTRATE
DISTURBING OTHERS	KEEP HANDS, FEET TO SELF

Collecting On-task Data

Date ____________________ Time ____________________

Student's Name: __________________________

Teacher: ________________________________

Grade: __________________________________

Initiating Appropriate Classroom Behaviors (On-task behaviors)

E eyes toward seatwork material or the chalkboard

G gathering materials, immediately followed by other on-task descriptors

W writing/drawing in conjunction with eyes on materials

R reading assigned materials

Inhibiting Inappropriate Classroom Behaviors (Off-task behaviors)

A out of classroom

M manipulating pencils, rulers, paper, scribbling, doodling

O out of seat

T talking with neighbors, whispering to someone else, motioning, making (unrelated to work) vocal noises

BM body movements (i.e., head on desk, head cupped in book, arms over head)

EN eyes not directed toward seatwork

C leaning out of desk, manipulating objects on floor, turned around in desk

Collecting On-task Data

Thirty-minute sessions—on- or off-task behaviors recorded every ten seconds. Coding scheme on previous page may be used if finer distinctions are desired.

1 ____	26 ____	51 ____	76 ____	101 ____	126 ____	151 ____
2 ____	27 ____	52 ____	77 ____	102 ____	127 ____	152 ____
3 ____	28 ____	53 ____	78 ____	103 ____	128 ____	153 ____
4 ____	29 ____	54 ____	79 ____	104 ____	129 ____	154 ____
5 ____	30 ____	55 ____	80 ____	105 ____	130 ____	155 ____
6 ____	31 ____	56 ____	81 ____	106 ____	131 ____	156 ____
7 ____	32 ____	57 ____	82 ____	107 ____	132 ____	157 ____
8 ____	33 ____	58 ____	83 ____	108 ____	133 ____	158 ____
9 ____	34 ____	59 ____	84 ____	109 ____	134 ____	159 ____
10 ____	35 ____	60 ____	85 ____	110 ____	135 ____	160 ____
11 ____	36 ____	61 ____	86 ____	111 ____	136 ____	161 ____
12 ____	37 ____	62 ____	87 ____	112 ____	137 ____	162 ____
13 ____	38 ____	63 ____	88 ____	113 ____	138 ____	163 ____
14 ____	39 ____	64 ____	89 ____	114 ____	139 ____	164 ____
15 ____	40 ____	65 ____	90 ____	115 ____	140 ____	165 ____
16 ____	41 ____	66 ____	91 ____	116 ____	141 ____	166 ____
1 ____	42 ____	67 ____	92 ____	117 ____	142 ____	167 ____
18 ____	43 ____	68 ____	93 ____	118 ____	143 ____	168 ____
19 ____	44 ____	69 ____	94 ____	119 ____	144 ____	169 ____
20 ____	45 ____	70 ____	95 ____	120 ____	145 ____	170 ____
21 ____	46 ____	71 ____	96 ____	121 ____	146 ____	171 ____
22 ____	47 ____	72 ____	97 ____	122 ____	147 ____	172 ____
23 ____	48 ____	73 ____	98 ____	123 ____	148 ____	173 ____
24 ____	49 ____	74 ____	99 ____	124 ____	149 ____	174 ____
25 ____	50 ____	75 ____	100 ____	125 ____	150 ____	175 ____

176 ____ 177 ____ 178 ____ 179 ____ 180 ____

CSI: Student Evaluation

1. In the last four weeks I have talked to myself more at school? *Yes or No*
2. In the last four weeks, I have felt more control over my school behavior. *Yes or No*
3. In the last four weeks, I have finished my work more often. *Yes or No*
4. In the last four weeks, the teacher has had to remind me to be a good worker at school. *Yes or No*
5. I am responsible for the way I behave at school. *Yes or No*
6. What do I say to myself to stop myself when I am playing around the room or at my desk?
7. What do I say to myself to remind myself to stay on task?
8. What do I say to myself to remind myself to raise my hand?
9. What do I say to myself to remind myself to stay in my seat?
10. What do I say to myself to remind myself to keep hands and feet to self?
11. What do I say to myself to remind myself to listen?
12. What do I say to myself to remind myself to stop daydreaming or staring around the room?
13. What do I say to myself to remind myself to stop jumping up/getting out of my seat?
14. What do I say to myself to stop myself from shouting out?
15. What do I say to myself to stop myself from disturbing others?

CSI: Parent Survey Form

Directions: Please think about your child's home behavior during the last month. Please circle the desired response to each item.

A. In the last month, have you noticed improvement in your child's ability to:

1. Concentrate for longer periods of time.
   a) Yes b) No c) Improvement Not Needed

2. Stick with a task until completion.
   a) Yes b) No c) Improvement Not Needed

3. Be more in control of self.
   a) Yes b) No c) Improvement Not Needed

4. Wait turn in family discussion.
   a) Yes b) No c) Improvement Not Needed

5. Talk to him or herself about responsibility (e.g., "I need to finish this").
   a) Yes b) No c) Improvement Not Needed

6. Take on more responsbility for family chores (e.g., keeping his or her room straightened).
   a) Yes b) No c) Improvement Not Needed

7. Try new tasks that he or she has not assumed before now.
   a) Yes b) No c) Improvement Not Needed

8. Be cooperative with sisters, brothers, or other family members.
   a) Yes b) No c) Improvement Not Needed

9. Begin home chores promptly.
   a) Yes b) No c) Improvement Not Needed

10. Respond quickly to parent responses (e.g., time for bed, bath, school, etc.).
   a) Yes b) No c) Improvement Not Needed

11. Listen attentively.
   a) Yes b) No c) Improvement Not Needed

12. Begin tasks without having to be reminded.
   a) Yes b) No c) Improvement Not Needed

(Published originally in Manning, 1988.)

Cognitive Analysis: Definition of Terms

Criterion variables The desired behaviors performed at a designated level to satisfy the requirements set forth by a teacher or educational researcher (e.g., students must be able to spontaneously produce cognitive self-instructional statements for five target behaviors).

Overt, faded, and covert self-instruction Exchange words for aloud (overt), whisper (faded), and silent (covert) self-talk in order to inform oneself.

Self-communication. A synonym of self-talk; however it connotes more meaning via the conversation with self.

Structured interviews Predetermined interviews, whereby the questions have been planned ahead of time and asked exactly as planned.

Target inhibitory The terminal (end result) behavior that needs to stop (e.g., shouting out answers) in order to restore a favorable classroom climate and/or improve classroom habits of individual students (e.g., persistence at a task).

Target initiatory The terminal (end result) behavior that needs to begin (e.g., respect for others) in order to foster a favorable classroom climate and/or improve classroom habits of individual students (e.g., improved concentration).

Cognitive Synthesis: A Summary

In the school setting, students are expected to learn predetermined content, at a predetermined rate (e.g., teachers must finish so much academic work by specific times). Partly due to this bureaucratic rigidity, some students are not motivated to learn, others lack the cognitive strategies required to manage the demands, others are not cognitively competent, and there are combinations of the above (Corno, 1987). In many students' cases, their most salient weakness is their lack of cognitive strategies needed to focus, follow through, and finish independent school tasks, even though they are motivated and competent. Our schools are full of students like this. And in too many cases, cognitive self-instruction for self-management is not addressed. If students exhibit cognitive deficits in self-management, the assumption is often that they are lazy and/or unmotivated. These students will either "get their act together" or fail in the school setting.

In this chapter a sequence of steps provided a programmatic way of incorporating CSI into the school curriculum. In addition a case study illustrated applying CSI for a particular student exhibiting poor self-management skills. Other CSI materials and aids are included. It is hoped that these suggestions will be sufficient for educators to become knowledgeable about how to help their population of learners who lack cognitive strategic knowledge required to meet the demands of classroom learning.

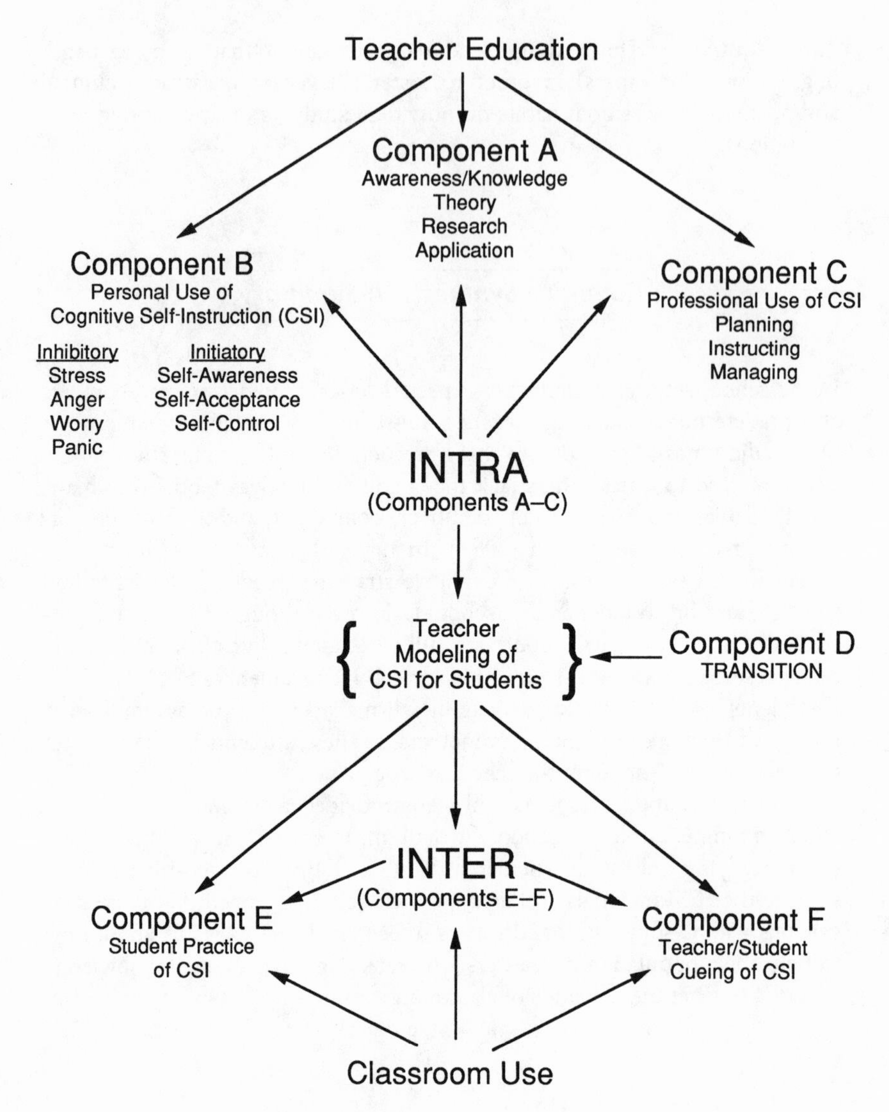

Figure 2 Metacognitive instruction

Summary of Part Three
Classroom Application of CSI

The synthesis of Part Three is illustrated in Figure 2. As is shown by this figure, CSI instruction begins in teacher education institutions as the ideal. When preservice and inservice teachers are well grounded in the theory, research, and application of CSI, they know metacognition, as related to learning. When they are taught to use, provided opportunities to use, and provided feedback about the use of CSI, then they have experienced a first-hand professional and personal use of the strategies. Therefore, they have more likely internalized the CSI skills and will be natural teachers of metacognitive strategies due to this internalization. It is more difficult to teach skills that are not an integral component of an individual's repertoire of skills. Therefore, one reason teachers do not often teach metacognitive/strategic knowledge and regulation of one's own learning is because they have not clearly articulated and internalized their own metacognitive/strategic knowledge.

To externalize this type knowledge, informed teachers model via "think aloud" their metacognitive awareness and regulation. The modeling teacher serves as the major vehicle for teaching and learning CSI. Modeling also serves as the transition between the intrapsychological functioning and the interpsychological functioning of the teacher. Teachers teach CSI directly as an interwoven part of academic subject matter instruction. Teachers also teach CSI as a separate instructional unit for fostering social responsibility and school work habits. Teachers provide for the practicing and cueing of CSI to firmly fasten down the skill into the students' repertoire of self-directed learning proficiency.

In Part Three, the information needed to move teachers from the intrapsychological use of CSI to the interpsychological exchange of CSI knowledge and skills from teacher to students was outlined. This section completes the picture of a theoretical base and the corresponding research documentation that structures a sound classroom application model of cognitive self-instruction for classroom processes.

Summary of Part Three
Classroom Application of CS

A FINAL WORD

An alarming number of students have little, if any, background or knowledge in the skills of cognitive self-guidance. Very few learners of school age can clearly articulate what it really means to listen, plan strategies for class work, monitor their ongoing work, and check their completed work. But students have within their grasp a powerful regulator of behavior: their own language. It is the responsibility of adults to become knowledgeable about directing the use of cognitive self-instruction to aid memory, comprehension, problem solving and self-control. Students must be taught why, what, how, and when to use CSI to foster appropriate regulation of action. As with many worthwhile educational endeavors, this procedure takes time, commitment, and energy. However, when students learn academic responsibility for self, they often simultaneously learn that expending efforts enhances their chances for academic excellence in performance. When students learn to manage their own classroom behavior, they often learn simultaneously that this feeling of being in charge of oneself is essential to a healthy self-concept. In my estimation, these results are worth the expenditure of human effort of both teachers and parents.

Ultimately some form of metacognitive instruction will offer valuable contributions to the core of educational curriculum. Decisions about problem-solving tasks in schools might then be based not only upon the content of the academic subjects, but also upon essential metacognitive skills. The differences may be noticeable diminishment of school failure and an addition of more responsible, self-directed students. Toward such an educational goal, this book has been written.

BIBLIOGRAPHY

Anderson, J. (1981). *Thinking, changing, and rearranging: Improving self-esteem in young people.* Eugene, OR: Timberline Press.

Anderson, L. M., & Prawat, R. S. (1983). Responsibility in the classroom: A synthesis of research on teaching self-control. *Educational Leadership,* April, 62–66.

Anderson-Inman, L. (1984). Neatness counts: Effects of direct instruction and self-monitoring on the transfer of neat-paper skills to nontraining settings. *Analysis and Intervention in Developmental Disabilities, 4*(2), 137–155.

Anohkin, P. K. (1969). Cybernetics and the integrative activity of the brain. In M. Cole & I. Maltzman (Eds.), *A handbook of contemporary Soviet psychology.* New York: Basic Books.

Asarnow, J. R., & Meichenbaum, D. (1979). Verbal rehearsal and serial recall: The mediational training of kindergarten children. *Child Development, 50,* 1173–1177.

Baker, L., & Brown, A. L. (1981). Metacognition and the reading process. In D. Pearson (Ed.), *A handbook of reading research.* New York: Plenum Press.

Bandura, A. (1977a). Self-efficacy: Toward a unifying theory of behavior change. *Psychological Review, 84,* 191–215.

Bandura, A. (1977b). *Social learning theory.* Englewood Cliffs, NJ: Prentice Hall.

Bandura, A. (1983). The psychology of chance encounters and life paths. *American Psychologist, 37,* 747–756.

Bandura, A., & Schunk, D. H. (1981). Cultivating competence, self-efficacy, and intrinsic interest through proximal self-motivation. *Journal of Personality and Social Psychology, 41,* 586–598.

Barclay, C. R. (1980). *On the relation between memory and metamemory.* Cortland: State University of New York Press.

Barling, J. (1980). A multistage multidependent variable assessment of children's self-regulation for academic performance. *Cognitive Behavior Therapy, 2,* 43–54.

Bartlett, F. C. (1932). *Remembering: A study in experimental and social psychology.* Cambridge, England: Cambridge University Press.

Bash, M., & Camp, B. (1975). *Think aloud program: Group manual.* Unpublished manuscript. University of Colorado Medical School.

Belmont, J. M., Butterfield, E. C., & Borkowski, J. G. (1978). Training retarded people to generalize memorization methods across memory tasks. In M. M. Gruneberg, P. E. Morris, & R. N. Sykes (Eds.), *Practical aspects of memory.* London: Academic Press.

Bem, S. (1967). Verbal self-control: The establishment of effective self-instruction. *Journal of Experimental Psychology, 74,* 485–491.

Bender, N. (1976). Self-verbalization versus tutor verbalization in modifying impulsivity. *Journal of Educational Psychology, 88,* 347–354.

Bereiter, C., & Bird, M. (1985). Use of thinking aloud in identification and teaching of reading comprehension strategies. *Cognition and Instruction,* 2, 131–156.

Berliner, D. C. (1987). Simple views of effective teaching and a simple theory of classroom instruction. In D. C. Berliner & B. V. Rosenshine (Eds.), *Talks to teachers.* New York: Random House.

Berne, E. (1964). *Games people play: The psychology of human relations.* New York: Grove Press.

Best, D. L., & Ornstein, P. A. (1979, March). *Children's generation and communication of organizational strategies.* Paper presented at the biennial meeting of the Society for Research in Child Development, San Francisco, CA.

Birch, D. (1966). Verbal control of nonverbal behavior. *Journal of Experimental Child Psychology, 4,* 266–275.

Bisanz, G. L., Vesonder, G. T., & Voss, J. T. (1978). Knowledge of one's own responding and the relation of such knowledge to learning: A developmental study. *Journal of Experimental Child Psychology, 25,* 116–128.

Bjorklund, D. F., & Zeman, B. R. (1982). Children's organization and metamemory awareness in their recall of familiar information. *Child Development, 53,* 799–810.

Blandford, B. J., & Lloyd, J. W. (1987). Effects of a self-instructional procedure on handwriting. *Journal of Learning Disabilities, 20*(6), 342–346.

Blick, D. W., & Test, D. W. (1987). Effects of self-recording on high school students' on-task behavior. *Learning Disability Quarterly, 10*(3), 203–213.

Bondy, E. (1984). *Thinking about thinking. Childhood Education, 60,* 234–238.

Borkowski, J., & Cavanaugh, J. (1979). Maintenance and generalization of skills and strategies by the retarded. In V. Ellis (Ed.), *Handbook of mental deficiency.* Hillsdale, NJ: Erlbaum.

Borkowski, J. G., Johnston, M. B., & Reid, M. K. (1987). Metacognition, motivation, and the transfer of control processes. In S. J. Ceci (Ed.), *Handbook of cognitive, social, and neuropsychological aspects of learning disabilities.* Hillsdale, NJ: Erlbaum.

Borkowski, J. G., & Krause, A. J. (1985). Metacognition and attributional beliefs. In G. d'Ydewalle (Ed.), *Cognition, information processing and motivation.* Amsterdam: North-Holland/Elsevier.

Borkowski, J. G., Reid, M. K., & Kurtz, B. E. (1983). Impulsivity and strategy transfer: Metamemory as mediator. *Child Development, 54,* 459–473.

Bornstein, P. H., & Quevillon, A. P. (1976). The effects of a self-instructional package on overactive preschool boys. *Journal of Applied Behavior Analysis, 9,* 179–188.

Bradley, J. (1984). I can manage myself club. *Instructor,* August, 113.

Brezin, M. J. (1980). Cognitive monitoring: From learning theory to instructional applications. *Educational Communication and Technology: A Journal of Theory, Research, and Development, 28,* 227–242.

Broden, M., Hall, R. V., & Mitts, B. (1971). The effect of self-recording on the classroom behavior of two eighth grade students. *Journal of Applied Behavior Analysis, 4,* 191–199.

Brookover, W., Beady, C., Flood, R., Schweitzer, J., & Wisenbaker, J. (1979). *School social systems and student achievement: Schools can make a difference.* New York: Praeger.

Brophy, J. (1984). Classroom management as instruction: Socializing self-guidance in students. *Theory Into Practice, 24*(4), 233–240.

Brophy, J., & Good, T. (1986). Teacher behavior and student achievement. In M. Wittrock (Ed.), *Third handbook of research on teaching.* New York: Macmillan.

Brown, A. L. (1975). The development of memory: Knowing, knowing about knowing, and knowing how to know. In H. W. Reese (Ed.), *Advances in child development and behavior* (Vol. 10). New York: Academic Press.

Brown, A. L. (1978). Knowing when, where, and how to remember: A problem of metacognition. In R. Glaser (Ed.), *Advances in instructional psychology* (Vol. 1). Hillsdale, NJ: Erlbaum.

Brown, A. L. (1987). Metacognition, executive control, self-regulation, and other more mysterious mechanisms. In F. E. Weinert & R. H. Kluwe (Eds.), *Metacognition, motivation, and understanding.* Hillsdale, NJ: Erlbaum.

Brown, A., Bransford, J., Ferrara, R., & Campione, J. (1983). Learning, remembering, and understanding. In Paul H. Mussen (Ed.), *Handbook of child psychology, 3.* New York: John Wiley and Sons.

Brown, A. L., Campione, J. C., & Barclay, C. R. (1979). Training self-checking routines for estimating test readiness: Generalization from list learning to prose recall. *Child Development, 50,* 501–512.

Brown, A. L., Campione, J. C., & Day, J. D. (1981). Learning to learn: On training students to learn from texts. *Educational Researcher, 10*(2), 14–21.

Brown, A. L., & DeLoache, J. S. (1978). Skills, plans, and self-regulation. In R. S. Siegler (Ed.), *Children's thinking: What develops?* Hillsdale, NJ: Erlbaum.

Brown, A. L., & Ferrara, R. A. (1985). Diagnosing zones of proximal development. In J. V. Wertsch (Ed.), *Culture, communication, and cognition: Vygotskian perspectives.* New York: Cambridge University Press.

Brown, A. L., & French, L. A. (1979). The zone of proximal development: Implications for intelligence testing in the year 2000. *Intelligence, 3,* 255–277.

Brown, A. L., & Lawton, S. C. (1977). The feeling of knowing experiences in educable retarded children. *Developmental Psychology, 13,* 364–370.

Brown, A. L., & Palincsar, A. S. (1982). Inducing strategic learning from text by means of informed, self-control training. *Topics in Learning and Learning Disabilities, 2,* 1–17.

Brown, A. L., & Smiley, S. S. (1978). The development of strategies for studying texts. *Child Development, 49,* 1076–1088.

Bruner, J. (1985). Vygotsky: A historical and conceptual perspective. In J. Wertsch (Ed.), *Culture, communication, and cognition: Vygotskian perspectives.* New York: Cambridge University Press.

Bruner, J. S. (1965). The growth of mind. *American Psychologist, 20,* 1007–1017.

Bryant, L. E., & Budd, K. S. (1982). Self-instructional training to increase independent work performance in preschoolers. *Journal of Applied Behavior Analysis, 13,* 259–271.

Bugenthal, D. B., Whalen, C. K., & Henker, B. (1977). Causal attributions of hyperactive children and motivational assumptions of two behavior change approaches: Evidence for an interactionist position. *Child Development, 48,* 874–884.

Burger, A. L., Blackmon, L. S., Holmes, M., & Zetlin, A. (1978). Use of active sorting and retrieval strategies as a facilitator of recall, clustering, and sorting by EMR and nonretarded children. *American Journal of Mental Deficiency, 83,* 253–261.

Burgio, L. D., Whitman, T. L., & Johnson, M. R. (1980). A self-instructional package for increasing attending behavior in educable mentally retarded children. *Journal of Applied Behavior Analysis, 13,* 443–450.

Buscaglia, L. (1986). *Bus 9 to Paradise.* New York: Slack, Inc.

Butler, P. E. (1981). *Talking to yourself: Learning the language of self-support.* San Francisco: Harper and Row.

Camp, B. W. (1977). Verbal mediation in young aggressive boys. *Journal of Abnormal Psychology, 86,* 145–153.

Camp, B. W., & Bash, M. A. S. (1981). *Think Aloud: Increasing social and cognitive skills: A problem-solving program for children.* (Primary level). Champaign, IL: Research Press.

Camp, B. W., & Bash, M. A. S. (1985). *Think Aloud: Increasing social and cognitive skills: A problem-solving program for children.* (Classroom Program, Grades 1–2.) Champaign, IL: Research Press.

Camp, B. W., Blom, G. E., Hebert, F., & Doorninck, W. J. (1977). "Think Aloud": A program for developing self-control in young aggressive boys. *Journal of Abnormal Psychology,* 3(2), 157–196.

Campione, J. C., & Brown, A. (1977). Memory and metamemory development in educable retarded children. In R. V. Kail, Jr., & J. W. Hagen (Eds.), *Perspectives on the development of memory and cognition.* Hillsdale, NJ: Erlbaum.

Cavanaugh, J. C., & Borkowski, J. G. (1979). The metamemory-memory "connection": Effects of strategy training and maintenance. *The Journal of General Psychology, 101,* 161–174.

Cawley, J. F., & Miller, J. H. (1986). Selected views on metacognition, arithmetic problem solving and learning disabilities. *Learning Disabilities Focus,* 2(1), 36–48.

Childs, C. P., & Greenfield, P. M. (1980). Informal modes of learning and teaching. In N. Warren (Ed.), *Advances in cross-cultural psychology* (Vol. 2). London: Academic Press.

Clark, C. M. & Lampert, M. (1986). The study of teachers' thinking: Implications for teacher education. *Journal of Teacher Education,* 37(5), 27–31.

Clark, C. M., & Peterson, P. L. (1986). Teacher's thought process. In M. Wittrock (Ed.), *Handbook of research on teaching* (3rd ed.). New York: Macmillan.

Clark, C. M., & Yinger, R. J. (1979). Teacher's thinking. In P. L. Peterson & H. J. Walberg (Eds.), *Research on teaching.* Berkeley, CA: McCutchan.

Cohen, R. (1989, March). *Toward computer coaching within children's mathematical microworlds.* Paper presented to the annual meeting of the American Educational Research Association. San Francisco, CA.

Cole, M. (1978). *Soviet developmental psychology: An anthology.* White Plains, NY: Sharpe.

Cole, M. (1985). The zone of proximal development: Where culture and cognition create each other. In J. V. Wertsch (Ed.), *Culture, communication, and cognition: Vygotskian perspectives.* New York: Cambridge University Press.

Corno, L. (1987). Teaching and self-regulated learning. In D. C. Berliner & B. V. Rosenshine (Eds.), *Talks to teachers.* New York: Random House.

Corno, L., & Mandinach, E. B. (1983). The role of cognitive engagement in classroom learning and motivation. *Educational Psychologist, 18,* 88–108.

Corno, L., & Rohrkemper, M. M. (1985). The intrinsic motivation to learn in classrooms. In C. Ames & R. Ames (Eds.), *Research on motivation in education: The classroom milieu.* Orlando, FL: Academic Press.

Corno, L., & Snow, R. E. (1986). Adapting teaching to individual differences among learners. In M. C. Wittrock (Ed.), *Third handbook of research on teaching.* New York: Macmillan.

Corsini, D. A., Pick, A. D., & Flavell, J. H. (1968). Production deficiency of non-verbal mediators in young children. *Child Development, 39,* 53–58.

Costa, A. L. (1984). Mediating the metacognitive. *Educational Leadership,* November, 57–62.

Cox, G. L., & Paris, S. G. (1979, March). *The nature of mnemonic production deficiencies: A lifespan analysis.* Paper presented at the biennial meeting of the Society for Research in Child Development, San Francisco.

Cross, D. R., & Paris, S. G. (1988). Developmental and instructional analysis of children's metacognition and reading comprehension. *Journal of Educational Psychology, 80*(2), 131–142.

Dagley, P. L. (1988). *The utility of cognitive self-instruction in altering teacher expectations and locus of control orientations.* Unpublished doctoral dissertation. University of Georgia, Athens.

Davey, B. (1983). Think aloud—modeling the cognitive processes of reading comprehension. *Journal of Reading,* October, 44–47.

Davydov, V. V., & Radzikhovskii, L. A. (1985). Vygotsky's theory and the activity-oriented approach in psychology. In J. V. Wertsch (Ed.), *Culture, communication, and cognition: Vygotskian perspectives.* New York: Cambridge University Press.

DeCorte, E., & Verschaffel, L. (1981). Children's solution processes in elementary arithmetic problems: Analysis and improvement. *Journal of Educational Psychology, 73*(6), 765–779.

DeLoache, J. S. (1985). Precursors of mnemonic strategies in very young children. *Child Development, 56*(1), 125–137.

Dempster, L. (1984). An exchange of views on the place of reading in science instruction. *Journal of Reading, 27,* 583–584.

Derry, S. J., Hawkes, & L. W., Zeigler, U. (1989). *Characterizing the poor problem solver: A system for on-line error detection.* Paper presented to the annual meeting of the American Educational Research Association. San Francisco.

Dewey, J. (1910). *How we think.* Boston: Heath.

Dewitz, P., Carr, E. M., & Patberg, J. P. (1987). Effects of inference training on comprehension and comprehension monitoring. *Reading Research Quarterly,* 22(1), 99–119.

Dirkes, M. A. (1985). Metacognition: Students in charge of their thinking. *Roeper Review, 8*(2), 96–100.

Douglas, V., Parry, P., Martin, P., & Garson, C. (1976). Assessment of a cognitive training program for hyperactive children. *Journal of Abnormal Child Psychology, 4,* 389–410.

Drabman, R., Spitalnik, R., & Spitalnik, K. (1974). Sociometric and disruptive behavior as a function of four types of token economies. *Journal of Applied Behavior Analysis, 7,* 93–101.

Dyer, W. (1978). *Pulling your own strings.* New York: Thomas Y. Crowell Co.

Edson, B. A. (1986, February). *Communicating intrapersonally about stress: The dynamics on self.* Paper presented at the annual meeting of the Western Speech Communication Association, Tucson, AZ.

Edwards, D., & Middleton, D. (1987). Conversation and remembering: Bartlett revisited. *Applied Cognitive Psychology, 1,* 77–92.

Egeland, B. (1974). Training impulsive children in the use of more efficient scanning techniques. *Child Development, 45,* 165–171.

Eisner, E. W. (1967). Educational objectives: Help or hindrance. *School Review, 75,* 250–266.

Ekanayake, N. (1986). *The effects of cognitive self-instruction on preservice teachers' locus of control.* Unpublished doctoral dissertation, University of Georgia, Athens.

Elig, I., & Frieze, I. (1975). A multi-dimensional scheme for coding and interpreting perceived causality for success and failure events: The CSPC. *JSAS Catalog of Selected Documents in Psychology, 5*(313) (Manuscript #1069).

Elkind, D. (1981). *The hurried child: Growing up too fast, too soon.* Reading, MA: Addison-Wesley.

Elliott, S. N. (1980). *Sixth grade and college students' metacognitive knowledge of prose organization and study strategies.* Paper presented at the annual meeting of the American Educational Research Association, Boston.

Ellis, A. (1962). *Reason and emotion in psychotherapy.* New York: Lyle Stuart.

Ellis, A. (1975). *How to live with a neurotic.* New Yorks: Crown.

Ellis, A. (1976). *Reason and emotion in psychotherapy.* New York: Lyle Stuart.

Ellis, A., & Harper, R. A. (1975). *A new guide to rational living.* CA: Wilshire Book Co.

Ellis, D. E. (1976). The assessment of self-instructional training in developing self-control of aggressive behavior in impulsive-aggressive boys (Doctoral dissertation, North Carolina State University-Raleigh). *Dissertation Abstracts International, 37,* 3070–B. (University Microfilms No. 76–28475).

Epictetus. (1899). *The works of Epictetus.* Boston: Little, Brown.

Ericsson, K. A., & Simon, H. A. (1980). Verbal reports as data. *Psychological Review, 87,* 215–251.

Ernst, K. (1973). *Games students play, and what to do about them.* Melbrae, CA: Celestial Arts.

Evertson, C. M., Emmer, E. T., Clements, B. S., Sanford, J. P., & Worsham, M. E. (1989). *Classroom management for elementary teachers.* Englewood Cliffs, NJ: Prentice Hall.

Fennema, E. (1985). Attribution theory and achievements in mathematics. In S. R. Yussen (Ed.), *The growth of reflection in children.* New York: Academic Press.

Feuerstein, R. (1980). *Instrumental enrichment.* Baltimore, MD: University Park Press.

Fischer, P. M., & Mandl, H. (1982). Metacognitive regulation of text processing: Aspects and problems concerning the relation between self-statements and actual performance. In A. Flammer & W. Kintsch (Eds.), *Discourse Processing.* Amsterdam: North Holland.

Fish, M. C., & Pervan, R. (1985). Self-instruction training: A potential tool for schools psychologists. *Psychology in the Schools, 22,* 83–91.

Fisher, K. M., & Lipson, J. I. (1986). Twenty questions about student errors. *Journal of Research in Science Teaching, 23,* 783–803.

Flavell, J. H. (1964). *Private speech.* Paper presented at the annual meeting of the American Speech and Hearing Association. San Francisco, CA.

Flavell, J. H. (1971). First discussants comments: What is memory development the development of? *Human Development, 14,* 272–278.

Flavell, J. H. (1976). Metacognitive aspects of problem solving. In L. Resnick (Ed.), *The nature of intelligence*. Hillsdale, NJ: Erlbaum.

Flavell, J. H. (1977). *Cognitive development*. Englewood Cliffs, NJ: Prentice Hall.

Flavell, J. H. (1979). Metacognition and cognitive monitoring. *American Psychologist, 34*, 906–911.

Flavell, J. H. (1987). Speculations about the nature and development of metacognition. In F. E. Weinert and R. H. Kluwe (Eds.), *Metacognition, motivation, and understanding*. Hillsdale, NJ: Erlbaum.

Flavell, J. H., & Wellman, H. M. (1977). Metamemory. In R. V. Kail, Jr. & J. W. Hagen (Eds.), *Perspectives on the development of memory and cognition*. Hillsdale, NJ: Erlbaum.

Flavell, J. H., Beach, D. H., & Chinsky, J. M. (1966). Spontaneous verbal rehearsal in memory tasks as a function of age. *Child Development, 37*, 283–299.

Flavell, J. H., Friedrichs, A. G., & Hoyt, J. D. (1970). Developmental changes in memorization processes. *Cognitive Psychology, 1*, 324–340.

Forman, S. C. (1982). Stress management for teachers: A cognitive behavioral program. *Journal of School Psychology, 20*, 180–187.

Fox, D. E. & Kendall, P. C. (1983). Thinking through academic problems: Application of cognitive behavior therapy to learning. In T. Kratochwill (Ed.), *Advances in School Psychology*, Vol. 3. Hillsdale, NJ: Erlbaum.

Freed, A. M. (1971). *TA for kids (and grown-ups too)*. Sacramento, CA: Jalmar Press.

Freed, A. M. (1973). *TA for teens (and other important people)*. Sacramento, CA: Jalmar Press.

Friday, N. (1977). *My mother, myself*. New York: Delacorte Press.

Friedling, C., & O'Leary, S. G. (1979). Effects of self-instructional training on second and third grade hyperactive children: A failure to replicate. *Journal of Applied Behavior Analysis, 12*, 211–219.

Frieze, I. H. (1976). Causal attributions and information seeking to explain success and failure. *Journal of Research in Personality, 10*, 293–305.

Fry, P. S. (1975). Affect and resistance to temptation. *Developmental Psychology, 11*, 466–472.

Fyans, L. J., & Maehr, M. L. (1979). Attributional style, task selection, and achievement. *Journal of Educational Psychology, 71*, 499–507.

Gallimore, R., & Dalton, S., & Tharp, R. G. (1986). Self-regulation and interactive teaching: The effects of teaching conditions on teachers' cognitive activity. *The Elementary School Journal, 86*(5), 613–631.

Garner, R. (1988). Verbal-report data on cognitive and metacognitive strategies. In C. E. Weinstein, E. T. Goetz, & P. A. Alexander (Eds.), *Learning and study strategies.* New York: Academic Press.

Gelzheiser, L. M. (1984). Generalization from categorical memory tasks to prose by learning disabled adolescents. *Journal of Educational Psychology, 76,* 1128–1138.

Genshaft, J. L., & Hirt, M. L. (1980). The effectiveness of self-instructional training to enhance math achievement in women. *Cognitive Therapy and Research, 4,* 91–97.

Gettinger, M. (1985). Effects of teacher-directed versus student directed instruction and cues versus no cues for improving spelling performance. *Journal of Applied Behavior Analysis, 18,* 167–171.

Gick, M. L. (1986). Problem solving strategies. *Educational Psychologist, 21*(1 & 2), 99–120.

Glasser, W. (1984). *Take effective control of your life.* New York: Harper and Row.

Glynn, E. L., & Thomas, J. D. (1974). Effect of cueing on self-control of classroom behavior. *Journal of Applied Behavior Analysis, 7,* 299–306.

Glynn, E. L., Thomas, J. D., & Shee, S. M. (1973). Behavioral self-control of on-task behavior in an elementary classroom. *Journal of Applied Behavior Analysis, 6,* 105–113.

Goldin, S. E., & Hayes-Roth, B. (1980). *Individual differences in planning processes.* (Tech. Rep. N–1488–ONR). Santa Monica, CA: The Rand Corporation.

Goldman, S. (1982). Knowledge systems for realistic goals. *Discourse Processes, 5,* 279–303.

Good, T. L., & Brophy, J. R. (1984). *Looking in classrooms.* New York: Harper & Row.

Goodlad, J. I. (1984). *A place called school: Prospects for the future.* New York: McGraw-Hill.

Goodwin, S. E., & Mahoney, M. J. (1975). Modification of aggression through modeling: An experimental probe. *Journal of Behavioral Therapy and Experimental Psychiatry, 6,* 200–202.

Gordon, J. (1974). *T.E.T.: Teacher effectiveness training.* New York: David McKay.

Gottman, J. M., & McFall, R. M. (1972). Self-monitoring effects in a program for potential high school drop-outs: A time series analysis. *Journal of Consulting and Clinical Psychology, 39,* 273–281.

Goudena, P. P. (1987). The social nature of private speech of preschoolers during problem solving. *International Journal of Behavioral Development, 10*(2), 187–206.

Goulet, L. R., & Hoyer, W. J. (1969). The effects of verbalization on verbal discrimination learning and associative recall in young children and adults. *Journal of Experimental Child Psychology, 7,* 434–439.

Grimm, J., Bijou, S., & Parson, J. (1973). A problem solving model for teaching remedial arithmetic to handicapped young children. *Journal of Abnormal Child Psychology, 7,* 26–39.

Guralnick, M. J. (1976). Solving complex perceptual discrimination problems: Techniques for the development of problem solving strategies. *American Journal of Mental Deficiency, 81,* 18–25.

Gwynn, C. (1987). The well-read textbook. *The Science Teacher, 54*(3), 38–40.

Haggard, M. R. (1985). An interactive strategies approach to content reading. *Journal of Reading, 29*(3), 204–210.

Hallahan, D., Lloyd, J. W., & Stoller, L. (1982). *Improving attention with self-monitoring: A manual for teachers.* Unpublished manuscript, University of Virginia Learning Disabilities Research Institute.

Haller, E. P., Child, D. A., & Walberg, H. J. (1988). Can comprehension be taught? A quantitative synthesis of "metacognitive" studies. *Educational Researcher, 17*(9), 5–8.

Harris, A. (1979). Historical development of the Soviet theory of self-regulation. In G. Zivin (Ed.), *The development of self-regulation through private speech.* New York: John Wiley and Sons.

Harris, T. A. (1969). *I'm OK—you're OK: A practical guide to transactional analysis.* New York: Harper and Row.

Hartig, M., & Kanfer, F. H. (1973). The role of verbal self-instructions in children's resistance to temptation. *Journal of Personality and Social Pscyhology, 23,* 1–5.

Hasher, L., & Zacks, R. T. (1979). Automatic and effortful processes in memory. *Journal of Experimental Psychology, 108,* 356–388.

Hawkins, J., & Pea, R. D. (1987). Tools for bridging the cultures of everyday and scientific thinking. *Journal of Research in Science Teaching, 24,* 291–307.

Hayes, D. S., Scott, L. C., Chemelski, B. E., & Johnson, J. (1987). Physical and emotional states as memory-relevant factors: Cognitive monitoring by young children. *Merrill Palmer Quarterly, 33*(4), 473–487.

Hayes-Roth, B., & Thorndyke, P. W. (1980). *Decision making during the planning process.* (Tech. Rep. N–1213–ONR). Santa Monica, CA: The Rand Corporation.

Hazareesingh, N. A., & Bielawski, L. L. (1989, March). *Modifying student teachers' perceptions of control during lesson planning using cognitive self-instruction.*

Paper presented to the annual meeting of the American Educational Research Association, San Francisco.

Heider, F. (1958). *The psychology of interpersonal relations.* New York: John Wiley and Sons.

Helmstetter, S. (1986). *What to say when you talk to yourself.* New York: Simon and Schuster.

Helmstetter, S. (1987). *The self-talk solution.* New York: William Morrow and Company.

Hormuth, S. E. (1986). The sampling of experiences *in situ. Journal of Personality, 54*(1), 262–293.

Hubbard, L. R. (1985). *Dianetics: The modern science of mental health.* Los Angeles: Bridge Publications.

Hughes, C. A., & Hendrickson, J. M. (1987). Self-monitoring with at-risk students in the regular class setting. *Education and Treatment of Children, 10*(3), 225–236.

Hughes, J. N. (1985). Parents as cotherapists in think aloud. *Psychology in the Schools,* 22, 436–443.

Humpreys, M. S., & Revelle, W. (1984). Personality, motivation, and performance: A theory of the relationship between individual differences and information processing. *Psychological Review, 91,* 153–184.

Istomina, Z. M. (1975). The development of voluntary memory in preschool-age children. *Soviet Psychology, 13,* 5–64.

Jackson, P. W. (1968). *Life in classrooms.* New York: Holt, Rinehart, and Winston.

Jensen, A. R. (1971). The role of verbal mediation in mental development. *Journal of Genetic Psychology, 118,* 39–70.

Johnston, M. B. (1983). *Self-instruction and children's math problem solving: A study of training, maintenance, and generalization.* Unpublished doctoral dissertation. University of Notre Dame. Notre Dame, IN.

Johnston, R. S., Johnson, C., & Gray, C. (1987). The emergence of the word length effect in young children: The effects of overt and covert rehearsal. *British Journal of Developmental Psychology, 5*(3), 243–248.

Justice, E. M. (1981). *The development of metamemory concerning memory strategies and its relationship to memory behavior.* Unpublished manuscript, Old Dominion University, Norfold.

Kagen, J., Rosman, B. L., Day, D., Albert, J., & Phillips, W. (1964). Information processing in the child: Significance of analytic and reflective attitudes. *Psychological Monographs,* 78 (1, Whole No. 578).

Kanfer, F. H. (1970). Self-regulation. In C. Neuringer, & J. L. Michael (Eds.), *Behavior modification in clinical psychology.* New York: Appleton-Century-Crofts.

Kanfer, F. H., & Zich, J. (1974). Self-control training: the effects of external control on children's resistance to temptation. *Developmental Psychology, 10*(1), 108–115.

Kantrowitz, B., & Wingert, P. (1989). How kids learn. *Newsweek,* April, 50–55.

Karoly, P. (1977). Behavioral self-management in children: Concepts, methods, issues, and directions. In M. Herson, R. M. Eisler, & P. M. Miller (Eds.), *Progress in behavior modification,* (Vol. 5). New York: Academic Press.

Kazdin, A. E. (1974). Reactive self-monitoring: The effects of response desirability, goal setting, and feedback. *Journal of Consulting and Clinical Psychology, 42,* 704–716.

Keeny, T. J., Cannizzo, S. R., & Flavell, J. H. (1967). Spontaneous and induced verbal rehearsal in a recall task. *Child Development, 38,* 953–966.

Kendall, C. R., Borkowski, J. G., & Cavanaugh, J. C. (1980). Metamemory and the transfer of an interrogative strategy by EMR children. *Intelligence, 4,* 255–270.

Kendall, P. C. (1982). Individual versus group cognitive-behavioral self-control training: One year follow-up. *Behavior Therapy, 13,* 241–247.

Kendall, P. C. (1984). Cognitive-behavioral self-control therapy for children. *Journal of Child Psychology and Psychiatry and Allied Disciplines, 25,* 173–179.

Kendall, P. C., & Braswell, L. (1982). Cognitive behavioral self-control therapy for children: A component analysis. *Journal of Consulting and Clinical Psychology, 50,* 672–689.

Kendall, P. C., & Finch, A. (1978). A cognitive-behavioral treatment for impulsivity: A group comparison study. *Journal of Consulting and Clinical Psychology, 46,* 110–118.

Kendall, P. C., & Zupan, B. A. (1981). Individual versus group application of cognitive-behavioral self-control procedures with children. *Behavior Therapy, 12,* 344–359.

Kendler, I. S., Kendler, H. H., & Wells, D. (1960). Reversal and nonreversal shifts in nursery school children. *Journal of Comparative Physiological Psychology, 53,* 56–60.

Keniston, A. H., & Flavell, J. H. (1979). A developmental study of intelligent retrieval. *Child Development, 50,* 1144–1152.

Knaus, W. J. (1975). *Rational Emotive Education.* New York: Institute for Rational Living, Inc.

Kohlberg, L., Yaeger, J., & Hjertholm, E. (1968). Private speech: Four studies and a review of theories. *Child Development, 39,* 691–736.

Kramer, J. J., & Engle, R. W. (1981). Teaching awareness of strategic behavior in combination with strategy training: Effects on children's memory performance. *Journal of Experimental Child Psychology, 32,* 513–530.

Kreutzer, M. A., Leonard, S. C., & Flavell, J. H. (1975). An interview study of children's knowledge about memory. *Monographs of the Society for Research in Child Development, 40* (1, Serial No. 159).

Kuhl, J., & Beckmann, J. (Eds.) (1985). *Action control: From cognition to behavior.* Berlin: Springer-Verlag.

Kunz, G. C., Drewniak, U., & Schott, F. (1989). *On-line and off-line assessment of self-regulation in learning from instructional text and picture.* Paper presented to the annual meeting of the American Educational Research Association. San Francisco.

Kurtz, B. E., & Borkowski, J. G. (1984). Children's metacognition: Exploring relations among knowledge, process, and motivational variables. *Journal of Experimental Child Psychology, 37,* 335–354.

Kurtz, B. E., Reid, M. K., Borkowski, J. G., & Cavanaugh, J. C. (1982). On the reliability and validity of children's metamemory. *Bulletin of the Psychonomic Society, 19,* 137–140.

Lampert, M. (1984). Teaching about thinking and thinking about teaching. *Journal of Curriculum Studies, 16*(1), 1–18.

Lawson, M. J., & Fuelop, S. (1980). Understanding the purpose of strategy training. *British Journal of Educational Psychology, 50,* 175–180.

Leal, L. (1987). Investigation of the relation between metamemory and university students' examination performance. *Journal of Educational Psychology, 79*(1), 35–40.

Ledger, G. W. (1985). Pictograph reading: Metacognition and deliberate strategic control. *National Reading Conference Yearbook, 34,* 219–226.

Lee, B. (1985). Intellectual origins of Vygotsky's semiotic analysis. In J. Wertsch (Ed.), *Culture, communication and cognition: Vygotskian perspectives.* New York: Cambridge University Press.

Leon, J. A., & Pepe, H. J. (1983). Self-instructional training: Cognitive behavior modification for remediating arithmetic deficits. *Exceptional Children, 50*(1), 54–61.

Levin, J. R., Yussen, S. R., DeRose, T. M., & Pressley, M. (1977). Developmental changes in assessing recall and recognition memory capacity. *Developmental Psychology, 13,* 608–615.

Lindquist-Sandmann, A. (1987). A metacognitive strategy and high school students: Working together. *Journal of Reading, 30*(4), 326–332.

Lloyd, J. (1980). Academic instruction and cognitive behavior modification: The need for attack strategy training. *Exceptional Education Quarterly, 1*(1), 53–63.

Lockhead, J., & Whimbey, A. (1987). Teaching analytical reasoning through thinking aloud pair problem solving. *New Directions for Teaching and Learning, 30,* 68–72

Long, N. J. (1984). Teaching self-control and pro-social behavior by using therapeutic signs and sayings in classrooms for emotionally disturbed people. *The Pointer, 28*(4), 36–39.

Lovaas, O. I. (1964). Cue properties of words: The control of operant responding by rate and content of verbal operants. *Child Development, 35,* 246–256.

Lovitt, T. C. (1973). Self-management projects with children with behavioral disorders. *Journal of Learning Disabilities, 6,* 138–150.

Lovitt, T. C., & Curtiss, K. A. (1968). Effects of manipulating antecedent events on math response rate. *Journal of Applied Behavioral Analysis, 1,* 329–333.

Lowenthal, B. (1986). Planning abilities to aid metacognition. *Academic Therapy,* 22(2), 199–203.

Luria, A. R. (1957). The role of language in the formation of temporary connections. In B. Simon (Ed.), *Psychology in the Soviet Union.* Stanford: Stanford University Press.

Luria, A. R. (1961). *The role of speech in the regulation of normal and abnormal behavior.* J. Tizard (trans.). New York: Liveright.

Luria, A. R. (1979). *The making of a mind: A personal account of Soviet psychology,* edited by M. Cole and S. Cole. Cambridge, MA: Harvard University Press.

MacDonald, J. B. (1965). Myths about instruction. *Educational Leadership, 22,* 571–576, 609–617.

Mahoney, M. & Mahoney, K. (1976). *Permanent weight control.* New York: W. W. Norton.

Manning, B. H. (1984a). A self-communication structure for learning mathematics. *School Science and Mathematics, 84*(1), 43–51.

Manning, B. H. (1984b). Problem solving instruction as an oral comprehension aid for reading disabled third graders. *Journal of Learning Disabilities, 17,* 457–461.

Manning, B. H. (1988). Application of cognitive behavior modification: First and third graders self-management of classroom behaviors. *American Educational Research Journal, 25*(2), 193–212.

Manning, B. H. (1990a). Cognitive self-instruction for an off-task fourth grader during independent academic tasks: A case study. *Contemporary Educational Psychology, 15,* 36–46.

Manning, B. H. (1990b). Self-talk and learning. *Teaching K–8,* April, 56–58.

Manning, B. H. (1990c). An educology of cognitive behavior modification: Applying Meichenbaum's cognitive behavior modification to regular education students exhibiting inappropriate classroom conduct. *International Journal of Educology, 4*(2), 112–121.

Manning, B. H. (accepted). Cueing classroom self-control. *Teaching K–8.*

Manning, B. H. (accepted). A categorical analysis of children's self-talk during independent school assignments. *Journal of Instructional Psychology.*

Manning, B. H., & Payne, B. D. (1989a). A cognitive self-direction model for teacher education. *Journal of Teacher Education, 40*(3), 27–32.

Manning, B. H., & Payne, B. D. (1989b). Verbal introspection: A contrast between preservice and inservice teachers. *Teacher Education Quarterly, 16*(3), 73–84.

Manning, B. H., & Payne, B. D. (1989c). Analysis of preservice teachers' private speech. *Educational Research Quarterly, 12*(3), 46–50.

Manning, B. H., & Reiff, J. C. (1989). Grade level and modality preference of elementary students taught to employ cognitive self-instruction. *Education, 109*(3), 361–366.

Manning, B. H., & White, C. S. (accepted). Task-relevant private speech as a function of age and sociability. *Psychology in the Schools,* October, 1990.

Markman, E. M. (1977). Realizing that you don't understand: A preliminary investigation. *Child Development, 46,* 986–992.

Markman, E. M. (1978, October). *Comprehension monitoring.* Paper presented at the meeting of the Conference on Children's Oral Communication Skills, University of Wisconsin.

Markman, E. M. (1979). Realizing that you don't understand: Elementary school children's awareness of inconsistencies. *Child Development, 50,* 643–655.

Markman, E. M. (1981). Comprehension monitoring. In W. P. Dickson (Ed.), *Children's oral communication skills.* New York: Academic Press.

Marshall, J. C., & Morton, J. (1978). On the mechanics of EMMA. In A. Sinclair, R. J. Jarvella, & W. J. M. Levelt (Eds), *The child's conception of language.* Berlin: Springer.

Masters, J. C., & Binger, C. G. *Inhibitive capability in young children: Stability and development.* Minneapolis: University of Minnesota Press. (ERIC Document Reproduction Service No. ED 130 787).

Masur, E., McIntyre, L, & Flavell, J. H. (1973). Developmental changes in apportionment of study time among items in a multi-trial free recall task. *Journal of Experimental Child Psychology, 15,* 237–246.

Maultsby, M. C. (1975). *Help yourself to happiness through rational self-counseling.* New York: Institute for Rational Living, Inc.

McCombs, B. L. (1988). Motivational skills training: Combining metacognitive, cognitive, and affective learning strategies. In C. E. Weinstein, E. T. Goetz, & P. A. Alexander (Eds.), *Learning and study strategies: Issues in assessment, instruction, and evaluation.* New York: Academic Press.

McMahan, I. D. (1973). Relationships between causal attributions and expectancy of success. *Journal of Personality and Social Psychology, 28,* 108–114.

McNair, K. (1978). Capturing inflight decisions: Thoughts while teaching. *Educational Research Quarterly, 3*(4), 26–42.

Meacham, J. A. (1973). Verbal-motor interactions during sequences of motor activity. (Doctoral dissertation, University of Michigan, 1972.) *Dissertation Abstracts International, 33,* 5545B. (University Microfilms No. 73–11, 205)

Mead, G. H. (1934). *Mind, self, and society.* Chicago: University of Chicago Press.

Meichenbaum, D. (1969). The effects of instruction and reinforcement on thinking and language behaviors of schizophrenics. *Behavior Research and Therapy, 7,* 101–114.

Meichenbaum, D. (1971). Examination of model characteristics in reducing avoidance behavior. *Journal of Personality and Social Psychology, 17,* 298–307.

Meichenbaum, D. (1972). Cognitive modification of test anxious college students. *Journal of Consulting and Clinical Psychology, 39,* 370–380.

Meichenbaum, D. (1974). Self-instructional training: A cognitive prosthesis for the aged. *Human Development, 17,* 273–280.

Meichenbaum, D. (1975a). Enhancing creativity by modifying what subjects say to themselves. *American Educational Research Journal, 12,* 129–145.

Meichenbaum, D. (1975b). Theoretical and treatment implications of developmental research on verbal control of behavior. *Canadian Psychological Review, 16,* 22–27.

Meichenbaum, D. (1976a). A self-instructional approach to stress management. A proposal for stress inoculation training. In C. Spielberger and I. Sarason (Eds.), *Stress and anxiety in modern life.* New York: Winston and Sons.

Meichenbaum, D. (1976b). Cognitive factors as determinants of learning disabilities: A cognitive-functional approach. In R. Knights and D. Bakker (Eds.), *The neuropsychology of learning disorders: Theoretical approaches.* Baltimore, MD: University Park Press.

Meichenbaum, D. (1977). *Cognitive behavior modification: An integrative approach.* New York: Plenum Press.

Meichenbaum, D. (1980). A cognitive-behavioral perspective on intelligence. *Intelligence, 4,* 271–283.

Meichenbaum, D. (1984). Teaching thinking: A cognitive-behavioral perspective. In R. Glaser, S. Chipman, and J. Segal (Eds.), *Thinking and learning skills (Vol. 2): Research and open questions.* Hillsdale, NJ: Erlbaum.

Meichenbaum, D. (1989, November). *Cognitive behavior modification: Effective interventions with adults, children, and adolescents.* Seminar presented through the Institute for the Advancement of Human Behavior, Atlanta, GA.

Meichenbaum, D., & Asarnow, J. (1979). Cognitive-behavioral modification and metacognitive development: Implications for the classroom. In P. C. Kendall and S. D. Hollon (Eds.), *Cognitive-behavioral interventions: Theory, research, and procedures.* New York: Academic Press.

Meichenbaum, D., & Cameron, R. (1973). Training schizophrenics to talk to themselves: A means of developing attentional controls. *Behavior Therapy, 4,* 515–534.

Meichenbaum, D., & Goodman, J. (1969). The developmental control of operant motor responding by verbal operants. *Journal of Experimental Child Psychology, 7,* 553–565(b).

Meichenbaum, D., & Goodman, J. (1971). Training impulsive children to talk to themselves: A means of developing self-control. *Journal of Abnormal Psychology, 77,* 115–126.

Meichenbaum, D., & Goodman, S. (1979). Clinical use of private speech and critical questions about its study in natural settings. In G. Zivin (Ed), *The development of self-regulation through private speech.* New York: John Wiley and Sons.

Middleton, J. L. (1985). I just can't take tests! *The Science Teacher, 52*(2), 34–35.

Miles, C. (1988). Cognitive learning strategies: Implications for college practice. In C. E. Weinstein, E. T. Goetz, and P. A. Alexander (Eds.), *Learning and study strategies.* New York: Academic Press.

Miller, G. E. (1985). The effects of general and specific self-instruction training on children's comprehension monitoring performances during reading. *Reading Research Quarterly, 20*(5), 616–627.

Miller, I., & Norman, W. (1979). Learned helplessness in humans: A review and attribution-theory model. *Psychological Bulletin, 86,* 93–118.

Miller, P. H., & Weiss, M. G. (1982). Children's and adult's knowledge about what variables affect selective attention. *Child Development, 53*(2), 543–549.

Mischel, W. (1974). Processes in delay of gratification. In L. Berkowitz (Ed.), *Advances in experimental social psychology* (Vol. 7). New York: Academic Press.

Mischel, W., & Baker, N. (1975). Cognitive appraisals and transformations in delay behavior. *Journal of Personality and Social Psychology, 31*, 254–261.

Mischel, W., & Patterson, C. J. (1976). Substantive and structural elements of effective plans for self-control. *Journal of Personality and Social Psychology, 34*, 942–950.

Monahan, J., & O'Leary, K. D. (1971). Effects of self-instruction on rule-breaking behavior. *Psychological Reports, 29*, 1059–1066.

Morgan, M. (1987). Self-monitoring and goal-setting in private study. *Contemporary Educational Psychology, 12*, 1–6.

Moss, E. (1985). *Information content of verbal exchanges between mothers and gifted preschoolers.* Paper presented at the biennial meeting of the Society for Research in Child Development, Toronto.

Muth, K. D., Glynn, S. M., Britton, B. K., & Graves, M. F. (1988). Thinking out loud while studying text: Rehearsing key ideas. *Journal of Educational Psychology, 80*(3), 315–318.

Neely, A. M. (1986). Planning and problem solving in teacher education. *Journal of Teacher Education, 37*(3), 29–33.

Neilans, T. H., & Israel, A. C. (1981). Towards maintenance and generalization of behavior change: Teaching children self-regulation and self-instructional skills. *Cognitive Therapy Research, 5*, 189–195.

Nelson, R. O. (1977). Methodological issues in assessment via self-monitoring. In J. D. Cone and R. P. Hawkins (Eds.), *Behavioral assessment: New directions in clinical psychology.* New York: Bruner/Mazel.

Newell, A., & Simon, H. A. (1972). *Human problem solving.* Englewood Cliffs, NJ: Prentice Hall.

Nicholls, J. G. (1983). Conceptions of ability and achievement motivation: A theory and its implications for education. In S. G. Paris, G. M. Olson, & H. W. Stevenson (Eds.), *Learning and motivation in the classroom.* Hillsdale, NJ: Erlbaum.

Nicholls, J. G. (1984). Achievement motivation: Conceptions of ability, subjective experience, task choice, and performance. *Psychological Review, 91*, 328–346.

Nielsen, L. (1984). Teaching adolescents the skills of self-management. *Clearing House*, September, 32–35.

Novaco, R. (1975). *Anger control: The development and evaluation of an experimental treatment.* Lexington, MA: Heath and Company.

Novaco, R. (1978). A stress inoculation approach to anger management in the training of law enforcement officers. *American Journal of Community Psychology, 5*, 68–71.

Novak, J. D., & Gowin, D. B. (1984). *Learning how to learn.* Cambridge, England: Cambridge University Press.

Nowicki, S., & Strickland, B. (1973). A locus of control scale for children. *Journal of Consulting and Clinical Psychology, 40,* 148–154.

O'Leary, K. D. (1968). The effects of self-instruction on immoral behavior. *Journal of Experimental Child Psychology, 6,* 297–301.

Palincsar, A. S. (1985, April). *The unpacking of a multi-component, metacognitive training package.* Paper presented at the annual meeting of the American Educational Research Association, Chicago, IL.

Palincsar, A. S. (1986). Metacognitive strategy instruction. *Exceptional Children, 53*(2), 118–124.

Palincsar, A. S., & Brown, A. L. (1984). Reciprocal teaching of comprehension-fostering and comprehension-monitoring activities. *Cognition and Instruction, 1,* 117–175.

Palincsar, A. S., Brown, A. L., & Campione, J. C. (1989, March). *Discourse as a mechanism for acquiring process and knowledge.* Paper presented to the annual meeting of the American Educational Research Association, San Francisco.

Palkes, H., Stewart, M., & Kahana, B. (1968). Porteus maze performance after training in self-directed verbal commands. *Child Development, 39,* 817–826.

Palmer, D., & Goetz, E. (1983). *Students' perceptions of study strategy attributes as a mediator of strategy use.* Paper presented at the meeting of the American Educational Research Association, Montreal, Canada.

Paris, S. G., & Oka, E. R. (1986). Children's reading strategies, metacognition, and motivation. *Developmental Review, 6*(1), 25–36.

Paris, S. G., Cross, D. R., & Lipson, M. Y. (1984). Informed strategies for learning. A program to improve children's reading awareness and comprehension. *Journal of Educational Psychology, 76,* 1239–1252.

Paris, S., Newman, R., & McVey, K. (1982). Learning the functional significance of mnemonic actions. Microgenetic study of strategy acquisition. *Journal of Experimental Child Psychology, 34,* 409–509.

Parrish, J. M., & Erickson, M. T. (1981). A comparison of cognitive strategies in modifying the cognitive style of impulsive third grade children. *Cognitive Therapy Research, 5,* 7–84.

Patterson, C. J., & Mischel, W. (1975). Plans to resist distraction. *Developmental Psychology, 11,* 369–378.

Patterson, C. J., & Mischel, W. (1976). Effects of temptation-inhibiting and task-facilitating plans on self-control. *Journal of Personality and Social Psychology,* 33(2), 209–217.

Pavlov, I. (1927). *Conditional reflexes*. London: Oxford University Press.

Payne, B. D., & Manning, B. H. (1988). The effect of cognitive self-instructional strategies on preservice teachers' locus of control. *Contemporary Educational Psychology, 13*, 140–145.

Payne, B. D., & Manning, B. H. (accepted). Cognitive self-direction methodological model. *Teacher Education Quarterly.*

Payne, B. D., & Manning, B. H. (accepted). The effect of cognitive self-instructions on preservice teachers' anxiety about teaching. *Contemporary Educational Psychology.*

Pellegrini, A. D. (1981). The development of preschoolers' private speech. *Journal of Pragmatics, 5*, 278–292.

Pellegrini, A. D. (1984). The development of the functions of private speech: A review of the Piaget-Vygotsky debate. In A. Pellegrini and T. Yawkey (Eds.), *The development of oral and written language in social contexts.* Norwood, NJ: Ablex.

Perkins, D. N. (1985). The fingertip effect: How information processing technology shapes thinking. *Educational Researcher, 14*, 11–17.

Peterson, P. L., & Clarke, C. M. (1978). Teachers' reports of their cognitive processes during teaching. *American Educational Research Journal, 15*, 555–565.

Peterson, P. L., Marx, R. W., & Clark, C. M. (1978). Teacher planning, teacher behavior, and student achievement. *American Educational Research Journal, 15*(3), 417–432.

Petti, M. (1986). Help for the hot-tempered kid. *Instructor,* March, 56–57, 60.

Pitkanen, L. (1974). The effect of simulation exercises on the control of aggressive behavior in children. *Scandinavian Journal of Psychology, 15*, 169–177.

Poindexter, C. A., & Prescott, S. (1986). A technique for teaching students to draw inferences from text. *The Reading Teacher, 39*(9), 908–911.

Popham, J. W., & Baker, E. L. (1970). *Systematic instruction.* New York: Prentice Hall.

Posansky, C. J. (1978). Age and task relevant differences in the use of category size information for retrieval of categorized items. *Journal of Experimental Child Psychology, 26*, 373–382.

Posner, M. I., & Snyder, C. R. R. (1974). Attention and cognitive control. In R. L. Solso (Ed.), *Information processing and cognition: The Loyola Symposium.* Hillsdale, NJ: Erlbaum.

Powell, D. E. (1984). Teaching self-control to high risk students in an urban environment. *The Pointer, 28*(4), 20–24.

Pressley, M. (1979). Increasing children's self-control through cognitive interventions. *Review of Educational Research, 49*(2), 319–370.

Pressley, M., & Levin, J. R. (1977). Developmental differences in subjects' associative learning strategies and performance: Assessing a hypothesis. *Journal of Experimental Child Psychology, 24*, 431–439.

Pressley, M., Borkowski, J. G., & O'Sullivan, J. T. (1984). Memory strategy instruction is made of this: Metamemory and durable strategy use. *Educational Psychologist, 19*, 94–107.

Pressley, M., Borkowski, J. G., & O'Sullivan, J. T. (1985). Children's metamemory and the teaching of memory strategies. In D. L. Forrest-Pressley, G. E. MacKinnon, & T. G. Waller (Eds.), *Metacognition, cognition, and human performance*. Orlando, FL: Academic Press.

Pressley, M., Levin, J. R., & Ghatala, E. S. (1984). Memory-strategy monitoring in adults and children. *Journal of Verbal Learning and Verbal Behavior, 23*, 270–288.

Reese, H. W. (1962). Verbal mediation as a function of age level. *Psychological Bulletin, 59*, 502–509.

Reeve, R. A. (1987). *The functional significance of parental scaffolding as a moderator of social influence on children's cognition.* Paper presented at the biennial meeting of the Society for Research in Child Development, Baltimore, MD.

Reid, M. K., & Borkowski, J. G. (1987). Causal attributions of hyperactive children: Implications for training strategies and self-control. *Journal of Educational Psychology, 79*, 296–307.

Renshaw, P. D., & Garner, R. (1987). *Parental goals and strategies in teaching contexts: An exploration of "activity theory" with mothers and fathers of preschool children.* Paper presented at the biennial meeting of the Society for Research in Child Development, Baltimore, MD.

Rest, S. (1976). Schedules of reinforcement: An attributional analysis. In J. H. Harvey, W. J. Ickes, & R. F. Kidd (Eds.), *New directions in attribution research* (Vol. 1). Hillsdale, NJ: Erlbaum.

Revelle, G. L., & Karabenick, J. D., & Wellman, H. M. (1981, April). *Comprehension monitoring in preschool children.* Paper presented at the meeting of the Society for Research in Child Development, Boston, MA.

Ridberg, E., Park, R., & Hetherington, E. (1971). Modification of impulsive and reflective cognitive styles through observation of film-mediated models. *Developmental Psychology, 3*, 369–377.

Riley, J. F. (1981). Creative problem solving and cognitive monitoring as instructional variables for teacher training in classroom problem solving. *Dissertation Abstracts International*, (University Microfilms, No. 81–07, 943)

Ringel, B. A., & Springer, C. (1980). On knowing how well one is remembering: The persistence of strategy use during transfer. *Journal of Experimental Child Psychology, 29*, 322–333.

Roberts, R. N., & Dick, M. L. (1982). Self-control in the classroom: Theoretical issues and practical applications. In T. Kratochwill (Ed.), *Advances in school psychology*, Vol. 2. Hillsdale, NJ: Erlbaum.

Robin, A., & Schneider, M., & Dolnick, M. (1976). The turtle technique: An extended case study of self-control in the classroom. *Psychology in the Schools, 13*(4), 449–453.

Robin, A. L., Armel, S., & O'Leary, K. D. (1975). The effects of self-instruction on writing deficiencies. *Behavior Therapy, 6*, 178–187.

Rogers, B. C. (1983). Metacognition: Implications for training teachers of the gifted. *Roeper Review, 6*, 20–21.

Rohrkemper, M. M., & Bershon, B. L. (1984). The quality of student task engagement: Elementary school students' reports of the causes and effects of problem difficulty. *Elementary School Journal, 85*, 127–147.

Rooney, K. (1985). The use of self-monitoring procedures with low I.Q. learning disabled students. *Journal of Learning Disabilities, 18*(7), 384–389.

Rose, J. S., & Medway, F. J. (1981a). Measurement of teachers' beliefs in their control over student outcomes. *Journal of Educational Research, 74*, 185–190.

Rose, J. S., & Medway, F. J. (1981b). Teacher locus of control, teacher behavior, and student behavior as determinants of student achievement. *Journal of Educational Research, 75*, 375–381.

Rosenbaum, M. S., & Drabman, R. S. (1979). Self-control training in the classroom: A review and critique. *Journal of Applied Behavior Analysis, 12*, 467–485.

Rosenshine, B. V. (1987). Explicit teaching. In D. C. Berliner and B. V. Rosenshine (Eds.), *Talks to teachers*. New York: Random House.

Rotter, J. B. (1966). Generalized expectancies for internal versus external control of reinforcement. *Psychological Monographs, 80*(1, Whole No. 609).

Ryan, E. B., Short, E. J., & Weed, K. A. (1986). The role of cognitive strategy training in improving the academic performance of learning disabled children. *Journal of Learning Disabilities, 19*, 521–529.

Ryan, R. M., Connell, J. P., & Deci, E. L. (1985). A motivational analysis of self-determination and self-regulation in education. In C. Ames & R. Ames (Eds.), *Research on motivation in education, Vol. 2: The classroom milieu*. Orlando, FL: Academic Press.

Sacerdoti, E. D. (1974). Planning in a hierarchy of abstraction spaces. *Artificial Intelligence, 5*, 115–136.

Sadowski, C. J., & Woodward, H. R. (1983). Teacher locus of control and classroom climate: A cross lagged correlational study. *Psychology in the Schools, 20,* 506–509.

Sadowski, C. J., Blackwell, M., & Willard, J. L. (1985). Locus of control and student teacher performance. *Education, 105,* 391–393.

Salatas, H. & Flavell, J. H. (1976). Behavioral and metamnemonic indicators or strategic behaviors under remember instructions in first grade. *Child Development, 47,* 81–89.

Sarason, I., & Sarason, B. (1981). Teaching cognitive and social skills to high school students. *Journal of Consulting and Clinical Psychology, 49,* 908–918.

Sarason, I. G., & Stoops, R. (1978). Test anxiety and the passage of time. *Journal of Consulting and Clinical Psychology, 46,* 102–109.

Schallert, D. L., & Kleiman, G. M. (1979). *Some reasons why the teacher is easier to understand than the text book* (Reading Education Report No. 9). Urbana: University of Illinois, Center for the Study of Reading. (ERIC Document Reproduction Service No. ED 172 189)

Schewel, R. H. & Waddel, J. G. (1986). Metcognitive skills: Practical strategies. *Academic Therapy, 22*(1), 19–25.

Schleser, R., Meyers, A. W., & Cohen, R. (1981). Generalization of self-instructions: Effects of general versus specific content, active rehearsal, and cognitive level. *Child Development, 52,* 335–340.

Schmitt, M. C., & Baumann, J. F. (1986). How to incorporate comprehension monitoring strategies into basal reader instruction. *The Reading Teacher,* 35(10), 28–31.

Schneider, M. (1974). Turtle technique in the classroom. *Teaching Exceptional Children, 7,* 22–24.

Schneider, W. (1985). Developmental trends in the metamemory-memory behavior relationship: An integrative review. In D. L. Forrest-Pressley, G. E. MacKinnon, & T. G. Waller (Eds.), *Metacognition, cognition, and human performance.* Orlando, FL: Academic Press.

Schneider, W., & Shiffrin, R. M. (1977). Controlled and automatic human information processing: Direction, search, and attention. *Psychological Review, 84,* 1–66.

Schunk, D. H. (1981). Modeling and attributional effects on children's achievement: A self-efficacy analysis. *Journal of Educational Psychology, 73,* 93–105.

Schunk, D. H. (1982–83). Progress self-monitoring: Effects on children's self-efficacy and achievement. *Journal of Experimental Education,* Wi, 89–93.

Schunk, D. H. (1986). Verbalization and children's self-regulated learning. *Contemporary Educational Psychology, 11*, 347–369.

Schunk, D. H., & Cox, P. D. (1986). Strategy training and attribution feedback with learning disabled students. *Journal of Educational Psychology, 8*, 201–209.

Scribner, S. (1985). Vygotsky's uses of history. In J. V. Wertsch (Ed.), *Culture, communication, and cognition: Vygotskian perspectives.* New York: Cambridge University Press.

Seaman, J. M., & Sloane, H. N. (1984). Evaluation of a cognitive interpersonal problem solving program. *Education and Treatment of Children, 7*(1), 33–47.

Seligman, M. E. P. (1975). *Helplessness: On depression, development, and death.* San Francisco: Freeman.

Shavelson, R. J., & Stern, P. (1981). Research on teachers' pedagogical thoughts, judgments, decisions, and behavior. *Review of Educational Research, 52*(4), 455–498.

Shepp, M. S., & Jensen, B. F. (1983). A comparison of the treatment effects of an operant strategy, a cognitive strategy, and a combined approach with a hyperactive boy. *School Psychology Review, 12*, 199–204.

Shiffrin, R. M. (1975). The locus and role of attention in memory systems. In P. M. A. Rabbitt & S. Dornic (Eds.); *Attention and performance.* New York: Academic Press.

Short, E. J., & Ryan, E. B. (1984). Metacognitive differences between skilled and less skilled readers: Remediating deficits through story grammar and attribution training. *Journal of Educational Psychology, 76*(2), 225–235.

Shure, M. B., & Spivack, G. (1978). *Problem-solving techniques in child rearing.* San Francisco: Jossey-Bass.

Siegel, B. S. (1986). *Love, medicine and miracles.* New York: Harper and Row.

Smith, D. D., & Lovitt, T. C. (1975). The use of modeling techniques to influence the acquisition of computational arithmetic skills in learning disabled children. In E. Ramp and G. Semb (Eds.), *Behavioral analysis: Areas of research and application.* Englewood Cliffs, NJ: Prentice Hall.

Smith, J. A. (1975). The effect of self-instructional training on children's attending behavior. (Doctoral dissertation, University of Toledo.) *Dissertation Abstracts International, 36*, 5285B. (University Microfilms No. 76–8364)

Sodian, B. (1986). Recall, clustering, and metamemory in young children. *Journal of Experimental Child Psychology, 41*(3), 395–410.

Spivack, G., & Shure, M. B. (1974). *Social adjustment of young children.* San Francisco: Jossey-Bass.

Spring, H. T. (1985). Teacher decision-making: A metacognitive approach. *The Reading Teacher, 39,* 290–295.

Stefanek, M. E., Olledick, T. H., Baldock, W. P., Francis, G., & Yaeger, N. J. (1987). Self-statements in aggressive, withdrawn, and popular children. *Cognitive Therapy and Research, 11*(2), 229–239.

Sternberg, R. J. (Ed.) (1982). *Handbook of human intelligence.* Cambridge, England: Cambridge University Press.

Szykula, S. A., & Hector, M. A. (1978). Teacher instructional behavior change through self-control. *Psychology in the Schools, 15*(1), 87–94.

Taba, H. (1962). *Curriculum development, theory and practice.* New York: Harcourt, Brace, and World.

Thomas, J. W., Strage, A., & Curley, R. (1988). Improving students' self-directed learning: Issues and guidelines. *The Elementary School Journal, 88*(3), 313–326.

Thorndike, E. L. (1917). Reading as reasoning: A study of mistakes in paragraph reading. *Journal of Educational Psychology, 8,* 323–332.

Thrackway, D., Meyers, A., Schlesser, R., & Cohen, R. (1985). Achieving generalization with general versus specific self-instruction: Effects on academically deficient children. *Cognitive Therapy and Research, 9,* 297–302.

Tice, L. (1980). *New age thinking for achieving your potential.* Seattle, WA: The Pacific Institute, Inc.

Toner, I. J., Moore, L. P., & Ashley, P. K. (1978). The effect of serving as a model of self-control on subsequent resistance to deviation in children. *Journal of Experimental Child Psychology, 26,* 85–91.

Torrance, E. P., & Myers, R. E. (1970). *Creative learning and teaching.* New York: Harper and Row.

Trimbur, J. (1987). Beyond cognition: The voices in inner speech. *Rhetoric Review, 5*(2), 211–220.

Turk, D. (1975). *Cognitive control of pain: A skills training approach for the treatment of pain.* Unpublished Masters thesis, University of Waterloo, Ontario, Canada.

Turkewitz, H., O'Leary, K. D., & Ironsmith, M. (1975). Generalization and maintenance of appropriate behavior through self-control. *Journal of Consulting and Clinical Psychology, 43,* 577–583.

Tyler, R. W. (1950). *Basic principles of curriculum and instruction.* Chicago: University of Chicago Press.

Urbaine, E. S., & Kendall, P. C. (1980). Review of social-cognitive problem solving interventions with children. *Psychological Bulletin, 88*(1), 109–143.

Vygotsky, L. S. (1934/1962). *Thought and language.* Cambridge, MA: MIT Press.

Vygotsky, L. S. (1978). *Mind in society: The development of higher psychological processes.* Cambridge, MA.: Harvard University Press. (Original work published 1930, 1933, and 1935)

Vygotsky, L. S. (1987). Thinking and speech. In *The collected works of L. S. Vygotsky: Vol. 1 Problems of general psychology.* New York: Plenum Press. (Original works published in 1934)

Waters, H. S. (1982). Memory development in adolescence: Relationships between metamemory, strategy use, and performance. *Journal of Experimental Child Psychology, 33,* 183–195.

Weaver, R. L., Cotrell, H. W., & Churchman, E. C. (1988). Destructive dialogue: Negative self-talk and positive imaging. *College Student Journal,* Fall, 230–240.

Weiner, B. (1979). A theory of motivation for some classroom experiences. *Journal of Educational Psychology, 71,* 3–25.

Weiner, B., Nirenburg, R., & Goldstein, M. (1976). Social learning (locus of control) versus attributional (causal stability) interpretations of expectancy of success. *Journal of Personality and Social Psychology, 44,* 52–68.

Weinert, F. E., & Kluwe, R. H. (1987). *Metacognition, motivation, and understanding.*Hillsdale, NJ: Erlbaum.

Wellman, H. M. (1977). The early development of intentional memory behavior. *Human Development, 20,* 86–101.

Wellman, H. M. (1977). Tip of the tongue and feeling of knowing experiences: A developmental study of memory monitoring. *Child Development, 48,* 13–21.

Wellman, H. M. (1983). Metamemory revisited. In M. Chi (Ed.), *What is memory development the development of? A look after a decade.* Basel: Karger.

Wertsch, J. V. (1978). Adult-child interaction and the roots of metacognition. *Quarterly Newsletter of the Institute for Comparative Human Development, 1,* 15–18.

Wertsch, J. V. (1979a). The regulation of human action and the given-new organization of private speech. In G. Zivin (Ed.), *The development of self-regulation through private speech.* New York: John Wiley and Sons.

Wertsch, J. V. (1979b). *The social interactional origins of metacognition.* Paper presented at the meeting of the Society for Research in Child Development, San Francisco, CA.

Wertsch, J. V. (1980). The significance of dialogue in Vygotsky's account of social, egocentric, and inner speech. *Contemporary Educational Psychology, 5,* 150–162.

Wertsch, J. V. (1981). *The concept of activity in Soviet psychology.* Armonk, NY: Sharpe.

Wertsch, J. V. (1985a). *Vygotsky and the social formation of mind.* Cambridge, MA: Harvard University Press.

Wertsch, J. V. (1985b). *Culture, communication, and cognition: Vygotskian perspectives.* New York: Cambridge University Press.

Wertsch, J. V. & Stone, C. A. (1985). The concept of internalization in Vygotsky's account of the genesis of higher mental functions. In J. Wertsch (Ed.), *Culture, communication and cognition: Vygotskian perspectives.* New York: Cambridge University Press.

Wertsch, J. V., McNamee, G. D., McLane, J. B., & Budwig, N. A. (1980). The adult-child dyad as a problem solving system. *Child Development, 51,* 1215–1221.

Wertsch, J. V., Minick, N., & Arns, F. J. (1984). The creation of context in joint problem-solving: A cross-cultural study. In B. Rogoff and J. Lave (Eds.), *Everyday Cognition.* Cambridge, MA: Harvard University Press.

Wham, M. A. (1987). Metacognition and classroom instruction. *Reading Horizons,* Winter, 95–101.

White, P. (1980). Limitations on verbal report of internal events: A refutation of Nisbett and Wilson and of Bem. *Psychological Review, 87,* 105–112.

Wippich, W. (1981). Does a shopping situation improve the prediction of memory in preschool children? *Zeitschrift fur Entwicklungspychologie und Padagogische Psychologie, 13,* 280–290.

Wittrock, M. C. (1988). A constructive review of research on learning strategies. In C. E. Weinstein, E. J. Goetz, and P. A. Alexander (Eds.), *Learning and study strategies: Issues in assessment, instruction, and evaluation.* New York: Academic Press.

Wolfgang, C. H., & Glickman, C. D. (1986). *Solving discipline problems: Strategies for classroom teachers.* Boston: Allyn and Bacon, Inc.

Wong, B. Y. L. (1985). Metacognition and learning disabilities. In D. Forrest-Pressley, G. E. MacKinnon, & T. G. Waller (Eds.), *Metacognition, cognition, and human performance.* Orlando, FL: Academic Press.

Wong, B. Y. L., & Jones, W. (1982). Increasing metacomprehension in learning disabled and normally achieving students through self-questioning training. *Learning Disability Quarterly, 5,* 228–240.

Wood, D., & Middleton, D. (1975). A study of assisted problem-solving. *British Journal of Psychology, 66,* 181–191.

Wood, D., Bruner, J. S., & Ross, G. (1976). The role of tutoring in problem solving. *Journal of Child Psychology and Psychiatry, 17,* 89–100.

Wordan, P. E., & Sladewski-Awig, L. J. (1982). Children's awareness of memorability. *Journal of Educational Psychology, 74,* 341–350.

Wozniak, R. J. (1972). Verbal regulation of motor behavior—Soviet research and non-Soviet replications. *Human Development, 15,* 13–57.

Yussen, S. R., & Berman, L. (1981). Memory predictions for recall and recognition in first, third, and fifth grade children. *Developmental Psychology, 17,* 224–229.

Yussen, S. R., Matthews, S. R., Buss, R. R., & Kane, P. T. (1980). Developmental changes in judging important and critical elements of stories. *Developmental Psychology, 16,* 213–219.

Zabrucky, K., & Ratner, H. H. (1986). Children's comprehension monitoring and recall of inconsistent stories. *Child Development, 57,* 1401–1418.

Zahorik, J. A. (1975). Teachers' planning models. *Educational Leadership, 33,* 134–139.

Zentall, S. S., & Kruczek, T. (1988). The attraction of color for active attention problem children. *Exceptional Children, 12*(4), 193–212.

Zimmerman, B. J. (1986). Becoming a self-regulated learner: Which are the key subprocesses? *Contemporary Educational Psychology, 11,* 307–313.

Zimmerman, B. J. & Schunk, D. H. (1989). *Self-regulated learning and academic achievement: Theory, research, and practice.* New York: Springer-Verlag.

Zinchenko, V. P. (1985). Vygotsky's ideas about units for the analysis of mind. In J. V. Wertsch (Ed.), *Culture, communication and cognition: Vygotskian perspectives.* New York: Cambridge University Press.

Zivin, G. (1979). Removing common confusions about egocentric speech, private speech, and self-regulation. In G. Zivin (Ed.), *The development of self-regulation through private speech.* New York: John Wiley and Sons.

Zivin, G. (1979). *The development of self-regulation through private speech.* New York: John Wiley and Sons.

Zumwalt, K. K. (1988). Are we improving or undermining teaching? In L. Tanner (Ed.), *Critical issues in curriculum: Eighty-seventh yearbook of the National Society for the Study of Education,* Part I. Chicago: The University of Chicago Press.

INDEX